People of the Book

MOSHE HALBERTAL

People of the Book

Canon, Meaning, and Authority

HARVARD UNIVERSITY PRESS
Cambridge, Massachusetts
London, England
1997

Library of Congress Cataloging-in-Publication Data

Halbertal, Moshe.
    People of the book : canon, meaning, and authority / Moshe Halbertal.
        p.   cm.
    Includes bibliographical references and index.
    ISBN 0-674-66111-7 (cloth : alk. paper). —ISBN 0-674-66112-5
    (paper : alk. paper)
    1. Bible.   O.T.—Criticism, interpretation, etc., Jewish.
    2. Bible.   O.T.—Canon.   I. Title.
BS1186.H23   1997
296.1—dc21   97-18945

For Tova

Acknowledgments

I began writing the book in the years I spent as a fellow at the Society of Fellows at Harvard. I wish to thank my colleagues at the society for their intellectual companionship, and especially Burton Dreben, who was then its chairman, and Diana Morse, its secretary; they made the unique environment of the society possible. I wish to give thanks as well to may colleagues at the Center for Ethics and the Professions at Harvard and to its director, Dennis Thompson, for a valuable year I spent at the center.

In Jerusalem I have benefited a great deal from ongoing discussions with my colleagues at the Shalom Hartman Institute for Advanced Jewish Studies. The community of scholars and students at the institute, and their commitment to creativity and honesty, have been a most valuable source of intellectual inspiration and companionship. I wish especially to thank David Hartman, the director of the institute, for his great and warm support, advice, and encouragement throughout the writing of this book.

Rogers Brubaker, Jonathan Cohen, Menachem Fisch, Billy Flesch, Moshe Idel, Steven Kipnes, Menachem Lorberbaum, Sanford Levinson, Jonathan Malino, Avishai Margalit, Sidney Morgenbesser, Adi Ofir, Laura Quinny, Amelie Rorty, Avi Sagi, Noam Zion, and the anonymous readers of Harvard University Press read the manuscript and offered

no
Jay
Harris

valuable comments. I wish to thank them for their friendship and advice. I with to thank Lindsay Waters, executive editor at Harvard University Press, for his generous support and advice, and the copy editor, Anita Safran, for her patient reading and valuable comments. And last, I owe special gratitude to my wife, Tova, to whom this book is dedicated, for an ongoing partnership, care, and love.

Contents

People of the Book

Introduction

Canonical Text and Text-Centered Community

Years ago a teacher of mine introduced me to a new concept of heaven and hell. "Don't think that hell is where people are consumed by fire for their sins or that heaven is where they are rewarded with pleasures for their piety. What really happens is that God gathers everybody in one large hall. Then He gives them the Talmud and commands them to start studying. For the wicked, studying Talmud is hell. For the pious, it's heaven." Clearly, the role of the sacred text in Jewish life is so profound that even the afterlife cannot be imagined without it.

The two main axes of this book are the canonical text and the text-centered community. In particular, I seek to understand the Jewish tradition as a text-centered tradition, not in its ideas about life after death but as this centrality affects life on earth. Rather than searching for the essence of Judaism in shared beliefs and practices that remain constant though they take superficially diverse forms, I have chosen to focus on the shared commitment to certain texts and their role in shaping many aspects of Jewish life and endowing the tradition with coherence.

In the Jewish tradition the centrality of the text takes the place of theological consistency. Jews have had diverse and sometimes opposing ideas about God: the anthropomorphic God of the Midrash, the Aristotelian unmoved mover of Maimonides and his school, the Kabbalah's image of God as a dynamic organism manifested in the complexity of his varied aspects, the *sefirot.* These conceptions of God have little in common and they are specifically Jewish only insofar as each is a genuine interpretation of Jewish canonical texts.

Not only does the text provide a common background for various ideas and practices; text-centeredness itself has deeper implications. Some of the major developments in Jewish tradition can be understood through the community's notions of its relation to text, of what text is, and how text functions in its midst. Text is thus more than a shared matrix for a diverse tradition—it is one of the tradition's central operative concepts, like "God" or "Israel."

The general classification of Judaism as a "book religion" is well known to students of comparative religion.[1] As in many other religions, among them Islam and Christianity, Scripture is at its center,[2] but the function, development, and implications of the centrality of text for the shape of Judaism are yet to be investigated. As I hope to show, focusing on text-centeredness will highlight the main distinctions between rabbinic Judaism and biblical religion. What made the Torah the main source of religious authority—the locus of religious experience and divine presence and the object of ongoing reflection—is what gave Judaism the form that persists to this day.

This book is not a full historical and chronologically ordered account of canonization within the Jewish tradition. My discussion is organized thematically, referring to different historical moments and to the various canons as they relate to the theme at hand. The first chapter discusses relationships between canon and meaning. The second treats tensions and competing ideas about the notion of authority of texts and interpreters, while the problem of the value of text and curriculum is discussed in the third chapter. Each chapter deals with a different canon within the Jewish tradition: the first focuses on the canonization of the Bible and its effects on Jewish trends in its interpretation; the second analyzes the canonization of the Mishnah and subsequent codes in the Jewish tradition as they relate to the problem of authority and controversy; and the third deals with the struggle accompanying the rise of the Talmud as the main text in the Jewish curriculum from the Middle Ages onward. Although the intense production of different Jewish canons over such a long time span does not receive a systematic historical treatment, the accumulated total does serve as a continuous resource for dealing with problems of canons and their relation to meaning, authority, and value within the Jewish tradition. The conceptual approach to issues of canonization within the Jewish tradition can also be of value to other fields of research such as law and literature, in which similar problems concerning canons arise. It is essential therefore to clarify the two principal concepts: canonical texts and text-centered communities. They are described in the sections below.

❧ KINDS OF CANONS

"Canonical" as an adjective describing a text refers to the text's special status, one that can have many guises. Texts form a *normative* canon; they are obeyed and followed, as, for example, are Scriptures and legal codes. They can also be canonical as a constitutive part of a curriculum; such texts are not followed in the strict sense but are taught, read, transmitted, and interpreted. These texts establish a *formative* canon, and they provide a society or a profession with a shared vocabulary. The importance of this kind of canonization is manifest in text-centered societies or institutions in which familiarity with certain texts is a precondition for membership. In yet another sense of the word, which will not be discussed in this book, canonical texts serve as paradigmatic examples of aesthetic value and achievement: models for imitation which set the criteria for what is regarded as a higher form of art. These constitute an *exemplary* canon. In a much narrower sense of canonization, texts can become exemplars of schools and trends; they highlight the characteristics of the genre lucidly and forcefully, though they do not necessarily represent the best of that genre but rather what most typifies it.

Different kinds of canonization occasionally converge in a single text. For example, the Talmud in Jewish tradition fulfills two canonical functions: it establishes the norms of behavior in many aspects of life and serves a formative function as the fundamental text in the traditional Jewish curriculum, the focus of endless interpretations and debates. (As we shall see, this dual nature of the canonicity of the Talmud was sometimes challenged by Jewish mystics and philosophers who maintained that the Talmud is authoritative in all matters of the law but is not a text worthy of exclusive, ongoing reflection and study).

Not all canonical texts enjoy equal status. Legal tracts are meant to be obeyed but do not form a central part of the curriculum—they are not regarded as "cultural assets." The Talmud, although it is canonical in these two senses—it is meant to be obeyed and studied—is not paradigmatic and did not set a standard for the formation of future texts. Few interpreters of the Talmud tried to imitate it; they did not write more Talmud; they just wrote about the Talmud.[3] Texts can therefore exert influence in many realms: they are followed and obeyed, studied and read; they are imitated and revered; and they set a standard and bestow value. They control action, thought, and creativity. It is this whole range of the power and function of texts that we wish to capture with the term "canonization." The distinction among these functions is of special importance to the discussion in the third chapter of the book.

The political dimension of the study of canonization is related to the question of status. Texts issue binding norms, and in many cases expertise in a canonical text underlies a claim to political authority and power. Reference to it is a source of legal and moral justification. The establishment of a curriculum and the definition of values involve strong acts of censorship. Canons are both exclusive and inclusive. They create monopolies and define who is worthy of being heard and who is not. In some situations, disagreement about what is included in the canon can divide a community. The connection between canon and censorship and canonization and crisis, as well as issues of authority and the authoritative interpreter, will be discussed in the second chapter.

Canonization fulfills a demarcating function, as in the example of the fixing of the Christian canon in the second century. The historical background of the canonization of the New Testament is still debated. Some scholars tend to see the process as mainly connected to internal developments in the early Church, others understand it as a powerful reaction to Marcion, a second-century Gnostic.[4] Marcion claimed that the Old Testament and the Gospels alike distorted the true teaching of Christ. These books were too "Jewish," he said, and he excluded them from the authoritative body of Christian teachings. In his view, holy Scripture contained only the Paulinian material of the New Testament and some parts of the Gospels. At the other extreme, the Jerusalem Church, which adhered at least partially to the Old Testament law, accepted the Gospels and challenged Paul's authority because of his rejection of the law.

The Christian Church, not yet fully defined, was torn between radically different religious outlooks which expressed the inner tension of its own message. Out of the existing sacred material a fixed canon was formed in response to both the Marcionites' challenge and to the challenge from the more traditional branch in Jerusalem. The establishment of a fixed Christian canon demarcated believers from heretics and erected boundaries between Christians and Gnostics. The logic of fixing a canon as an act of creating boundaries requires the existence of groups that it excludes; canon and heresy are twins.[5]

Since canonical texts have many functions, various arguments are advanced concerning their authority. A text can be authoritative because it claims origin from a unique source such as God, the king, or an expert in the field. Sometimes the authority of texts may be independent of the superior will that instituted them. For H. L. A. Hart the law is authoritative because legal norms were constructed according to the appropriate procedure. This procedure is defined by the legal system itself through a set of high-order rules which dictate that laws should be formed through the Parliament and the like.[6] The authority of a text can also derive from its unique intrinsic merit, like that of a great book. These claims to authority can be challenged on several grounds.

If a text is authoritative, then the issue of who may interpret it is of enormous importance. It is then necessary to explain what justifies the authority of the text and who is authorized to interpret it. These issues are connected to the broader question of what sort of text becomes canonized and for what reason. Is it the text as a potential source of meanings, a specific reading of the text, or is it an institution that defines the meaning of the text? For example, when the Constitution of the United States was made authoritative, was it the specific intention of the writers of the Constitution that was canonized, that is, one particular reading of the text, or was it future readings, that is, any reading that can be justified as a "reading" of the text, so we can say that the text "as such" was canonized? A third option is that only readings produced in the proper institution constitute the true canon. In the case of the Constitution, the Supreme Court's reading is the canonized meaning. Much of the debate about constitutional law revolves around this issue, reflecting internal tensions in the canon's authority.[7]

Since the meanings of texts are sometimes undetermined, variant interpretations may be used to undermine the practices, beliefs, and institutions that are grounded by reference to canonical texts. Thus canonical texts can easily become subversive texts. Consequently, they have often been kept safe and out of sight of the very people over whom the texts assert authority. For example, the early writings of Marx were not available in Communist regimes. Likewise, before the Reformation, the Church often argued that the public should learn Scripture from pictures, usually on the walls of the local church, while the texts themselves should be kept from the community.[8] Cardinal Newman defends the Catholic preference of traditional over nontraditional interpretation of Scripture as follows: "being withdrawn from public view [the tradition] could not be subjected to the degradation of a comparison [with the text of the New Testament], on the part of inquirers and half-Christians."[9] The apostolic tradition was protected from the public eye in an effort to keep it pure and uncontaminated, unlike the New Testament in the hands of the Protestants. In the history of many religious traditions the sacred texts have proved to be as much sources of heresy as sources of faith. "No heretic without a text" is a proverb Spinoza quotes in his *Treatise* as he describes the widespread sectarianism of the seventeenth century.[10] The canonical text with all of its prestige and authority—precisely because of that prestige and authority—must be protected; its readers should be screened and its meanings controlled.

▰ TEXT-CENTEREDNESS

Various aspects of the relationship between the Jewish community and its canonized texts are indicative of text-centered communities in general. First, expertise in the text is a source of power and prestige, both religious and political. Religious authority need not rest on expertise in the text; it can be derived from an individual's exclusively ordained role in ritual (priesthood), or from his unique charisma (prophecy). The idea that expertise in the text is a source of authority—an idea that gives rise to the centrality of the scholar in the Jewish hierarchy— defines an important feature of text-centeredness. Such expertise may become the main source of authority, and then priests and prophets are replaced by scholars. The leading role of the scholar constituted a revolutionary, postbiblical conception of religious authority within Judaism, challenging other conceptions.[11]

A second feature of text-centeredness in the Jewish tradition is that Torah study is considered a foremost religious ideal, indeed a commandment obligating all members of the community. Such a commandment makes membership in the community conditional upon familiarity with the text, and it makes the Torah an ongoing focus of attention. In radical versions of this idea, the Torah is the only focus of attention and thought. The text is an object of reflection, to be explored in depth so that its hidden meanings may be discovered. For when the text moves to the center of attention, it expands its meanings and dimensions.

Both aspects of text-centeredness—the relationship between expertise and authority and the centrality of study—raise questions of access to the text, and whether knowledge of the text is equally distributed among members of the community.

Knowledge of and access to the text are affected by many factors. Literacy can be restricted, as can knowledge of the language in which the text is written. Monopolistic control over the power derived from familiarity with the text can thus be achieved at the basic level of linguistic differentiation,[12] as was the case with Roman Catholicism: the clergy knew Latin and the laity mostly did not. When there is a gap between the language of the text and that of the community, the rules controlling the translation of the text become crucial. However, in the absence of linguistic barriers, access to the text may be controlled by other measures, such as restrictions on dissemination of the text, restrictions on teaching it, or institutional control of education.

In the case of the Torah, making it public knowledge is emphasized as an obligation in the text itself; the laws are supposed to be read in a public ceremony and made known to the community at large.[13] While some first-century rabbinic authorities advocated limiting the teaching of Torah to the sons of "good families," the main trend was democratic and the study of Torah was restricted by neither wealth nor lineage.[14]

Popular participation in the text was a crucial aspect of the emergence of the text-centered community. Access to knowledge was limited to men, however. According to an opinion that became dominant, Torah may not be taught to women.[15] Since Jewish culture evolved through the interpretation of the canon, and authority was attached to knowledge of the Torah, this discrimination against women had far-reaching effects. The unequal distribution of knowledge deprived women of the opportunity to gain the power and influence resulting from engagement with the text. Women hardly participated in shaping the culture, and their voices were unrecorded. In text-centered com-

munities, policies of distribution and access to the text are therefore
crucial.

A third aspect of text-centeredness is that the text itself becomes a
locus of religious experience. The text serves not only to report sacred
events like the Exodus, in which God revealed himself in history, but
the very reading of the text becomes a religious drama in and of itself.
God is present in the sacred text and studying is thus tantamount to
meeting God; it is a moment of great religious intimacy. The Torah
becomes a portable Temple, the sacred territory of scholars. The earliest formulation of such an approach to the Torah appears in one of
the late Psalms (119:19):"I am a stranger on the earth: do not hide thy
commandments from me." The second half of the verse employs a
common formula—"do not hide your face from me"—usually used in
reference to God in the Psalms, to address the Torah.[16] God and Torah
become interchangeable in this Psalm, and this phenomenon marks the
beginning of the great rabbinic idea of the text as the center of religious drama.

A fourth aspect of text-centeredness is that agreement on a common
text defines the boundaries of the community and makes it cohesive.
The shared text may be a source of conflicting beliefs and practices,
but the community recognizes that it alone must be used to justify
them all. While members of the community may disagree about specific beliefs and practices, they do agree about what is the proper way
of justifying them. It is a procedural agreement that all practices,
beliefs, or institutions, whatever they may be, are to be justified in reference to the text, as an interpretation of the text. In a text-centered
community such as the Jewish one, along with other forms of justification such as local traditions and customs, court enactments, and rulings based on reasoning independent of interpretation, interpretation
becomes the main and central form of justification. Legal practice is
similarly bounded by such procedural agreement. Courts can produce
radically opposing rulings; what binds them together is agreement
about the text that is the ground for the rulings.

A shared text is binding under various circumstances. In one case
there may be agreement about an interpretation, an agreement which
is more than procedural. In cases where concrete interpretations differ,
we look for a procedural agreement, that is, we would agree that in
order to come to a decision we have to interpret a common text. On
the procedural level, one can imagine a case in which there is agree-

ment on the text to be interpreted, but still a disagreement about the interpretive procedure. Hence we should distinguish between two kinds of procedural agreements: agreement about what counts as interpretation, even if there is disagreement about the interpretation itself; agreement only about the text that should be interpreted, but disagreement even on what counts as interpretation. In the legal sphere, judges occasionally argue about what should be interpreted in the text. One party claims that the intention of the legislator should be the object of interpretation, while others search for something else; for example, the best case that can be made out of the text. This is an instance of loose procedural agreement to interpret the same text, but not agreement about what counts as the procedure called "interpretation."

The unifying role of a text in the legal system appears in text-centered communities in stronger and weaker versions. The split between Karaites and Rabbinites in the eighth century had to do with the establishment of the Talmud as the text of reference. The Karaites, who did not accept the Talmud, formed a separate community, unraveling the common bond of text even in its loose form. Although both communities were bound by a common text—the Bible—the canonization of the Oral Law transmitted in the Mishnah and the Talmud as the proper reading of the Bible narrowed the inclusiveness of the community, making the schism between the Karaites and Rabbinites inevitable.[17]

After its canonization the Talmud functioned as the binding text, and we can well suppose that canonizing a future interpretation of the Talmud would create another split. When the loss of the common text is compensated by an appeal to other forms of unity that bind communities together, the community stops being text-centered. Until the "emancipation," the Jewish community—with its radical linguistic and geographical diversity, and a certain plurality of practices and beliefs— was a text-centered community united by at least procedural agreement concerning a shared text. The rise of a modern national Jewish identity, stressing other elements of commonality, is in many ways a sign of the loss of the centrality of the text as the binding force.

The Jews became the "people of the book" after a long history that defined the relationship of the community toward the canonized texts and established the diverse functions of texts. What turned the Jews into a text-centered community, with all the repercussions mentioned above, was a deeply rooted revolution that began at the start of the Second Temple period.[18] During this period text-centeredness manifested itself more forcefully and affected the nature of authority, the basic institutions of society, and spiritual life as a whole. This transformation, as we will see in the pages that follow, is related to the process and understanding of canonization within the rabbinic tradition.

CHAPTER 1

Canon and Meaning

An intuitive way to make the distinction between canonical and non-canonical works is to classify them according to the authority and value that a community ascribes to certain texts above others. In this sense, canonization is defined in terms of the element added to the text—sacredness, authority, value, prestige, and so on. However, canonization should be viewed not only as the addition of status to an accepted meaning but as a transformation of meaning itself. In modern approaches to meaning much has been said about the effect of context, and canonizing a text clearly involves viewing the text in a certain context. Unlike other texts, canonical texts are read with special commitments and expectations. In other words, canonization affects not only the status of a text but the way it is perceived and read.

A text can be read, recited, kept as a testimony, interpreted, studied, transmitted, rehearsed, told, performed, and so on. Not all texts are studied and not all texts become objects of reflection and interpretation. A prayer book is recited, a contract is something one signs and keeps as a proof and a reminder, a story is something one tells. The multiplicity of the functions of texts applies also to the role of Scripture in different religious traditions. Sacred texts can have performative and informative functions. In the case of the Indian Vedas, the power of the sacred recitation of the text is independent of whether the reciter understands them.[1] William Graham has emphasized the aural aspect of sacred words, analyzing the importance of recitation of the Qura'n in the Islamic tradition. In the preprint era most believers heard the words of the Scriptures before they saw them in a written form. As Graham has shown, in many religious traditions the primacy of the ear over the eye in regard to the sacred word had enormous effect on the function of these texts. When the ear has primacy, only on rare occasions will an individual meditate upon the words in isolation, facing the written text, and the recitation of the text includes many nondiscursive aspects.[2] Because Scripture serves such an array of functions in different religions, scholars of comparative religion have concluded that it would be fruitless to seek a general conception that will encompass the role of Scriptures in world religions.[3]

One of the primary acts of canonization is to establish the particular function for the canonized book. The published letters of a great person are read differently from the way they were read by their original recipients. A diary when published serves totally different functions than when it is written, and a book can become a "textbook." Thus canonization often involves not only adding authority or status to a text, but assigning a function to that text.

The plurality of the functions of texts is strikingly visible in the biblical use of the term "book" *(sefer)*. In the Bible "book" covers a wide range of meanings—in fact, the range covered by our use of the broader term "text." A book in the Bible can be a document. In Deut. 24:1–3, a bill of divorce is called a book of divorce *(sefer kritut)*. A book can be a contract; Jeremiah calls a contract of purchase "the book of purchase" *(sefer ha-mikna,* Jer. 32:11–16). A letter is also called a book, such as the one David sent to Yoav—a letter with instructions (2 Sam. 11:14, 2 Kings 5:5, Esther 3:13). In light of this variety of functions the word "book" performs in Hebrew and especially in the Bible, the "book of Torah" is a formulation that must be examined carefully. Let us assume that we are at the stage when the Israelites had a more or less fixed version of it. What is the function of the "book of the Torah"— what are its ritualistic or nonritualistic uses—from the point of view of the Torah itself, and why was this specific text written?

The earliest reference to the Torah as a book is found in Deuteronomy. In the earlier parts of the Torah there is no mention of the book as a whole. Instead we have different texts, written on different occasions, that integrate the book of Torah. In Exodus we encounter "the book of the covenant" *(sefer ha-brit)*. This is a legal document, a contract, to remind a party of the obligation he has taken upon himself. Moses gives to the people the laws he heard from God, the people accept them, and he subsequently writes them in a book which is called "the book of the covenant":

> And Moses wrote all the words of the Lord . . . And he took the book of the covenant, and read in the hearing of the people, and they said: "All that the Lord has said will we do, and obey." And Moses took the blood, and sprinkled it on the people, and said: "Behold the blood of the covenant which the Lord has made you concerning all these words."
> (Exod. 24:4–8)

The writing and the reading of the book is part of a covenant-sealing ceremony that includes the ritual spilling of the blood of the sacrifice and throwing the blood on both parties to the contract: Israel and the altar which represents God. (The term "book" is used in the same context in Josh. 24:26.) This contract was placed in the temple, as was common procedure with treaties of suzerainty between kings and vassals. Such treaties were kept in temples dedicated to the gods, who would punish the party that violated the contract.[4]

The same pattern carries over into a more secular context, when Israel accepted a new form of government, kingship, and Saul was enthroned. Samuel, much against his will, "told the people the rules of the kingdom and wrote them in a book and laid it up before the Lord" (1 Sam. 10:25). In the covenantal context, writing is a sign of commitment; texts are a physical embodiment of will, objects of consent. They also serve to remind people of their promise. God asked Moses to write in a book, as a reminder, that war against Amalek is everlasting till the total destruction of the Amalekites (Exod. 17:14). In the book of Joshua the covenant was first read aloud to all the people of Israel, and the words were then engraved in stone. In this way they become *"edut,"* a testimony written on immutable stone (Josh. 8:31-35). The text of the Torah in this case does not function as an object to be studied and reflected upon. Rather, it is meant to be an embodiment of commitment, a testimony that is publicly read in covenant rituals and kept in front of God.

Here the function of the sacred text, from the point of view of the text itself, is to serve as the physical statement of a commitment, and it is kept as a testimony to this commitment, with all the implied sanctions if the covenant is violated. Writing the text is part of a covenantal ritual, and the function of text is defined in that context. What is important about this use of the text is that the people who committed themselves to the text may very well be illiterate. Moses told the Israelites the laws, which they accepted and fully understood orally; only then did he write down the laws.[5]

The pedagogic function of the book of the Torah is first mentioned in Deuteronomy, which uses the expression "book of the Torah" and the verb "to learn" or "study" used in reference to it.[6] "Learning" has a special sense in this context. In many verses in which learning is mentioned, the people become acquainted with the book and thus "learn" to fear God and to keep his commandments. When teaching is equivalent to announcing and telling, studying is therefore listening. One learns from the book but one does not learn the book.

The activities of learning and repeating resemble other mnemonic activities such as placing the text on the doorpost of the house, binding the text upon one's arm and between one's eyes, or carrying the text around.[7] In those contexts learning does not mean reflecting or discovering. The text is not an object of art with many meanings and layers; it has surface rather than depth, and one must listen to it again and again in order to overcome forgetfulness. Used in this manner, the text is not problematized. It has no contradictions to resolve, hints to follow, or allusions to grasp. Even as a contract it is not self-referential, in the way we relate to contracts today.

This is not, by any means, meant to imply that the text of the Torah is not artistically and carefully constructed. The text was definitely produced and guarded by a group of priestly scribes. Moreover, there is clear evidence that earlier materials were recycled and used by different authors, and those sources are quoted and subtly rephrased to produce the later layers. Michael Fishbane argues that we can find cases of internal biblical interpretation in which a discernible effort is made to overcome contradictions existing in the earlier stages.[8] But these findings must be accepted with some reservations. The distinction between rewriting and interpreting is not maintained at this stage, and no assumption is made that a sealed text exists—a finished product to be interpreted but not to be amended. The later strata of the text rewrite and rephrase the older ones, producing a new one. Even later, in the Dead Sea Scrolls, an intermediary stage between internal biblical interpretation and rabbinic interpretation, the distinction between text and interpretation is blurred. In the Temple Scroll the interpretation is inserted into the text and the book of Deuteronomy is rewritten. The editor and the interpreter are still one and the same, constructing a new text out of the old one rather than interpreting the old one.[9]

Thus "the book of the Torah" displays multiple functions within the Torah itself. In Exodus, books are not to be learned; they are to be signed and kept. Deuteronomy presents the Torah as something to be learned and read. Even the king, for example, is obligated to write out a copy of the Torah and to read the Torah all his life; this is so that he will learn to fear God and follow his laws. At this stage it is not the text as such that is the object of learning: one does not learn the text, one learns from the text.[10]

In the Bible the clearest formulation of the idea of Torah as a constant object of inquiry and reflection appears in later materials. As mentioned in the introduction, in Psalm 119 (which is dated by scholars to the second century B.C.) learning is a constant source of joy and religious intimacy; the Torah becomes interchangeable with God. Another even earlier manifestation of this understanding of the Torah appears in the descriptions of Ezra's activities and his role as a scribe. A new verb is used to describe Ezra's way of studying: *doresh be-Torat Moshe.* The verb *lidrosh* means to search or to inquire. The application of this verb to the study of Torah implies a notion of the text as something that requires probing, not only reciting or reading; it contains allusions and hints; it is a subtle code.[11] The transformation of the function of the text to an object of contemplation in the full sense of the word is therefore a later development. The Torah moves from being the basic contract—the text which is the core of obligation—to being the center of curriculum, a text that is studied and contemplated.

This is one of the major shifts in the function of the text leading to a text-centered community. The change in function also entails change in meaning and in the way the text is read, in the expectations and demands that readers bring to the text. It becomes an object with depth, something to be discovered; and it becomes self-referential. Questions about the law come to be answered in reference to the law itself. Studying moves beyond reminding and reciting; it takes on the aspects of inquiring, investigating, contemplating.

The shift in the function of the text and justification of the new concept of its dimensions are achieved through the new reading of the text itself, in which the text proclaims its new function as if it had been there forever. It is part of that new meaning that such a shift should be effected by appealing to the text itself. This great revolution in interpretation is directly connected with the formation of a text-centered society, the rise of the scholar as an authority figure, the end of prophecy, and the decline of the priesthood—and all these changes are related to the act of sealing the canonical text.

?• THE SEALED CANON

There are two basic types of canon: open and sealed. In the open one all the elements are canonical, and other canonical texts may be added at any time. An example of an open canon is a system of legislation that permits the addition of new laws whose legal status will be as binding as the existing law. In a sealed canon, by contrast, the status of the textual elements is exclusive, and no new texts of equal importance may be added. Not all Scriptures are bound and closed; in the Hindu tradition the sacred texts are by far more fluid and open than others.[12] The Bible is the most prominent example of a sealed and exclusive canon.

The chronology of the sealing the Bible is complex. The first aspect of this process is agreement on the list of canonical books, and the second involves the time when those books reached a relatively fixed version. As late as the generation after the destruction of the Second Temple, around 90 C.E., the Sages of Yavneh argue about the place of some books of the canon, although these disputes, for the most part, concern the writings rather than the prophets. There is also testimony of dispute over the book of Ezekiel and its place in the canon at the end of the Second Temple period.[13] Nonetheless the canon seems to have been established during the Second Temple era, apparently during the late Persian or early Hellenistic period, perhaps as early as 150 B.C. Remnants of all the biblical books (aside from the book of Esther) were found among the Dead Sea Scrolls, and Josephus mentions the existence of twenty-two books of the Bible prior to the rabbinic debates over the canon.[14]

The disagreements among the Sages, recorded in the Mishnah in the Tractate *Yadaim*, are about whether to exclude books already part of the canon, and not whether to include new items in the canon. Interestingly, none of the opinions censoring the existing canon was accepted. According to rabbinic tradition, the criterion for inclusion in Scripture depends upon whether or not the book was divinely inspired. (From a rabbinic perspective this is a necessary but not sufficient condition. Thus not every prophecy was included in the Bible, only those that were relevant to future generations.) Since, according to rabbinic tradition, prophecy ceased during the Persian period, any book after that time would by definition be excluded from the canon. Yet the cessation of prophecy is not a likely reason for the exclusion of the Apocrypha from the canon. Perhaps the need to exclude any possible additions to the canon explains how the rabbis determined when prophecy ceased and not vice versa.

It is also very difficult to establish criteria for judging whether a book was divinely inspired, aside from its acceptance as such by the community. Nothing in the book of Ben Sira is particularly problematic, yet it is excluded from the rabbinic canon because of its late date. We can therefore assume that in the rabbinic circles the canon was regarded as sealed before the time of Yavneh, and its sealing is connected to a general view concerning the cessation of prophecy.[15]

On the other hand, although remnants of most of the existing canon were found among the Dead Sea Scrolls at least a century prior to Yavneh, additional authoritative texts were also found there, indicating that the Judean Desert sect might have had a larger canon. Some scholars claim that those texts, such as the Damascus Document and the various *pesharim*, are inspired interpretations of the established canon and not additions to the canon. Others maintain that at least the Temple Scroll is not only an interpretation of Scripture but a new version of Scripture revealed to the members of the sect.[16] In addition, there is good reason to assume that some apocalyptic material that was excluded from the rabbinic canon, such as the Book of Jubilees, was included in the Dead Sea canon.

In addition to the difficulty of dating the sealing of the canon within rabbinic tradition, it possible that other Jewish groups might have had different canons. We lack sufficient historical knowledge to resolve this issue, however, and I do not intend to add speculation to existing conjectures concerning the chronology of the canon. I will focus on a different problem: the consequences of the sealing of the canon for the formation of the text-centered community.

Rabbinic tradition speaks of the dual sealing of the Scriptures; on the one hand the Torah of Moses, the first five books of the Bible, and on the other, the sealing of the prophetic books and the writings that make up the rest of the Bible. The difference between the two sealing lies not only in the attribution of the Pentateuch to Moses, the greatest of the prophets, but also and primarily in a qualitative difference between the status of the Law of Moses and that of other prophecies. In the view of the Sages, the Torah of Moses is the only legislation allowed through prophecy. The *Sifra* comments on the verse "These are the commandments": "from this we learn that from now on no prophet can add anything new."[17] The other prophets speak out on numerous subjects, but they do not enact new law. A prophet is not permitted to introduce a new festival, although he is allowed to foretell surrender or revolt against a Babylonian king. According to the Sages, if a prophet seems to create a new law it is in fact either a reform enacted without the authority of prophecy or a law emerging from an interpretation of the Law of Moses. The internal sealing of the Torah within the Scriptures served to restrict prophetic activity to a nonlegislative realm, or to put it more extremely, as Maimonides understood it, this internal sealing confined the prophets to the task of admonishing the people to obey the Law of Moses.[18]

Before considering the question of sealing the canon and its implications for authority, we must discuss what happens to the meaning of a text after it is sealed. Does the meaning of an already canonical but unsealed text change when it is sealed? And does there ensue a fundamental difference in the way this text is regarded?

The Book of Numbers 15:32–36 recounts the story of a man who is found gathering sticks on the Sabbath and brought before Moses. Moses does not know what to do and waits for God to judge for him; finally he receives a response. Had Moses been one of the Sages, or had such a problem arisen after Moses' death, the solution would have been reached through a consideration of the meaning of "work," which the Torah forbids on the Sabbath. Questions like these are raised by the hundreds in the Talmud. Knowing that the sole texts prescribing conduct on the Sabbath were the Ten Commandments and isolated passages of the Bible, the rabbis were compelled to undertake a campaign of interpretation in order to respond to such questions. Thus the sealing of these texts endowed them with increased breadth and depth. Henceforth the texts themselves would have to be probed to provide solutions to all possible questions. In our example the term "work" in the verse "You shall not do any work" becomes amplified to contain most of the information about the laws of the Sabbath.

The sealed text is laden with an unprecedented burden, and it is no wonder that with the passage of time the literal meaning of expressions gradually deteriorated, just as a hook on which too much is hung eventually snaps under the weight. The rabbis themselves comment upon the relationship between the profusion of laws concerning the Sabbath and the brevity of the biblical text: "The laws of the Sabbath are mountains suspended on a hair, for the verses are few and the laws many" (Mish. *Hagigah*, 1:8).

When prophecy as legislation ended and the text was sealed as a consequence, text became self-referential in a circular way. The sealed text not only acquires the status of exclusivity but new information can be gained mainly through interpreting the text, and the problems that arise are resolved by the text itself. The self-referential text is the exclusive container of any future rulings. According to the Bible itself, Torah study means memorizing the text and passing it on to subsequent generations. But after the sealing of the text, the Scriptures became also an object of interpretation and contemplation, like an artistic creation. As the sealed text acquires new dimensions, Torah study acquires different meaning.

?◆ AUTHORITY AND SEALING

Looking at the distinction between open and sealed canons, the position of the sealed canon seems to be stronger at first glance. Besides being canonical, the text is also the sole authority. But the sealing of the text engenders both the bestowal and the removal of authority. The sealing of Scripture arrested the prophetic activity that had been instrumental in its formulation and, by awarding absolute authority to previous prophecies, dissipated the power of contemporary prophecies. The moment the text was sealed, authority was removed from the writers of the text and transferred to its interpreters; denied to the prophets and awarded to the Sages. "Henceforth you must incline your ear to the works of the learned."

The sealing of the Scriptures does indeed indicate recognition of the exclusive authority of these texts, but at the same time the authority is redistributed. Thus the sealing of the Scriptures instigates a comprehensive upheaval within the Jewish community. The new leadership model of the Torah scholar arises, the religious ideal of Torah study becomes central, and new institutions such as the *beit midrash* acquire a prestigious position in the community. A new genre of writing also develops, that of interpretative texts linked to biblical verses.

In addition, other texts knock on the doors of the canon. Once the gates were locked, the texts still claiming to be part of the Scriptures became Apocrypha. A severe act of censorship seems to be a concomitant of the act of sealing. Not only does the bearer of authority change; the very source of authority changes as well. The rabbis do not derive their authority from direct, personal experience of revelation but rather from being the interpreters of the sealed revelation.[19] As David Weiss Halivni formulated the rise of Midrash: "Canonization (even in its early, imperfect state) dried up the flow of direct information from God to man (or was it the other way around, that the drying up was responsible for the canonization?), forcing man to rely on Midrash and intellectual endeavor that anchors the preset in the past."[20]

The sealing of the Scriptures transformed both the structure and the source of authority. It is important to note that this change in the conception of authority, although it dominates the central current of Judaism, was not fully accepted. Within the talmudic corpus we still find attempts to draw authority from revelation or divine inspiration, a practice that continued through the Middle Ages and later.[21] Other techniques for answering legal questions, such as the use of dreams, omens, and revelations, persisted alongside strict legal reasoning, but these were marginalized.

The following story from the Babylonian Talmud, Tractate *Temurah*, exemplifies the transition from inspiration to interpretation. The story appears with other stories whose central motif is the halakhic situation immediately after the death of Moses, and it attempts to fill the gap in continuity found in the opening verses of the book of Joshua: "Now after the death of Moses the servant of the Lord it came to pass that the Lord spoke to Joshua the son of Nun, Moses' minister, saying 'Moses my servant is dead; now therefore arise, go over the Jordan, thou and all this people to the land which I do give to them, to the children of Israel.'"

What happened between the death of Moses and the injunction to Joshua to cross the Jordan? The simplest answer is that Moses was forbidden to enter the Promised Land, so after his death God ordered Joshua to lead the people there. Yet such an answer does not satisfy the exegetical flair with which gaps in the biblical narrative can be filled. According to the Midrash, this is what occurred, in those very words:

> Rav Judah reported in the name of Rav: when Moses departed this world for the Garden of Eden he said to Joshua: "Ask me concerning all the doubts you have." He replied to him: "My master, have I ever left you for one hour and gone elsewhere? [that is, I have no doubts]. Did you not write concerning me in the Torah: 'But his servant Joshua departed not out of the Tabernacle'" (Exod. 33:11). Immediately the strength of Moses weakened [that is, he took offense at Joshua's remark, which implied Joshua no longer had need of him] and Joshua forgot 300 laws and there arose 700 doubts concerning laws. Then all the Israelites rose up to kill him. The Holy One blessed be He then said to him: "It is not possible to tell you [these laws]. Go and occupy their attention in war," as it says: "Now after the death of Moses the servant of the Lord, it came to pass that the Lord spoke." (Josh. 1:1)

This story appears with other stories relating to the death of Moses and to forgetting. On the same page of the Talmud there is another example of the same preoccupation:

> Rav Judah reported in the name of Samuel: 300 traditional laws were forgotten during the period of mourning for Moses. They said to Joshua, "Ask"; he replied: "It is not in heaven" (Deut. 03:12). They [the Israelites] said to Samuel: "Ask"; he replied "These are the commandments" (Num. 36:13) [implying that since the promulgation of these commandments no prophet has the right to introduce anything new].

God refrains from answering the halakhic questions posed to Him. He thus refuses to help Joshua, the conceited pupil who has forgotten the teaching, and will not give him a response that will ease all the doubts that have beset him. Instead of a halakhic answer, Joshua receives a bit of Machiavellian advice from God: if you wish to escape the fury of the people alive, go and distract them with political problems.

This is an interesting view of the war that was fought to conquer the land, implying that it began because of Joshua's failure as a Torah scholar. Had Joshua correctly answered the questions posed in the *beit midrash*, he would not have become the military commander who started a war to save his own skin. This *midrash* thus reflects the transition from prophets to rabbis at the moment when prophecy becomes halakhically forbidden, and it also expresses implicit pride in the new figure of the Torah scholar and his superiority over the man of war.[22]

Thus there is latent tension in the sealing of the canon which does not exist in an open canon. This tension originates in the paradoxical outcome of the sealing itself: the act of awarding exclusive authority places out of reach the activity which first created the canon. This does not occur in the case of an open canon. When a canon is sealed, one can expect an all-encompassing change in the conception of authority, its source, and its bearers. As in the case discussed above, the movement from prophet to scholar and from prophecy to interpretation accompanies a new conception of the text, allowing for the variety of interpretation initiated by scholars.

The movement from prophet to the commentator is accompanied by another shift, no less drastic, from priest to scholar. This aspect of the change in the conception of authority was due to the rise of the expert-interpreter. From the second century B.C.E., and perhaps even earlier, a new religious elite began to emerge: that of the Sages. Their relative influence and impact on the rest of the community waxed and waned over time, and their power was institutionalized to varying degrees in different eras. Before the destruction of the Temple in 70 C.E., the Sages seem to have been a totally uninstitutionalized force, and historians debate the extent of power and influence they exerted on the Jewish masses.[23] After the destruction of the Temple, the Sages emerged as the only existing elite, and in the third and fourth centuries they reached the height of their influence and institutionalized power, although their actual impact on the general population still needs careful evaluation. Among the most interesting changes that came with the rise of the Sages was the decline of priestly leadership. According to one view, the priests had been the primary force in the transmission and interpretation of the tradition, and the decline of priestly leadership followed the destruction the Temple. Hence it began only in 70 C.E., and even after this date priests continued to hold a broader leadership role. According to another view the shift began before the destruction of the Temple, as early as the Hellenistic period in the second century B.C.E., for the Sages had already formed a popular and influential alternative to the priesthood while the Temple was still in existence.

Detailed analysis of the historical problem is beyond the scope of this work; we will refer only to sources from the end of the second century C.E., which articulate the normative consequences of this shift.[24] In this striking example of setting priorities for saving lives when sacrifices are inevitable, the Mishnah expresses its preference for scholars over priests: a bastard scholar must be saved before an ignorant high priest. Scholarship with defective lineage is thus preferable to ignorance with the best lineage.[25] Unlike the authority of the priest, that of the scholar does not rest on a monopoly over ritual. Priestly authority rests on the claim that a certain group has the exclusive right to perform a variety of rituals. The priests alone can atone for the people in the Temple; the priests alone maintain the order of nature by continuing the daily ritual routine in the Temple. The well-being of the community is therefore dependent upon individuals who have exclusive control over these cardinal religious goods. This exclusivity is guarded by exclusivity of lineage and is the source of priestly power. Unlike priests, scholars in the rabbinic tradition have no unique role in the ritual. Every ritual performed by them can also be performed by the rest of the community. Even more, in institutions formed by the rabbis for the performance of ritual, such as the synagogue, the priests have very limited monopoly on ritual. Any Jew can blow the *shofar*; any Jew can read the Torah, and so on. The expert's authority is derived not from his exclusive role in the ritual but from his skills as interpreter of the sealed text.

?◆ THE MEANING OF THE CANONICAL TEXT

Clearly, the status of the book changes when as part of the Scripture it becomes authoritative, but does its meaning also change, and if so, in what way? A case in point is the book of Ecclesiastes, whose composition has been dated to the third century B.C.E. and whose text reflects a deeply skeptical position typical of early Hellenistic philosophy.[26] Traditional motifs such as Divine Providence and revelation are absent in Ecclesiastes, and it contains more than a hint of heresy. God, though omnipotent, is quite arbitrary: "In my own brief span of life, I have seen both these things: sometimes a good man perishes in spite of his goodness, and sometimes a wicked one endures in spite of his wickedness" (7.15). Piety, therefore, is not recommended: "So do not overdo goodness and do not act the wise man to excess . . ." (7.16). A nihilistic mood pervades the book in its meditations on the meaninglessness of man's deeds and efforts, and the hedonistic conclusion it reaches derives in part from this feeling: "There is nothing worthwhile for a man but to eat and drink and afford himself enjoyment within his means" (2.24). The tenet that is probably most central to biblical faith, the meaningfulness of history, is rejected by Ecclesiastes, where history is described as a recurring cycle of meaningless events. The sons reenact the deeds of the fathers, and there is nothing new under the sun.

The book of Ecclesiastes, which not only contradicts the beliefs represented in the Bible but also expresses a radically different temperament and consciousness, is bound together with the rest of the Bible, just as the Epistle of James in the New Testament is found alongside the other Epistles.

When Ecclesiastes was introduced into the body of the Scriptures, however, it was required to give up its unique and heretical message. The moment it became part of the scriptural canon, the exegete was obligated to make it consistent with the rest of the Scriptures. This new reading means implicitly that its original meaning will be lost. Thus it is too general and essentially useless to say merely that canonization imbues the book with authority, for the authority is conditional upon a specific way of reading the text. After the act of canonization, the expositor is no longer called upon to justify his views in accordance with Ecclesiastes. On the contrary, Ecclesiastes must be justified in the eyes of the expositor. The reader, more than the text itself, becomes the bearer of authority.

The Midrash deals with the heretical elements of the book in the following manner:

> Rabbi Benjamin ben Levi stated [that] the Sages wanted to inter the book of Ecclesiastes, for they found in it ideas that leaned toward heresy. They argued, was it right that Solomon should have said the following: "Rejoice, O young man, in thy youth and let thy heart cheer thee in the days of thy youth" (Eccles. 11:9). Moses said, "Go not about after your own heart and your own eyes" (Num. 15:39), but Solomon said, "Walk in the ways of thy heart and in the sight of thine eyes" (Eccles. 11:9). What then? Is all restraint to be removed? Are there neither judges nor justice? When, however, he said, "But know then that for all these things God will bring thee into judgment," they admitted that Solomon had spoken well.

Rabbi Samuel ben Nahmani stated [that] the Sages intended to inter the book of Ecclesiastes because they found ideas in it that leaned toward heresy. They said, "Should Solomon have uttered the following: 'What profit hath man of all his labor'?" This might imply, might it not, that labor in the study of the Torah was also included? On the other hand, they argued, if he had said "of all labor" and left it at that, we might have thought that he meant to include labor as well in the study of Torah. However, he does not say this but "of all his labor," implying that it is in his own labor that man finds no profit, but that he does find profit in the labor of studying Torah. R. Judah explained that "under the sun" he has no profit but above the sun [in heaven] he has. (Midrash *Rabbah Leviticus*, XVIII)

This *midrash* addresses the two central themes of Ecclesiastes: the sentiment of the futility of human expectations and its hedonism. The feeling of hopelessness endangers man's motivation to perform the commandments, for they seem to be among those things that offer no profit. Thus the interpreter annotates the phrase "all of his labors" and explains that it does not include the labor of Torah. In this way the feeling of despair expressed in Ecclesiastes is transferred to the realm of secular life and is even transformed into an encouraging voice urging the fulfillment of the precepts and labor in Torah study. The advocacy of hedonism in Ecclesiastes becomes a threat: know that God will be the judge of your indulgence.

The new reading is applied throughout Ecclesiastes *Rabbah*, and is exemplified by the following general rule which appears in that text:

"I know that there is nothing better for them than to rejoice, and to get pleasure so long as they live. But also that every man should eat and drink" (Eccles. 3:12:f). R. Tanhuma in the name of R. Nahman, the son of R. Samuel b. Nahman, and R. Menahem [in another version: R. Jeremiah and R. Mayasha in the name of R. Samuel b. R. Isaac] said: "All the eating and drinking mentioned in this book refer to Torah and good deeds." (Eccles. R. 3:12)

The hedonistic message becomes a metaphor; whenever Ecclesiastes tells you to eat and drink, know that what he means is "go and do good deeds and study Torah." The book of Ecclesiastes thus pays dearly for the everlasting fame it wins by being canonized; renown comes at the expense of distortion and effacement of its unique and radical message.

The accommodation of the text to the canon was made possible not only by reinterpretation but by additions to the text itself. The closing verses seem to have been added to alter the general nature of the book: "The sum of the matter, when all is said and done: Revere God and observe His Commandments! For this applies to all mankind. That God will call every creature to account for everything unknown, be it good or bad." How different this is compared to what seems to have been the original ending, seven verses earlier: "Utter futility—said Koheleth—All is futile!" (12:9).

The canonization of a book is not tantamount to an acceptance of its meaning as authoritative. The inclusion of the Song of Songs in the canon does not give courtship and love the status of an obligation. Rather, the canonical position of this poem compels a metaphorical reading of it, making the love described there a metaphor for the relationship between man and God. The same is true for the book of Esther. It is not the canonization of a comedy about courtly life in a kingdom of Persia, as the book may be read and as Luther did in fact read it, hence refusing to make it canonical. In the Jewish canonization of Esther the absence of God's name (which does not appear once in the entire book) acquires religious meaning: it represents the concealment of the Divine Presence from Israel, and the miracle which occurs is also concealed in a series of events that seem completely coincidental.[27] Paradoxically, then, the canonization of a work sometimes serves to suppress its most plausible readings. Moreover, the implications of the particular kind of reading that allows for inclusion in the canon may be far-reaching and also pose a certain danger. Because the canonization of a book is in fact the canonization of a very specific reading of it, one must make certain the reader does indeed read it that way. Otherwise, the book becomes a blessing and a curse: it becomes renowned as an authoritative and holy book yet could lead to heretical conclusions. It is easy to imagine a reader who, knowing the Ecclesiastes is a holy book and its message obligatory by virtue of being canonical, reads the recommendations of hedonism without interpreting every mention of eating and drinking as a metaphorical expression of Torah and good deeds. In that reader's hands Ecclesiastes is clearly a dangerous book, and his reading must be mediated by outside influences. The same is true every time the commentary on a book of the Scriptures becomes distant from the text itself.

໕ CANON AND THE PRINCIPLE OF CHARITY

In short, canonization of a text may at times serve to take the authority away from its original meaning, allowing the commentator to choose the meaning that will be deemed authoritative. In reality, he wields authority over the text. In the interpretation of Esther and other books, the text is read in the "best" possible light in order to redeem it—a light that is consistent with what the interpreter believes is expressed in the rest of Scriptures.

This phenomenon in the interpretation of a canonical text is an example of what Willard Quine has called "the principle of charity," a topic that promises to broaden our perspective on the subject of canonization. The principle of charity is an interpretative method that would yield an optimally successful text. For example, although a person's words might be read as self-contradictory and thus meaningless, they should not be interpreted in that way. If someone tells us he feels good and bad, we should not take his statement as meaningless but rather understand by this that sometimes he feels good and sometimes bad, or that his feelings are mixed.[28]

In Quine's usage, the principle entails quite a limited amount of charity. He discusses problems of translation that involve the use of basic logical rules. In cases of radical translation a charitable attitude is adopted so that a speaker's words will make sense and the sentence he utters can have meaning, any meaning. Charity is not used here to interpret the other's statements in the best possible light, but simply to shed some light on them. The other limit of charity is that use of the principle is not based on any assumptions of the speaker's talent and capability but is simply the precondition for understanding any discussion. Charity amounts to seeing the other as a user of a language, and it is necessary for holding a conversation.

The following example will help clarify the distinction between the level of charity required for shedding any light at all on a sentence and the level of placing it in the best light. A given conversation might be fraught with suspicion; for various reasons the speaker may think that his interlocutor is lying and is therefore totally uncharitable in this sense. Sometimes we just take it for granted that the other is lying, so we apply the principle of "liar until proved truthful." But even so, we must employ the sort of charity that Quine defines, for in order to tell a lie, the other must make sense and speak a shared language.

Ronald Dworkin extends Quine's principle of charity in interpretation to the second level. Dworkin claims that the choice between competing interpretations is governed by the criterion of which interpretation shows the work in the best light. In literary interpretation we will choose the one that accounts for all the aspects of the narrative. An interpretation that seems to leave a portion of the story unconnected and therefore superfluous will be ruled out. In legal interpretation the standard for the best possible interpretation is not aesthetic but moral. We will select the interpretation that makes the best moral case of the legal material. According to Dworkin, even those who claim that we must discover the original intention of the legislator base their opinion on the belief that this is the best possible way of reading a legal text. The writer's intention does not provide an independent criterion for establishing the meaning of the text; Dworkin rejects that standard and argues that those who adopt it do so for political reasons. In their view, this is the only way that the legal system can achieve stability and be freed from the arbitrariness of the interpreter—the judge. Their prime guiding principle of interpretation is a value judgment concerning the optimal interpretative strategy, not an objective standard for interpretation. Moreover, according to Dworkin, in reconstructing the writer's intention we attempt to present it in the best possible light. Interpretation is thus closely linked to evaluation, and value serves as the ultimate standard for interpretation.[29]

Dworkin seems to claim that this attitude defines the activity of interpretation in general, and it certainly does apply to canonical texts. With regard to many ordinary texts, however, there is no commitment to presenting the text in the best possible light. In court, lawyers seek to interpret the law not in the best possible moral light but in the manner that will best serve their clients.[30] And literary critics sometimes strive to represent works in the worst possible light. By contrast, the commitment of the judge is to make the best moral case, and it demands a unique attitude toward the text. The judge's position is not always grounded in his belief that the text he is interpreting is morally perfect, but rather in his role in the system. From his point of view the canonization of the legal text not only endows it with authority but also requires a commitment to make the best of it. At other times the reverse will be true: the same attitude will be derived not from the role in the system but from belief in the intrinsic value of the canonical work. What defines the consideration of an artistic work as canonical will be that attitude of presenting it in the best possible aesthetic light.

In the case of a sacred text the speaker is God and it is thus by definition perfect; not only can no contradictions exist but the text is the best possible. Such an assumption naturally influences the way the text is read in relation to other sources that seem less perfect in comparison. Reading a holy text requires using the principle of charity as generously as possible in interpreting it, since it is inconceivable that such a text could err. We apply the principle of charity in our reading of a holy text not only to ensure its meaningfulness when literal interpretation creates an impression of meaninglessness, but also to ensure that it corresponds to the highest criteria of perfection. In the case of the Scriptures, there is an a priori interpretative commitment to show the text in the best possible light. Conversely, the loss of this sense of obligation to the text is an undeniable sign that it is no longer perceived as holy. Making use of the principle of charity, the following principle can be stipulated: the degree of canonicity of a text corresponds to the amount of charity it receives in its interpretation. The more canonical a text, the more generous its treatment.

A conscious expression of the principle of pure charity in reading of Scripture is found in Maimonides' declaration in the *Guide to the Perplexed*.

> Know that our shunning the affirmation of the eternity of the world is not due to a text figuring in the Torah according to which the world has been produced in time. For the texts indicating that the world has been produced in time are not more numerous than those indicating that the deity is a body. Nor are the gates of figurative interpretation shut in our faces or impossible of access to us regarding the subject of the creation of the world in time. For we could interpret them as figurative, as we have done when denying His corporeality. (II, 25)

Maimonides states that if it were clear to him in a metaphysical sense that in truth the world was eternal rather than created, he would interpret the Scriptures in harmony with this truth. He applied the same principle in his treatment of the expressions in the Bible describing God in corporeal terms: he interpreted them in accordance with the metaphysical truth that God is not material. He assumes that we are aware of proved metaphysical truths, and that Scripture, by definition, speaks the truth. Hence instances when two statements seem to contradict each other must be resolved by a metaphorical interpretation of the Scriptures, as in the numerous cases of corporealization found in the Bible. According to this approach, the canonical status of the text entails interpreting it with the maximum amount of charity.

However, Maimonides' teaching runs counter to the opposite intuition regarding the interpretation of Scripture, an intuition that introduces an entirely contrary hermeneutic principle and derives a different meaning from the canonical status of the text. Maimonides' view that a holy text necessitates maximal charity in its interpretation is opposed by the view that a holy text must be interpreted with minimal charity. If a scriptural expression appears to contradict commonly accepted metaphysical axioms—by implying the materiality of God, for example—then that metaphysical position must be abandoned. The interpreter must concede that what he had believed to be a metaphysical axiom is incorrect. Similarly in questions of justice: if he sees something in the text that seems unjust to him, rather than offer a more just explanation, he must revise his own concepts of justice.

This approach confronts the reader with two options, one more radical than the other. The more moderate one is that the reader must suspend his moral judgment facing the sacred text. The reader is not required to redefine his moral principles completely, but is forbidden to accommodate the text to these principles in the face of a contradictory commandment of God. According to the radical approach, it is the text that must determine the interpreter's concept of charity. He cannot postulate a conception of justice or truth that he formulated before his encounter with the text and still interpret the text in the best possible light. The holiness and authority of the text is so all-encompassing that it alone determines the concepts of good and evil, truth and falsity; no other criterion exists by which it can be interpreted.

The moderate approach does not entail a complete revaluation and negation of moral convictions and metaphysical knowledge which, according to the radical approach, ought to be constituted solely by the canonical text. Rather, it demands suspension of value and knowledge in cases of conflict and disallows the accommodation of the text to values and beliefs that were consistent with the previous conception of charity.

The radical position may also be expressed as follows: all that we know about God comes from revelation. In contrast, Maimonides declared that his knowledge of God was independent; He is not material, hence all corporeal descriptions will be explained in a metaphorical sense. This position is unacceptable in a theology that emphasizes that the distance between God and man can be bridged by revelation alone. Its adherents would agree that the text must be interpreted in the best possible light, but that would be an empty demand, for what is positive and negative can only be known from the text itself.

Interpretation of Scripture is thus divided into two opposing attitudes toward the principle of charity in interpretation. One claims that its nature as a sacred text demands a maximal, indeed nearly infinite, degree of charity in interpretation, while the other argues that the nature of a sacred text demands absolute abstention from the principle of charity, since the text alone determines what is charity.

NB !

These contrary attitudes regarding the principle of charity in interpretation of Scripture are related to the degree that the text is seen as making all-encompassing demands upon the interpreter. This in turn depends on whether the interpreter can refer to any sort of legitimate background for assistance in the exegesis of the Scriptures. In the view of the moderates such a background does exit, but the radicals, rejecting the principle of charity in interpretation of the Scriptures, would argue that there can be none, since all human knowledge is as naught compared to revelation, which establishes the entire fund of knowledge appropriate to its interpretation. The question of the exclusivity of the sacred text, which is implicit in this disagreement, came out into the open in Rabbi Elfakar's contestation of the *Guide to the Perplexed.*

Yehudah Elfakar, a rabbi from Toledo who participated in the debate over Maimonides' writings that erupted in the fourth decade of the thirteenth century, was critical of Maimonides' interpretative strategy. In his opinion, Maimonides was justified in denying corporealization in the Scriptures, but not because of arguments against corporealization in the philosophy of Aristotle, but because the Torah itself explicitly rejects corporealization. This is in fact the only legitimate argument that could be made in defense of a metaphorical interpretation of the materialist expressions.[31] Spinoza in his *Treatise* attacks Maimonides on the same point.[32] In Part II of the *Guide of the Perplexed*, Maimonides declared that if he had proof the world was eternal, he would interpret the Torah in conformity with that view of an eternal world, just as he did with expressions of corporeality. This declaration, according to R. Elfakar, demonstrates his bond to Aristotle rather than to the Torah. If you possess proof that the world is eternal and the Torah seems to say that the world is created, you must abandon that proof. He argues that no relevant external background information can serve as criterion for interpreting the Torah itself, whereas Maimonides accepts the independent truth of philosophy while denying that the Torah could possibly contradict it.

These two contrary positions on reading Scripture "with charity" share one assumption: what is written in Scripture is truth. The dispute between the view of Maimonides and that of Elfakar resides in their respective solutions to problems of apparent contradiction between Scripture and truth. In these cases, should Scripture be accommodated to the readers' beliefs about truth, or should those beliefs be accommodated to the meaning of Scripture?[33]

In scriptural interpretation, the religious conception of the distance between God and the reader is the central hermeneutical issue. The interpreter must either abnegate himself before God, setting aside the whole of his human consciousness as irrelevant, or allow his human consciousness to serve as a legitimate hermeneutical tool. At this juncture we face a fundamental tension affecting the act of reading canonical texts according to the principle of charity. The midrashic interpretation of that principle is exemplified in the passage from Ecclesiastes discussed earlier. The reading was based on knowledge originating within the Scriptures. That is, the rabbis reinterpreted the hedonistic words of Ecclesiastes in the light of Moses' injunction, "Go not about after your own heart and your own eyes."

Besides Maimonides, there are other instances of traditional scriptural readings that base the principle of charity on sources of authority external to the canonical corpus. To dwell on this question of external and internal influence would divert us from the problem of canonization, however, and lead us toward the problem of interpretation, and I wish to deal with the latter only in its connection with the former.[34]

ತಿ TEXTUAL CLOSURE AND HERMENEUTICAL OPENNESS

Canonizing a text results in increased flexibility in its interpretation, such as the use of complex hermeneutical devices of accommodation to yield the best possible reading. This phenomenon conflicts with the restrictive impulse of canonization itself, an act which creates boundaries and in many cases censors other texts and prevents them from becoming canonical. In addition, textual fluidity is often arrested with canonization. The legal and narrative material of canonized texts used to be transmitted in a number of traditional ways which were developed before the authoritative canon became fixed. In some cases, canonization does not mean a selection of the one and only version of the existing legal and narrative material. Rather, the older traditions are included in the canon and juxtaposed within it—contradicting and duplicating each other. Fixing a canon arrests the process of multiplicity of traditions, and it is usually accompanied by the establishment of a precise version of the text itself.

This tension between the hermeneutical openness created by canonizing a text and the restrictive tendency manifested by the canonization is revealed in a far more radical form when we examine two elements in Jewish hermeneutics which became central to the attitude towards a canonical, revealed text in the Middle Ages. The first is the concept of the multilayered text, which includes an esoteric and hidden layer. The second is the idea that a canonized text speaks a qualitatively different kind of language, and conventional hermeneutic devices are therefore incapable of uncovering its deepest layers. The concept of the Torah as a multilayered text hiding a secret esoteric meaning, and the claim that divine language necessitates unconventional modes of interpretation, enlarge the possibility of deriving meanings from the text almost endlessly.

The idea of the multilayered text with hidden esoteric meaning took root in Jewish hermeneutics as early as the first and second centuries, although it is not the organizing principle of the hermeneutical endeavor in midrashic literature.[35] This concept grew powerful in the Middle Ages, permitting new metaphysical and theological visions to be integrated into the Torah, a text which seemed superficially either alien or indifferent to these formulations. Both Kabbalah and Jewish philosophy were bold, innovative theological ventures, and they could be integrated in the tradition because they presented themselves as articulations of the Torah's hidden message. This grand interpretative move, which thoroughly transformed the most basic conceptions of Judaism, was sustained by complex theories of language and divine speech and by political and theological notions of esotericism. For one of the major achievements of both Kabbalah and Jewish philosophy was the development of new notions of Torah and language. These novel conceptions of the canon served in turn to integrate the other substantive innovations of Kabbalah and Jewish philosophy by means of complex hermeneutical systems. The emergence of new notions of Torah and the development of innovative interpretive techniques to expand and open the text enlarged the implications canonicity had for meaning.

Kabbalistic conceptions of the Torah have been discussed by several scholars, among them Gershom Scholem and Moshe Idel, in various thorough works on kabbalistic hermeneutics.[36] Within the Maimonidean tradition interpretation also received a thorough analysis.[37] A detailed account of the fascinating history of hermeneutics within these two movements is beyond the scope of this work. Instead, I will discuss two classical texts of each school: Maimonides' introduction to *The Guide of the Perplexed* and Nachmanides' introduction to his commentary of the Torah. In discussing the conception of canon of these two outstanding figures of medieval Jewish philosophy and Kabbalah, I endeavor to show how their conceptions opened the text to derive new forms of meaning and also wish to emphasize the connection between secrecy and nonconventional hermeneutics.

Why should a text hide anything, especially if the hidden meaning is the most important, revealing the true nature of God? Maimonides' idea of the necessity of esotericism is grounded in the deep cleavage between the enlightened elite and the ignorant masses. The noncorporeal abstract conception of God could not be disclosed to the masses exoterically, since they cannot grasp a nonmaterial existence. Furthermore, such a conception of God and a naturalistic theology accompanying it would endanger the social order, which depends upon belief in Divine Providence and retribution. A widespread belief in a personal God who rewards the righteous and punishes the wicked is the main motivation for maintaining the basic norms necessary for social stability. An Aristotelian naturalistic theology would be dangerous to the uninitiated.

These political arguments are the core of Maimonides' explanation for the need to conceal a philosophical understanding of God behind the anthropomorphic image presented at the surface of the biblical text. There is another, entirely apolitical explanation of esotericism which Maimonides ties to the elusive and ineffable nature of metaphysical truth. God's essence can be expressed only through indirect hints and allusions. It is not that the surface of the text is a coded message constructed intentionally by the prophets to hide its deeper layer. Rather, it is only the indirect means for expressing what is ineffable. This apolitical conception of esotericism is expressed in Maimonides' introduction to the *Guide* alongside the political argument:

> Know that whenever one of the perfect wishes to mention, either orally or in writing, something that he understands of these secrets, accordingly to the degree of his perfection, he is unable to explain with complete clarity and coherence even the portion that he has apprehended, as he could do with the other sciences whose teaching is generally recognized. Rather there will befall him when teaching another that which he had undergone when learning himself. I mean to say that the subject matter will appear, flash, and then be hidden again, as though this were the nature of this subject matter be there much or little of it. For this reason all the Sages possessing knowledge of God the Lord, knowers of the truth, when they aimed at teaching something of this subject matter, spoke of it only in parables and riddles.[38]

It would seem natural for the idea of the esoteric layer of the text to be connected with the claim that divine language is qualitatively different from ordinary language and thus in need of a nonconventional hermeneutic approach to unlock its meanings. Interestingly, Maimonides, one of the main exponents of the concept of a multilayered Torah, rejects the idea of a divine language. According to him, all languages, including Hebrew, the sacred language, are products of human convention. The sacredness of Hebrew as the language of the Torah does not derive from its unique ontological status as a divine, presocial, cosmic, and natural language, but from its social conventions, such as the lack of names for sexual organs in Hebrew.[39] The hidden layer of the text is thus revealed by conventional features that exist in any language. Maimonides describes the *Guide of the Perplexed* as a hermeneutical text:

> The first purpose of this Treatise is to explain the meanings of certain terms occurring in books of prophecy. Some of these terms are equivocal; hence the ignorant attribute to them only one or some of the meanings in which the term in question is used. Others are derivative terms; hence they attribute to them only the original meaning from which the

other meaning is derived. Others are amphibolous terms, so that at times they are believed to be univocal and at other times equivocal. . .

This Treatise also has a second purpose: namely, the explanation of very obscure parables occurring in the books of the prophets but not explicitly identified there as such. Hence an ignorant or heedless individual might think that they possess only an external sense, but no internal one.

All the terms Maimonides endeavors to explain denote more than one object or concept in the language. The existence of equivocal terms in language is a great source of confusion—among them taking a metaphor literally—especially when the very identification of metaphors demands prior metaphysical knowledge. This is the case with corporeal terms concerning God in the Torah, such as God's hand and many other terms which the ignorant take at face value, claiming that the Torah describes an anthropomorphic, corporeal God. Yet it is principally these equivocal terms and parables that make esotericism possible. Parables and equivocal terms make it possible to address two audiences simultaneously—the enlightened and the ignorant. The enlightened audience grasps the "internal" meaning of the equivocal term and the parable, and the ignorant, its surface. A language lacking equivocal terms—in which every word denotes only one object or concept—would be completely transparent and thus could not be prophetic, since it would be unable to address a heterogeneous community and speak to the two audiences in it. Esotericism is therefore both expressed and uncovered through a conventional feature of language, equivocation, a feature which is an impediment to communication though it has great political uses.[40] In the Maimonidean tradition the idea of the multilayered canon is thus supported by a view of the world that postulates the political and social need for esotericism, the equivocal nature of language which serves as a medium for both revealing and hiding, and a notion of the canon that addresses a heterogeneous community. This outlook deepened and broadened the interpretive possibilities of the Torah. With a detailed hermeneutic project—which reinterprets concepts as metaphors and narratives as allegories—the philosophical religious sensibility was presented as the hidden and deeper meaning of the canon.[41]

In the Kabbalah, in contrast, the idea of the multilayered text is supported by the notion of a presocial, cosmic, divine language which is qualitatively different from conventional language. Unlike the Maimonidean tradition, which regarded language, even the holy language, as a social convention, the kabbalists' view of Torah language enriched the interpretative possibilities to infinity.[42] The question of whether Scripture speaks in a qualitatively different language and hence must be approached with hermeneutic tools not applicable to human speech was debated within rabbinic Midrash from the second century onwards. According to the school of R. Ishmael, the Torah spoke in the language of humans. Thus it used conventional rhetorical devices such as doubling a term or a commandment to emphasize a point. According to R. Akiva, there is no redundancy in the text and any duplication is present in order to teach us something new.[43] Given their conception of Torah language as divine, the kabbalists' hermeneutics is a continuation of the trend of R. Akiva's school.

In his introduction to commentary of the Torah, Nachmanides writes that part of the Mosaic revelation was oral, and it included the knowledge of the whole chain of being from the lowest elements to the knowledge of the divine: "Fifty gates [degrees] of understanding were created in the world and all were transmitted to Moses with one exception, as it is said 'Thou hast made him but little lower [than] the angels.'" The last gate, not given to Moses, is the unknown essence of God. In the next paragraph Nachmanides states:

> Everything that was transmitted to Moses our teacher through the forty-nine gates of understanding was written in the Torah explicitly or by implication in words, in the numerical value of the letters or in the form of the letters, that is, whether written normally or with some change in form such as bent or crooked letters and other deviations, or in the tips of the letters and their crownlets.

The Torah implicitly includes all possible knowledge, and an interpreter armed with the proper hermeneutical key can lay bare those secrets.[44] King Solomon, according to Nachmanides, possessed the keys to such wisdom: "King Solomon, peace be upon him, whom God had given wisdom and knowledge, derived it all from the Torah, and from it he studied until he knew the secret of all things created, even of the forces and characteristics of plants so that he wrote about them even a Book of Medicine." Nachmanides claims that nonconventional hermeneutic devices—the numerical values of letters, the shape of the letters, and so on—are the way to attain knowledge. He justifies his claim on the grounds of the existence of rules and traditions prescribing the detailed forms of each letter in the Torah—including the tips of the letters and their crownlets. Since changes in the shape of letters presumably do not affect the conventional meaning of words, the insistence on particular shapes in writing a Torah scroll is a sign that each of them does make a difference—by conveying a coded message.[45]

Nachmanides develops the idea that the insistence on nonsemantic aspects in the preservation and transmission of the canonical text signifies the need to apply nonconventional hermeneutics to lay bare hidden layers of meaning; this leads him to support a far more radical interpretive kabbalistic tradition:

> We have yet another mystic tradition that the whole Torah is comprised of Names of the Holy One, blessed be He, and that the letters of the words separate themselves into Divine names when divided in a different manner . . . It is for this reason that a Scroll of the Torah in which a mistake has been made in one letter's being added or subtracted is disqualified [even though the literal meaning remains unchanged], for this principle obligates us to disqualify a scroll of the Torah in which one letter *vav* is missing from the word *otam*—of which there are thirty-nine fully spelled ones in the Torah [although the same word appears many times without a *vav*] . . . It is this principle which has caused the Biblical scholars to count every full and defective word in the Torah and Scripture and to compose books on the Masoretic text.

The existence of precise rules prescribing the preservation of particular letters whose addition or deletion does not make any difference in literal meaning supports the radical interpretative possibility that with a different division, the Torah would consist of a sequence of God's names. The existing division of words becomes only one possible reading of the text. The reason every letter in the present form of the Torah is prescribed, even those which make no difference in meaning, is that they would make a difference if the division into words were different. The interpretative potential of the text is extended significantly by the argument that other meanings can be drawn from the text by changing the division of the letters into words. In his own writings Nachmanides never practiced such a technique, but the enormous potential embodied in the deconstruction of the sequence of letters in the text was practiced in a radical fashion by Abraham Abulafia one generation after Nachmanides.[46] Nachmanides adds to the word-division notion the idea that the Torah in its original form, prior to the creation of the world, was written in an uninterrupted sequence, not divided into words, and this sequence is one long name of God. In its hidden primordial form, the Torah is a manifestation of God's essence, his name, which was turned into communicative revelation through certain ordering of letters into words.

Nachmanides' argument reveals an interesting reciprocal tension between consolidation of the canonical text and radical hermeneutical openness. The strict canonization of the Torah—not only its precise words in their proper sequence but also variations in shapes of letter, crownlets, and the addition or deletion of letters which make no literal difference—are taken as expanding the hermeneutical possibilities. Shapes of letters and their numerical values become bearers of meaning, and therefore the semantic field of the text is extended far beyond its straightforward surface meaning. Paradoxically, the canonical text, because it has been fixed to the last detail, becomes saturated with signifiers which, in principle, contain all knowledge—divine and natural.

The extension of the possibility of signification is accompanied by another paradoxical move in Nachmanides' introduction. According to him, the Torah in its primary condition, before it became a particular sequence of words, was a long name of God and therefore signified only one thing—God. The magnitude of signification of the Torah in its present form, which includes all knowledge, is reduced in the deeper primary level of the text to one object. It can even be said that in its deepest layer the text loses all its semantic quality, since God's name has no ordinary referential function. The name is a direct manifestation of God, and, in some kabbalistic traditions, identical with God. It is no accident that Nachmanides alludes to the magical uses of God's names that are hidden in the text, since they themselves bear divine powers.

This connection between Torah and God informs other esoteric conceptions of the Torah in which the surface serves as a complex symbolic language reflecting God's dynamic aspects—the *sefirot*. The conception of the Torah as a direct symbolic manifestation of God's inner life, sometimes as identical with God, provides a ground for esotericism vastly different from the one offered by Maimonides. Kabbalistic conceptions of esotericism are not political, and the hidden layer of the text is not an intentionally obscure message. It is a direct reflection of God's hidden, ineffable nature, to which one can only allude indirectly through a complex, symbolic language.

The rise of esotericism in the Middle Ages and the growing tendency to use nonconventional modes of interpretation, supported by innovative conceptions of the Torah, were the background for the introduction of two powerful world views into the canon—the philosophical and the kabbalistic. The complex hermeneutical endeavor, reflected in hundreds of commentaries written at the time, attests to a paradoxical situation in which the solid, authoritative, fixed canon came to be reinterpreted in a most radical fashion. Framing a text as canonical and, in our case, as divinely revealed opens hermeneutical possibilities that threaten to erode its "original" and straightforward core.

ᛞ UNCHARITABLE READINGS OF CANONS

Texts are given readings varying from a minimal degree of charity, which implies the effort to make sense, to the extreme charity that is typical of the reading of canonized texts. Loss of charity in its primary sense is a form of decanonization of the text. But there is a deeper version of decanonization which is intimately connected to the withdrawal of charity and may be called the principle of uncharity.

Paradoxically again, canonized works can elicit a radically uncharitable reading. "Uncharitable" here is not meant in Quine's sense of reading utterances uncharitably as meaningless; rather, the text is unmasked, as it is a conspiratorial device that conceals meaning. In this reading the canonical text makes perfect sense, but the sense it makes is in the service of an unjust cause.

One of the most fascinating cases of the principle of uncharity is the Gnostic reading of the Bible as a text given by a demiurge with evil intentions. The Gnostics believed that the power that created the universe was a demiurge—an evil god. A benevolent god is alien to this world, and the *gnosis* (knowledge) of his redemptive existence is the message of the believers. One of the many Gnostic groups active during the second century, followers of Marcion, identified the demiurge with the God of Israel, the giver of the Torah. This Christian Gnostic sect believed that some sections of the New Testament did constitute the revelation of the true benevolent God, while the rest of Scripture ought to be screened and condemned as the work of the demiurge.[47] The good God, according to the Gnostic text "The Testimony of Baruch," sent his angel Baruch to Moses bearing the good laws: "Baruch was now sent to Moses, and through him he spoke to the children of Israel that they should turn to the Good. But the third angel (in service of the demiurge), through the soul which since Eden dwells in Moses as also in all men, darkened the commandments of Baruch and brought it about that they should listen to his own."[48] The good God tried to reveal laws of righteousness to Moses, but the demiurge had control of the human soul so he distorted the righteous laws and darkened the commandments. Therefore the laws of Moses did not come from the good God.

Gnosticism was by no mean a unified phenomenon; it took many shapes and forms. It existed in both Jewish and Christian variants and had its followers within the Hellenistic pagan culture. Both in its Jewish and Christian forms Gnosticism developed a close and complex relationship to the Bible, and the plurality of Gnostic outlooks is manifested in the relationships of Gnostic texts to the Bible, which vary from total rejection to full acceptance.[49] Here I will focus on the rejectionists.

The Gnostic rejection of the world and its religious authorities and beliefs produced the most uncharitable reading of the Bible, the same Bible that was most charitably read by Christian and Jews alike. The Gnostic readings postulate an evil God-creator who gave the Torah to mankind as another shrewd device for its torment. It is the task of the Gnostic, he who has the knowledge of the supreme, benevolent, true, hidden, and alien God, to unmask the evil nature of the demiurge and expose his revelation. The manner in which the text is read is the polar opposite of the Jewish reading. The creation myth in Genesis, as unmasked by the Gnostics, reveals the true creation. In the story of the expulsion of Adam and Eve from Eden, the good character of the story is the serpent who wanted Adam and Eve to have knowledge of good and evil for their own benefit. Hence he advised them to eat from the Tree of Knowledge, while the demiurge deprived them of that benefit out of sheer jealousy. The Gnostics offered many explanations of how the demiurge was created out of the good God, but that is less relevant to our discussion than the creation of the world by this demiurge, a story that is heavily based on a negative reading of Genesis.[50]

After the demiurge himself was created and in his turn created a host of subsidiary powers, he realized that there is a superior god that endangers his existence. (According to some Gnostic sources, the demiurge became aware of God's existence when he saw God's beautiful image reflected on the water.) The demiurge wanted to enslave the righteous God (called Adam of Light) by creating a man in God's image and controlling him—in effect, using man as hostage since he bears God's likeness. The verse "Let us make an Adam in our image and likeness," which in Genesis refers to God's announcement of the creation of man, is interpreted in a Gnostic text as a conspiratorial plan offered by the demiurge to his angels:

> Yes, if you do not want him [the good God Adam of Light] to be able to ruin our work, come let us create a man out of earth according to the image of our body and according to the likeness of this being [that is, Adam of Light] to serve us; so that when he [Adam of Light] sees his likeness he might become enamored of it. No longer will he ruin our work; rather we shall make those who are born out of the light our servants.

The Gnostic reader focuses on the plural tense that appears in the biblical verse (Gen. 1:26) in which God says, "We shall make." The plural form is a sign of deliberate conspiracy, something invented and carried out by a group. The same plural pronoun also troubled other readers—charitable readers. The Midrash understood the plural as implying that God consulted with the angels in the creation of Adam. This consultation was interpreted as a lesson to future generations that even the great must seek advice from the humble. The plural subject that the Gnostics took as a sign of conspiracy is read by the charitable reader as a sign of humility on the part of God.[51]

The continuation of the creation story, according to this Gnostic document, is a series of conspiratorial acts carried out by the demiurge and his council, though they do not realize that the benevolent God turns every plan against the conspirators. The attacks and counterattacks by the good God are modeled according to the Biblical story, but with a revised evaluation. The Adam of Light, the benevolent God, sends Eve to rescue man after he was created by the demiurge; she gives life to Adam, who describes her as Mother of all living creatures. The demiurge, realizing that Eve is working against him, tries to defile her. To defend herself, Eve forges another image in her likeness, then she hides and becomes the Tree of Knowledge. The story goes on: "Then the seven of them together laid plans. They came up to Adam and Eve timidly: they said to him, 'the fruit of all the trees created for you in Paradise shall be eaten; but for the tree of knowledge, control your-

selves and do not eat from it. If you eat, you will die.'" At this moment
appears the serpent, the good adviser: "Then came the wisest of all creatures, who is called Beast. And when he saw the likeness of their mother
Eve and he said to her . . ." The serpent's speech from the Genesis story
is repeated here word by word until the last sentence, which makes all
the difference: "Indeed it was in jealousy that he said this to you, so
that you would not eat from it." In the Gnostic transvaluation, the two
characters who in the Bible are the cause of Adam's disobedience, Eve
and the serpent, are described as good instructors who are sent to rescue
Adam from the jealousy of the demiurge—the biblical God.

The expulsion from Eden is described in the same conspiratorial
mode: "Behold, Adam has come to be like one of us, so that he knows
the difference between the light and the darkness. Now perhaps he will
be deceived as in the case of the tree of knowledge and also will come
to the tree of life and eat from it and become immortal and become
lord and despise us and disdain us and all our glory. Then he will
denounce us along with our universe, come let us expel him from Paradise."[52] The devaluation continues across biblical sacred history. A
denunciation of biblical heroes appears in the Gnostic text "The Second
Treatise of the Great Seth":

> For Adam was a laughingstock since he was made a counterfeit type of
> man . . . And Abraham and Isaac and Jacob were a laughingstock since
> they, the counterfeit fathers, were given a name by the Hebdomad . . .
> Moses a faithful servant, was a laughingstock, having been named "the
> Friend," since they perversely bore witness concerning him who never
> knew me. . . . For the Archon (the Demiurge) was a laughingstock
> because he said: "I am God, and there is none greater than I."[53]

To use Nietzsche's term, this is a total transvaluation of values: what
the demiurge represents as worthy and good is exposed as bad. The
Gnostic reading thoroughly decanonizes the text. Instead of assuming
a charitable attitude towards the canon, the Gnostics adopt an extreme
uncharitable reading of it and make of it a religious obligation. From
a hermeneutical point of view, the relativism created by the shift of
perspective is fantastic. The identical text, read with radically opposing
attitudes, yields opposite meanings, yet both are coherent and the text
seems to contain them both. One reading gives us a text that is a sacred
gift from a benevolent God, while the other reads in the text a whole-
sale conspiracy of the demiurge.

The Gnostics seize upon a deep ambivalence in the biblical text: God creates Adam in his likeness yet prohibits him from becoming like God; this ambivalence gives rise to two different and opposing evaluations. In one of the most powerful passages from a Gnostic tract, "The Testimony of Truth," the author formulates the problem in the boldest possible terms:

> But of what sort is this God? First he maliciously refused Adam from eating of the tree of knowledge. And secondly he said, "Adam where are you?" God does not have foreknowledge; otherwise would he not know from the beginning? And afterwards he said, "Let us cast him out of this place, lest he eat of the tree of life and live forever." Surely he has shown himself to be a malicious grudge. And what kind of a God is this? For great is the blindness of those who read and they did not know him. And he said "I am the jealous God; I will bring the sins of the fathers upon the children until three and four generations." And he said, "I will make their heart thick and I will cause their mind to become blind that they might not know nor comprehend the things that are said." But these things he has said to those who believe in him and serve him.[54]

An interesting twist on the theme of jealousy was brought out in a passage from the Secret Book of John: "And when he saw the creation which surrounds him and the multitudes of angels around him which had come forth from him, he said to them, 'I am a jealous God, and there is no other God beside me.' But by announcing this he indicated to the angels that another God does exist; for if there were no other one, of whom would he be jealous?"[55] Modern biblical criticism, with all its loss of charity toward the sacred text, is mild compared to this ancient criticism and decanonization.

Since canonization determines the function of texts and affects the expectations of the community of readers, it has great impact not only on the status of texts but on their meaning. There is an interesting asymmetrical relation between canonization and hermeneutical openness. The more canonized the text, the broader interpretative possibilities it offers.

Authority, Controversy, and Tradition

ஃ AUTHORIAL INTENTION AND AUTHORITATIVE MEANING

The Mishnah, edited at the end of the second century by Rabbi Yehudah the Prince, is the first canon of its kind known to us, a canon that transmits the tradition in the form of controversy: the House (school) of Shammai said one thing, the House of Hillel said another, and so on. Some of the best modern scholars of the Mishnah are puzzled by its form. Is it an anthology of various opinions voiced by the rabbis, a legal code that includes dissenting opinions, or something in between?[1] By contrast, in the earlier canon, the Bible, debates are either repressed, concealed, or harmonized. There are different legal codes and they do disagree on some matters, but the Bible does not present them in opposition, saying for instance that P (the priestly code) advanced a certain argument while D (the Deuteronomist) disagreed. The same is true of postbiblical writings composed before the Mishnah. The Dead Sea Scrolls, for example, advance different opinions with never a canonization of two opinions side by side.

Ordinarily, canonical texts do not merely record existing traditions of a given period. They select and censor in order to create an authoritative body out of contending candidates. The Mishnah therefore, in its codification of controversy, represents a definite break with the pattern of canonization, choosing neither to censor minority opinions nor to harmonize them within the rest of the material. It is important to examine this deviation, especially if the assumption is correct that such an act is internally connected to every canonization.

The Karaite movement, which developed in the eighth century, denied the authority of the Mishnah. One of its main arguments against that tractate, advanced by Salomon Ben Jeroham in a vehement polemical work, focused on the peculiar nature of controversy in the Mishnah as a sign of its nonauthenticity:

> I have set the six divisions of the Mishnah before me. And I looked at them carefully with mine eyes. And I saw that they are very contradictory in content. This one mishnaic scholar declares a thing to be forbidden to the people of Israel, while that one declares it to be permitted. My thoughts therefore answer me, and most of my reflections declare unto me, that there is in it no Law of logic nor the Law of Moses the Wise.[2]

If the Mishnah is the interpretation of the Torah it must be trustworthy, which becomes problematic when contradictory interpretations are presented alongside one another. What is the hermeneutical conception that enabled the Mishnah's mode of canonization, and how does the canonization of controversies relate to the problem of truth in interpretation, especially when the word of God is concerned? If the Mishnah is based on an Oral Torah handed to Moses at Sinai and carried through a chain of sages, how did controversies evolve?

The peculiar and original form of the Mishnah as a canon gave rise to a variety of different and opposing conceptions of controversy, authority, and interpretation within subsequent rabbinic material. Among them we find an innovative attitude to the Torah as a canon based on a new approach to the Author's intention and to the proper way of discerning that intention; they produced the Mishnah's unique form. But before analyzing different approaches to the issue within the rabbinic material, I will introduce a conceptual argument concerning the problem of the author's intention and its status in the canon to illustrate the depth of the issue at stake.

The question of what exactly becomes canonized in a text was discussed in the introduction. One central claim is that the canon embodies the original intention of the author. This is the view expressed by some constitutional theorists, who argue that the authoritative meaning of the Constitution is the Framers' intention and nothing else.[3] The argument derives from a general conception of interpretation and meaning: thus E. D. Hirsch, for instance, contends that only the search for the author's intention can count as a genuine interpretation. Meaning is conceptually connected to intention, and the author's intention is the only valid criterion for judging between true and false readings.[4]

Such a general conception of meaning has been a target for much of modern philosophy. Critics point out that someone may intend to say something, yet according to the socially accepted conventions of language says something else. What then is the meaning of what was said? The very possibility of this occurring shows that meaning can be independent of the speaker's intentions and itself depend on social linguistic conventions.To pursue this point deeper, the speaker's own ability to express his intention depends on his mastering the conventional uses of language. This argument undermines the idea of priority of intention as something that precedes conventional rules of linguistic meaning.[5]

More interesting than the issue of intention and meaning is, for my purpose,the question of authority and intention. The argument is as follows. Even if the text has many meanings, and some of them are totally detached from the author's intention, the author's intention is what gives authority to the canon. The question is not what counts as an "interpretation," but which interpretation is faithful to the expression of authority. For example, in a system that obligates us to heed what our parents command, their intentions embodied in a written will are authoritative, and not the possible readings of the will. There is no specific obligation to obey parents' wills, but there is a general obligation to respect their wishes, and in this case those wishes took a written form. The same is true in the case of a canonical text. What is canonized, that is, what is authoritative, is an expression of will embodied in a written text.

In this version the authority of the text is intrinsically connected to the authoritative meaning that is its justification. If the authority of the text is claimed to derive from its source—the will of a legislator or some other superior will—then the canonized meaning is the intention of that will embodied in a text. In this view, canonical texts do not have authority as such; rather, they have authority insofar as they bear and express the author's voice.[6]

The argument for the exclusive canonicity of the writer's intention is especially strong when the text's authority derives from an appeal to a unique source. If the authority of the parent's will derives from its author's authority to command, then the text is simply a medium of expression of that authority. The authority of the text may be founded on an appeal to other claims, however, such as that proper procedure was followed its formation, or that it has intrinsic value; in those cases the detachment of authorial intention from the text's authoritative meaning could be defended. Interestingly, in the case of Scripture, where the authority of the text is grounded upon the appeal to its source and therefore should naturally be conceived as a pure medium, we can discern a trend among the options of rabbinic self-understanding which in fact detaches authoritative meaning from authorial intent. To enlarge upon this point it is necessary to make an additional distinction, between text as a medium for authority and text as authorized by authority.

OVEN
or
AKHNAI

A well-known story in the Talmud reports a controversy between Rabbi Eliezer and Rabbi Yehoshua.[7] After each side exhausted its arsenal of arguments with little success, and after attempts to adduce miracles and countermiracles as signs of vindication, Rabbi Eliezer appealed to God to intervene on his behalf. A voice immediately issued from heaven and ruled in favor of Rabbi Eliezer. In response Rabbi Yehoshua made a counterargument reminding God that He had said in the Torah itself that the Torah "is not in heaven," and, moreover, that "the majority should be followed." This argument can be read in two ways. The more moderate reading is that although R. Yehoshua rejected God's intervention, he agreed that God's intention is decisive. However, R. Yehoshua argued that prophecy offers unreliable access God's intention, since there is no clear criterion for the authenticity of prophets. Hence God's original intent can be reached only through the deliberation of the Sages. There is an even more radical reading, in which R. Yehoshua's argument is seen as implying that God had authorized the Torah as an independent text, divorced from his intention, and his own subsequent intervention in interpreting his own text would be prohibited. Thus the Torah is not the direct medium of expression of God's authority but rather an authorized text.

In his argument R. Yehoshua appealed to a higher-order intention of the source of the text's authority, independent of God's "personal" authorial intention. This higher-order intention was derived from the text itself, and the end of the talmudic story is that God acceded to Yehoshua's argument and agreed that the majority should be followed regardless of his "personal" intervention in the matter.

The Talmud relates that R. Nathan asked Elijah the prophet how God reacted when he heard the argument of R. Yehoshua, and Elijah replied that God smiled and said: "My sons have defeated me, my sons have defeated me." By conceiving the text not as the medium of authorial authority but as an authorized text, the Author's intention is detached from the text's authoritative meaning. Returning to the analogy of parents and their authority, in this position the Torah is like a text that parents have commanded their children to follow the way it is understood. They authorize the text rather than command through it.[8]

This is a broader conception of sealing than that discussed in Chapter 1. The sealing of Scripture serves not only to prohibit prophecy from adding material to Scripture; it also restricts prophecy as a mode of interpreting existing texts. The intimate access to the Author's intention achieved by a prophet cannot sanction him or her as the authoritative interpreter. If the Author's intention is not relevant to the interpretation of the Torah, then a prophet gains nothing by asking the Author to explain and determine the meaning of the text. The detachment of the authorized meaning from the Author's intention affects the nature of the authoritative interpreter's claim; prophetic access to intention does not legitimize an interpreter. A common and daring theme in the Midrash is that God studies the rabbis' interpretations of the Torah. Because the text is autonomous, its meaning unfolds through constant interpretations, and the Author himself must study and follow those interpretations in order to understand the future meanings of the text.[9]

This strong conception of sealing stands in radical opposition to that of the Dead Sea Scrolls (first century B.C.). In those texts divine inspiration is considered necessary for the interpretation of Scripture and serves as the very ground for the interpreter's authority. The interpreter here is an inspired reader, a person endowed with unique abilities to discover the "solution" *(pesher)* of the text's meaning, whereas the mainstream of the rabbinic tradition rejected prophecy as the ground for the interpreter's authority.[10]

These radically different conceptions of the authoritative meaning and the authoritative interpreter coexist, and both are open to dispute. Prophets may disagree with one another, and, indeed, disputes among prophets appear in the Bible. These are presented as disputes between true and false prophets. However, when prophecy is no longer the sole ground for interpretation, controversy among interpreters can become canonical. The revolution that detached authoritative meaning from authorial intention, thus making intimate access to the God's intention irrelevant to interpretation, engendered the canonization of controversy. The older, Dead Sea material acknowledges the continued authority of prophets and does not provide two opinions side by side, attributing one to Rabbi X and the other to Rabbi Y as in the Mishnah. But with the sealing of the prophetic voice in rabbinic Judaism, the Jewish canonized text acquires one of its striking features: the codification of controversy.

∾ CANON AND CONTROVERSY

The break between authoritative meaning and intimate access to the Author's intention is crucial to the possibility of controversy and therefore to the unique form the Mishnah took as a canon. The rise of the interpreter-scholar permitted codification of controversies without undermining the authority of the canon. Nevertheless, the question of what motivated the transmission of the tradition in such an innovative and peculiar way remains open.

This question must be qualified. Although the Mishnah is full of controversies, these controversies do not cover the full range of debate in Jewish life in that period. The Mishnah includes some controversies in the tradition but excludes others. Out of the radical plurality of Jewish sectarianism at the time, the Mishnah forms a canon composed of internal debates that arose within a particular sect. Absent are the Christian Jews of the time, the Gnostic Jews, the Essenes, the Zadokites. All of these movements had a definite relationship to the Bible, but they are not mentioned in the Mishnah as legitimate parties to the debate. The variety of Jewish cultures during the first two centuries of the common era is nearly inconceivable, yet many of these voices are absent from the Mishnah.[11] The various sects definitely rejected one another, for some of the differences between them made coexistence within a single tradition almost impossible. For example, the Dead Sea community rejected the rabbinic lunar calendar. As the two sects had no common calendar, cooperation in a unified community was clearly impossible.[12] The range of internal debate among the rabbis themselves is more restricted, but it sometimes reaches a degree that in other communities would have caused a radical schism. Disagreement about marriage and divorce laws is a case in point. The Mishnah reports cases in which, according to the House of Hillel, a woman was considered still married, while according to the House of Shammai she was considered divorced, or vice versa. Such disagreements threaten marriage contracts among people on opposite sides and could result in separation into two communities.[13] An analogous discrepancy in ruling exists in Jewish life today, and the Orthodox in Israel use it as an argument for retaining the monopoly of the official rabbinate on marriage and divorce. But in the Mishnah, disagreements about marriage rules are presented side by side. The Mishnah reports that these disagreements did not cause a schism between the houses of Shammai and Hillel, and their adherents intermarried freely. So the question remains: why is the tradition not presented in unified form in the Mishnah?

In a rare moment of self-reflection about the nature of the canon incorporated in the Mishnah, the rabbis engage in a disputation about over why disputes occur in the Mishnah: a controversy about controversy. In Tractate *Eduyot*, after listing the disagreements between Shammai and Hillel, a general question is raised about Mishnah's editorial policy: "And why do they record the opinion of the individual against that of the majority, whereas the Halakhah [the law] may be only according to the opinion of the majority? So that if a court approves the opinion of the individual it may rely upon him, since a court cannot annul the opinion of another court unless it exceeds it both in wisdom and in number."

The minority's opinion is preserved in the canonical transmission of tradition because, while not valid in the present, a future court may rely on this opinion and rule against the present majority. Thus the dissenting opinion is preserved in the corpus as an option that could be revived.

On the other hand, "R. Yehudah said: 'If so, why do they record the opinion of the individual against that of the majority when it does not prevail?' So that if one shall say, 'I have received such a tradition,' another may answer, 'Thou didst hear it [only] as the opinion of such-a-one.'" In this view a rejected individual opinion is preserved in order to prevent someone from reviving it with the claim that it is an autonomous and legitimate variant tradition. Documented as a minority view, the dissenting opinion is rejected in law forever.

We have, then, two opposing explanations for the practice of canonizing controversies in the Mishnah: one, that codifying minority
rulings preserves them as future options; two, that the dissenting view
is recorded so that another such opinion would be suppressed if it ever
arose again in the future. Documenting the losing side may have opposite effects: either it keeps the loser alive or it eternalizes him as the
loser.[14] Interestingly, the editor of the Mishnah presented the second
opinion as a minority opinion in the name of Rabbi Yehudah, whereas
the opinion that perceives the Mishnah as a flexible code was presented
as a majority opinion. The editor thus created a kind of a circular
paradox: according to the majority view, minority opinions were mentioned in the Mishnah so that they could be revived in the future;
whereas in the eyes of the minority, minority opinions were mentioned
so they could be rejected forever. None of the opinions presented in
the debate over the status of minority opinions in the Mishnah considers the Mishnah to be a mere selective anthology of diverse rab-
binical opinions. Both sides agree that the Mishnah is a code, and its
editor rules anonymously in favor of one party. The debate between
the majority in Mishnah of *Eduyot* and R. Yehudah is whether the
Mishnah is a flexible code which preserves minority opinion for a future
recall against its own ruling, or whether it is a closed code which preserves the minority opinion in order to freeze the rejection forever.
This controversy over controversy and over the nature of Mishnah as
a canon has enormous legal implications. Can a future court rely on
minority opinions in the Mishnah in order to diverge from the
Mishnah's own rulings, or not? It is fascinating that while the editor
of our Mishnah ruled that it is a flexible and tentative code, the editor
of the *Tosefta* ruled that it is a closed code. In the *Tosefta* the view that
the Mishnah is a flexible code is attributed to R. Yehudah and thus
stated as the minority opinion,[15] and the view that minority opinions
are mentioned only to be rejected is considered the majority view. We
are confronted with two radically different traditions over the nature
of controversy, and with two different traditions of ruling between
them.

Controversy pervades the canon concerning the function of canonizing disputes. While the tradition acknowledges that fact, it still needs
to explain it. Reflection on this question led the rabbis to divergent
views. One tendency saw controversy as a sign of deterioration: neglect
and irresponsibility had caused the diversity of tradition, which had

not been preserved in its purity and would have to be reconstructed carefully and preserved. "Said R. Yosef: 'At first there were no disputes in Israel. . . . Once the disciples of Shammai and Hillel who did not adequately serve their master became many, disputes multiplied in Israel, and they became two Torahs.' "[16]

The rabbis offered a different explanation. Controversy is not a sign of the downfall of tradition or of distance from the moment of receiving it; rather, it is part of the tradition, projected backward to the moment of revelation. In a striking passage that seems to anticipate the complaint of the Karaite Salmon Ben Jeroham, the rabbis present a different view of controversy:

> A man might think, "Since the House of Shammai declare unclean and the House of Hillel clean, this one prohibits and that one permits, why should I henceforward learn Torah?" Scripture says, "Words . . . the words . . . These are the words. . . ." All the words have been given by a single Shepherd, one God created them, one Provider gave them, the Lord of all deeds, blessed be He, has spoken them. So you build many chambers in your heart and bring into it the words of the House of Shammai and the words of the House of Hillel, the words of those who declare unclean and the words of those who declare clean.[17]

To secure tradition from the danger of error, even lacking clear knowledge of who is mistaken, revelation is portrayed as not fully determined. God gave the Torah with one reading and with the opposite one as well. No specific reading borne by tradition is the authorized one. Multiplicity in the tradition reflects the very nature of the canon as a text with many meanings. The search for the single authorial intention is futile because the text was intentionally given many meanings; the tradition reflects this fact, as does the work of selecting one certain meaning from among the many.[18]

> Said R. Yannai, "If the Torah were handed down cut and dried, we would not have a leg to stand on. What is the Scriptural basis for that statement? [It is] 'And the Lord spoke to Moses . . .' Moses said to Him: 'Lord of the World, teach me the law.' He said to him, 'follow the majority [to decide the law].' If the majority finds the accused innocent, find him innocent; if guilty, find him guilty. So the Torah may be expounded in forty-nine ways siding with a decision on uncleanness and in forty-nine ways favoring a decision of cleanness."[19]

The uniqueness of the Mishnah as a flexible code is made possible by
a new concept of multiple revelation, and by an innovative conception
of authoritative meaning and authorized interpreter.

The tension inherent in these two short passages describing controversy—one as decline caused by neglect, and the other as a mark of
open-ended revelation—was developed by medieval halakhists into several elaborate and radically opposite accounts of controversy and its
relations to tradition. Each approach took one of the contrasting
accounts in the talmudic material as its paradigm and developed a picture of controversy and tradition with far-reaching importance to the
understanding of authority and interpretation. Each began with a different historical explanation for the presence of controversy in the
Mishnah. Our analysis will focus on three divergent historical explanations: that of Abraham Ibn Daud, a twelfth-century Andalusian
thinker who follows a Geonic tradition; that of Maimonides, who differs with this tradition in major respects; and that of Nachmanides,
who does not offer a complete account of the problem but makes some
important comments leading in a new direction that was developed
further by his students.

ઝ⊷ THREE VIEWS ON CONTROVERSY AND TRADITION

Retrieval

The view I call the "retrieval model" was espoused by Abraham Ibn
Daud, who follows a long tradition among the Geonim. In it the
halakhic process is understood as the transmission from generation to
generation of an orally revealed body of Halakhah. Moses received the
entire Law, both written and oral, and at its source it was complete
and perfect. All of the Halakhah was then transmitted to us through
a continuous chain of scholars. Over time, due to forgetfulness and
carelessness (and also to harsh political circumstances), this knowledge
began to erode. Halakhic reasoning therefore became essential, not
merely to organize, justify, and transmit given knowledge, but as a
vital tool in the desperate attempt to reconstruct, through argumentation, the lost portions of a once complete body of knowledge. The
main advantage of such a view lies in the elimination of human creativity from the halakhic process, and the grounding of the oral Law
in God's revelation. From that perspective, there is no difference

between the sources of authority—both the oral and the written Torah are founded on direct revelation.[20] It is no wonder that anti-Karaite polemics gave rise to some of the most important articulations of this picture.[21]

This view of the history of halakhic knowledge also informs the project of writing a history of Halakhah. Such an undertaking is meant to establish the chain of transmission as uninterrupted from Moses to the author's own days, thus pursuing the present Halakhah to its source and grounding it in God's revelation to Moses. This aim is addressed in the programmatic statement made by Abraham Ibn Daud in his introduction to *Sefer ha-Kabbalah*:

> The purpose of this Book of Tradition is to provide students with the evidence that all the teachings of our rabbis of blessed memory, namely, the sages of the Mishnah and the Talmud, have been transmitted: each great sage and righteous man having received them from a great sage and righteous man, each head of an academy and his school having received them from the head of an academy and his school, as far back as the men of the Great Assembly, who received them from the prophets, of blessed memory all. Never did the sages of the Talmud, and certainly not the sages of the Mishnah, teach anything, however trivial, of their own invention, except for the enactments which were made by universal agreement in order to make a hedge around the Torah.

Sefer ha-Kabbalah seeks to establish the chain of transmission beyond any doubt and to prove that, aside from some *takanot* (rabbinic enactments), there is no human component in the Mishnah and Talmud. Ibn Daud's view is certainly connected to anti-Karaite polemics and continues a long trend in Geonic writings characterized by a shared view of the history of the Halakhah, the purpose of which is to attest to the unbroken chain of transmission. R. Shrira, the leading Gaon of the tenth century, structured his history of Halakhah on the same model, although his account goes beyond the mere mention of the links in the chain of tradition.

A question posed to R. Shrira Gaon by the North African community of Kiruan articulates the divisive issue. The sticking points are the overwhelming presence of R. Akiva's students in the Mishnah and the fact that the Mishnah was written as late as R. Yehudah the Prince, which would seem to support the Karaite challenge that the Mishnah is a late invention of the rabbis. In short, if the Mishnah is a received

tradition, why did the early Sages leave so much of the task of formu-
lating and presenting it to later generations? In his response, R. Shrira
Gaon cannot merely affirm the chain of transmission. He must address
the serious Karaite challenge to his view. The model he proposes is
thus complex. Although he adheres to the conviction already voiced
by Sa'adia that the Mishnah is a received tradition,[22] he claims that the
particular *halakhot* were ordered and formulated in different versions
by different schools and that R. Yehudah the Prince based his Mishnah
on R. Akiva's version. The *halakhot* taught by the various Sages were
essentially identical, but each had his own manner of presenting and
ordering them. The presence of Akiva's students in the Mishnah is not
a proof that the *halakhot* are their own invention but rather that their
version of the Mishnah serves as the basis of R. Yehuda's Mishnah.
According to R. Shrira Gaon, there is a human component to the oral
tradition of Halakhah, but this component affects only the wording of
the laws and the method of their organization, not their content.[23] By
modifying the strict notion of tradition, R. Shrira was able to explain
the preponderance of relatively late generations in the Mishnah.[24]

The main weakness of this model is the presence of controversy
within the body of Halakhah. For if Halakhah is independent of the
fluctuations of human legal reasoning, which naturally produce controversy, why are there controversies in the Mishnah and Talmud? Ibn
Daud raises this problem and explains that neglect at one point in the
chain gave rise to controversy:

> Now should anyone infected with heresy attempt to mislead you, saying:
> "It is because the rabbis differed on a number of issues that I doubt their
> words," you should retort bluntly and inform him that he is "a rebel
> against the decision of the court"; and that our rabbis of blessed memory
> never differed with respect to a commandment in principle, but only
> with respect to its detail; for they had heard the principle from their
> teachers, but had not inquired as to its details since they had not waited
> upon their masters sufficiently. As a case in point they did not differ as
> to whether or not it is obligatory to light the Sabbath lamp; what they
> did dispute was "with what it may be lighted and with what it may not
> be lighted." Similarly, they did not differ as to whether we are required
> to recite the Shema evenings and mornings; what they differed on was
> "from when may the Shema be recited in the evenings" and "from when
> may the Shema be recited in the mornings". This holds true of all of
> their discussions.[25]

In other words, Ibn Daud argues, all halakhic knowledge was available and explicit in the earliest stages of tradition, but certain students failed to clarify the complete details of all the rules with their teachers, and they are to blame for the crisis in the transmission of tradition and for the rise of controversy. Thereafter interpretation and halakhic reasoning evolved as an attempt to recover a body of knowledge lost because of students' neglect.

The presence of controversy obligates authors who advance the retrieval model to acknowledge that a crisis has occurred within the chain of transmission, and this poses an implicit danger to their position, for it casts doubt upon the credibility of the entire process of transmission. If neglect and forgetfulness could erode a given body of knowledge passed down from Moses, what guarantees the credibility of the core of tradition itself? Hence these authors tend to minimize the extent of controversy within the Mishnah in order to preserve the credibility of the chain of transmission. Ibn Daud claims that no controversy exists concerning the main body of Halakhah: "Our rabbis of blessed memory never differed with respect to a commandment in principle, but only with respect to its detail."

The version of the history of Halakhah presented by the Geonim recurs. In the second half of the seventeenth century, David Nieto's *Mateh Dan (ha-Kuzari ha-Sheni)* repeats the main elements of Ibn Daud's account. Nieto offers the same explanation for the talmudic passage which accounts for the emergence of controversy:

> When the disciples of Shammai and Hillel who had studied insufficiently increased in number, disputes multiplied in Israel and "the Torah became as two Torot" (T.B. *Sanhedrin* 88b). "They studied insufficiently," that is, they did not stay with their teachers long enough to receive the interpretation of the principles and thus controversy emerged." (p. 63)

An innovative element in Nieto's account—although it follows naturally from the internal logic of the scenario—is his conception of the authority of the ancients. To him early generations of Sages are more authoritative than the Sages of later generations because of their proximity to the first stages of the transmission, before the process of erosion accelerated. Nieto explicitly rejects the argument of the sixteenth-century scholar R. Joseph Karo that the authority of the Mishnah stems from the legally binding agreement made by the Amoraim not to argue with the Tanaim.[26] He contends instead that "since they [the Amoraim] thought that all the words of the Tanaim are received [*kabbalah*] and because the Tanaim had received them from earlier generations, there was no controversy in what they said" (*ha-Kuzari ha-Sheni*, p. 67).[27]

The retrieval model also maintains that the biblical text is only canonical insofar as it is mediated by a specific tradition. In the legal sphere, an analogy to such canonization is the claim that a court must take the Constitution into account with all its interpretation by previous courts, thus narrowing and controlling the way the text will be approached by future courts and limiting the freedom caused by the indeterminacy of the text. In the religious realm, this approach to shielding the canon is not confined to the rabbinic claims regarding the oral Law. The authority of tradition has often been invoked against arguments based on direct consultation of the text. The Church Fathers employed the authority of tradition against heretics, and the Catholics did the same against the Reformation's direct appeal to the text. Newman, who discovered tradition and converted to Catholicism, asserts that "a traditionary system of theology, consistent with but independent of Scripture, has existed in the Church from the Apostolic age."[28]

The community is bound to the text and to the tradition to which it is central. Those who challenge this tradition form a different community. A historical example of such a challenge to the mediating authority of the Jewish tradition was the Karaite schism. The Karaite ideology, which began in the eighth century, denied the oral tradition and rejected the Talmud. The Karaites called for individual responsibility in interpreting the Bible, which they regarded as the only recognized authoritative source. Karaite scholar Sahl ben Masliah, writing in the second half of the tenth century, states it as follows:

> Know, O our brethren, the children of Israel, that each one of us is responsible for his own soul. . . . Know that he who justifies himself by saying: "I have walked in the way of my fathers," will gain nothing by it, for did not our God say: "Be ye not as your fathers" (Zech. 1:4) and again: "And might not be as their fathers, a stubborn and rebellious generation" (Ps. 78: 8). This shows that there is no duty resting upon us to follow our fathers unconditionally. . . . If their words contradict the Law we must reject them and ourselves search and investigate, using the method of analogy, because the precepts and other things written in the Law of Moses are in no need of any sign or witness to testify whether they are true or not, whereas the words of the fathers require a sign and a trustworthy witness, that you may know whether or not they are true.[29]

This somewhat idealized version of Karaism totally rejects the idea of the "authoritative interpreter" and attacks the concept of the authority of tradition and of exclusive expertise in it. Tradition, says Sahl ben Masliah, should be criticized according to the plain meaning of the text. He does not claim that the Karaites have a monopoly on interpretation. The book is open, and it is the individual's responsibility to interpret the text. The rejection of the authority of tradition and the Oral Law and ultimately of the very idea of an authorized interpreter drove the Karaites out of the Jewish community. But in order to form a community of their own, they gradually accepted certain readers as authoritative and formulated a Karaite tradition. Later Karaite thinkers were compelled to justify these deviations from pure Karaite ideology.[30] Although the original split from the rabbinic tradition was achieved by appeal to an unmediated reading of the text, the formation of an alternative community, with shared common practices and ideals, necessitated some mediation of tradition and authorized readers.[31]

The retrieval model of the history of Halakhah, raised by the Geonim and articulated by Ibn Daud and later authors, entails a coherent attitude toward the halakhic process. It offers an explanation for the emergence of controversy as a crisis within the process of transmission of tradition. It has a clear conception of the authority of the ancients and of the Mishnah as a canon. Since all of the Halakhah was given at Sinai and tradition erodes through time, the earlier the stage of transmission the more authoritative the scholar; hence the authority of the Mishnah over the Talmud. This view also provides a definite secondary role for interpretation and halakhic reasoning which aims at restoring lost knowledge. All of these are challenged by Maimonides, who presents a different approach to the emergence of controversy in the Mishnah and consequently a different position on the nature of halakhic interpretation and authority.

The Cumulative View

Maimonides departs from both the Geonic picture of the history of Halakhah and from Ibn Daud's formulation.[32] He is the first to claim that the Sages introduced novel interpretations of the Torah of their own invention alongside the received tradition from Moses. Thus he views the halakhic process as cumulative, each generation adding substantive norms derived by their own reasoning to the given, revealed body of knowledge.[33] In the previous model, interpretation was an attempt to recover what initially been revealed or to attach received oral material to its source in the written Torah. In Maimonides' view, interpretation is derivation. From the given material of revelation— both oral and written—the Sages, equipped with rules of derivation, deduce new norms which in turn become part of the accumulative material of halakhic knowledge. Controversy emerges only regarding the newly derived *halakhot*, since these hermeneutical inferences are not strictly logical in the sense that a deduction necessarily follows from given premises.[34] According to Maimonides, there was never any controversy regarding the received normative material transmitted by the Sages of each generation; argumentation is restricted to the normative material newly derived by hermeneutical inferences.[35] On this point especially Maimonides diverges from Ibn Daud's account of the emergence of controversy, attacking it directly and bluntly:

> But the opinion of one who thought that also the laws wherein there is disagreement are received from Moses, and that disagreement took place due to an error in receiving the tradition or due to forgetfulness, i.e., that one [disputant] is correct in his tradition and the second errs in his tradition, or he forgot or he did not hear from his teacher all that he should have; and he [who holds this opinion] offers as evidence for this what they said, "When the disciples [of Shammai and Hillel who had insufficiently studied, increased in number, disputes multiplied in Israel and the Torah became as two Torot." Behold this, as God knows, is a despicable and very strange position, and it is an incorrect matter and not compatible with principles. And he [who holds this position] suspects people from whom we received the Torah and this is falsehood.

Maimonides uses harsh terms for Ibn Daud's model, since in his opinion controversy arises out of the inherent limitations of legal reasoning and not because of neglect in the transmission of tradition:

> And when the study of their students became less and the methods of argument became weakened for them in comparison to Shammai and Hillel, their teachers, disagreement befell them during the give-and-take on many issues, because each one of them reasoned according to the power of his intellect and according to the principles known to him. . . . And in this manner befell disagreement, not that they erred in their receiving of tradition and one's tradition is true and the other's false.

The problem that appears to concern Maimonides is that the attempt to ground the Mishnah and the Talmud upon the solid foundation of revelation and tradition calls tradition itself into question. By explaining controversy as neglect and forgetfulness in the process of transmission, proponents of the retrieval model cast doubt on its reliability. In Maimonides' own words, one who makes such a claim "suspects people from whom we received the Torah." Paradoxically, Ibn Daud's minimalization of human inventiveness in the history of the halakhic process ultimately undermined the authority of tradition. Conversely, Maimonides' attempt to guard the purity of the process of transmission in the history of Halakhah detaches much of the legal material of the Mishnah from its direct grounding in revelation and gives rise to a contingent foundation for the authority of the Oral Law.

According to Maimonides, while no argument can be raised against the received material of Halakhah, a later generation can in principle debate the *halakhot* newly derived from previous ones. The authority of the Mishnah cannot rest solely on tradition, since where there is debate there is no tradition; its authority rests instead on the fact that the Mishnah and the Talmud were widely accepted by the nation of Israel as a whole. Since, according to Maimonides, tradition is uncontaminated by forgetfulness, a text or a scholar gains no special privilege by being earlier and closer to the source. In relation to the revealed knowledge at Sinai, all generations have an equal claim. Theoretically, the Amoraim could have argued with their predecessors, the Tannaim, and the Geonim with the Amoraim, concerning the newly derived *halakhot* which constitute most of the Mishnah. Thus the authority of the Mishnah and Talmud is founded on the historically contingent fact of acceptance, a ground for authority that was rejected by later adherents to the Geonic approach.

The cumulative Maimonidean model carries certain implications regarding interpretation and its role in controversy and intergenerational authority. In this view interpretation is not meant to retrieve but to derive; controversy arises out of the process of derivation rather than through a crisis in transmission; and the authority of the Mishnah and Talmud is based not only upon the unbroken chain of tradition but also upon the historically contingent fact of widespread acceptance. These two conflicting explanations (Geonic versus Maimonidean) for the presence of controversy in the Mishnah also entail completely different understandings of the source of its authority and the role of interpretation.

It is important to stress that Ibn Daud and Maimonides alike considered that the spread of controversy was a failing, since both scholars—for completely different reasons—assume a notion of unitary truth in Halakhah. Ibn Daud's conception can be described as a simple correspondence theory of halakhic truth. A halakhic opinion is defined as true or false relative to the complete revelation of Sinai. For example, in a controversy concerning the proper time to recite the Shema in the evening, the determination of correctness depends on whether the opinion corresponds to the rule which was given at Sinai and was lost in the process of transmission. As we saw, Maimonides rejects this correspondence theory of halakhic truth, since he asserts that where there is controversy there was never a prior received tradition which can serve as a criterion to examine the correctness of the matter. Nevertheless, Maimonides does assume a conception of halakhic truth which is analogous to another theory: what in modern philosophy is called the coherence theory of truth. According to Maimonides, an area of debate is inevitable in human legal reasoning, since such reasoning is not conducted within the framework of strict logical deductions. Yet in principle strong deductive powers combined with shared premises and methods of deduction can yield a correct and agreed upon answer. Such an answer will be correct in the sense that it successfully coheres with the earlier premises upon which this new conclusion rests. Its correctness does not reside in the degree of its correspondence to a prior given halakhic tradition grounded in the complete revelation. According to Maimonides, it is for this reason that Hillel and Shammai, men who shared the deductive method and enjoyed deductive powers of high quality, had very few halakhic disputes,

> for when two people are identical in understanding and in study and knowledge of the principles from which they learn, there will not occur at all between them disagreement in what they learn by one of the hermeneutic principles, and if there will disagreements they will be few, just as we have never found disagreements between Hillel and Shammai other than in a few laws, for their methods of study in all they would learn by one of the principles were similar to one another, and also the correct general principles which were held by one were held by the other.

Maimonides then proceeds to explain why in the period of the students of Hillel and Shammai disputes increased. The students of Shammai and Hillel cannot be blamed for that situation, not in the way Ibn Daud implies. Unfortunately, there is a natural disparity in intellectual skills among scholars, and no one can be blamed for not reasoning above his skills. In contrast, when men of high intellectual capabili-

ties apply correct legal reasoning, disputes could be significantly minimized. The retrieval view of Ibn Daud and the cumulative approach
of Maimonides are different conceptions of what counts as a true, correct halakhic opinion.[36]

The Constitutive View
The third model can be traced to the writings of Nachmanides and his
students, fourteenth-century Catalonian scholars Yom Tov Ishbili,
known as Ritba, and Nissim Gerondi, also called the Ran. Their
approach, which I call the constitutive model, has its source in Nachmanides' rationale for obeying every legal ruling made by the court
even if it says "of the right that it is left and of the left that it is right":
". . . Scripture, therefore, defined the law that we are to obey the Great
Court. . . For it was subject to their judgment that He gave them the
Torah, even if it appears to you to exchange right for left."

According to this explanation there is no a priori right and left;
rather, the court itself defines what is right and what is left. In other
words, the court cannot be mistaken about the Halakhah, because its
members have the privilege, granted them by the Author, to constitute the very meaning of that text.[37] According to the constitutive view,
interpretation and legal reasoning do not retrieve a given lost body of
knowledge, nor do they derive new norms from a fixed body of transmitted tradition; they actually constitute those norms. Nachmanides'
explanation—"For it was subject to their judgment that He gave them
the Torah" recurs in the work of his students, who offer a new explanation of controversy. Both Ibn Daud and Maimonides had focused on
a passage which describes controversy as a sign of decline: "When the
disciples [of Shammai and Hillel] who had insufficiently studied,
increased in number, disputes multiplied in Israel and the Torah
became as two Torot." In contrast, Ritba refers to a talmudic statement expressing a different attitude toward argumentation:

"These and these are the words of the living God." The French Rabbis
of blessed memory asked how it were possible that both positions could
be the words of the living God when one prohibits and the other permits, and they answered: When Moses ascended to heaven to receive that
Torah they have shown him forty-nine reasons for prohibition and forty-
nine reasons for permission concerning each rule. He asked God about
this and God answered that the matter will be given to the sages of Israel
in each generation and the ruling will be as they decide.[38]

Nissim Gerondi raises the same issue in his *Derashot ha-Ran* and presents a full exposition of the constitutive account of the emergence of controversy in the Mishnah:

> It is a known fact that the entire Torah, written and oral, was transmitted to Moses, as it says in the Tractate *Megillah:* "R. Hiyya bar Abba said in the Name of R. Yohanan: The verse 'and on them was written according to all the words' teaches that the Holy One blessed be He showed Moses the details prescribed by the Torah and by the Sages, including the innovations they would later enact—and those concerning reading the Megillah." The "details" provided by the rabbis are halakhic disputes and conflicting views held by the Sages of Israel; all of them Moses learned by divine word with no resolution of every controversy in detail. Yet [God] also gave him a rule whose truth is manifest, i.e., "Favor the majority opinion," as the Sages of that generation saw fit, for the decision had already been transmitted to them, as it is written: "And you shall come to the priests, the Levites, and to the judge that shall be in those days" and "You shall not deviate."[39]

While Ibn Daud explained that controversy arose because of a crisis in transmission, both Ritba and Nissim Gerondi describe controversy as rooted in the very structure of revelation. The body of knowledge transmitted to Moses was not complete and final as Ibn Daud had described it, but open-ended, including all future controversies as well.[40] Moses passed on this multifaceted body of knowledge and left it to the court in each generation to constitute the norm. The process of the dissemination of knowledge is thus the reverse of Ibn Daud's model, which posits a complete and a clear-cut body of knowledge at the tradition's starting point, gradually eroding and becoming open-ended through neglect. In the Ritba and Ran's accounts the tradition is open-ended and multifaced at the start and over time becomes definitive, each generation constituting clear-cut norms out of the multiplicity of options transmitted to them. In this respect the constitutive model also differs from the Maimonidean cumulative approach and his argument that controversy arose through the attempt to derive newly reasoned norms from a clear-cut body of knowledge.

As well as providing a novel explanation of controversy, this approach offers an alternative view of interpretation. Interpretation is now employed neither to reconstruct and restore a lost, perfect moment, nor to derive new norms by way of induction from given clear premises. Rather, it constitutes and shapes an open-ended body of material.

This model also affects notions of authority. The authority of the scholars in matters of Halakhah no longer derives from their proximity to the source, which is open-ended in any case. Now it is based on a privilege granted to the Sages by the Torah itself, permitting them to set norms. A challenge to the interpretative process through an appeal to "true" meaning of the text is ruled out, since the court itself defines the meaning of the text out of the multiplicity of given options. Thus, not surprisingly, generational gaps are, in theory, not crucial in the constitutive view, as the Ran mentions in the continuation of the passage cited above: "Permission has been granted to the rabbis of each generation to resolve disputes raised by the Sages as they see fit, even if their predecessors were greater or more numerous. And we have been commanded to accept their decisions, whether they correspond to the truth or to its opposite."[41]

Nachmanides was the first halakhist to introduce the bold conception that the Torah was given, "subject to their [the Sages] judgment that He gave them the Torah." This statement provided the foundation for the constitutive approach of his school. Yet it is important to stress that the statement was understood differently by Ritba and the Ran. It even received a third explication by another author who belonged to Nachmanides' school: the anonymous author of *Sefer ha-Chinukh*. Ritba understood revelation as completely open-ended and pluralistic, attributing from God's point of view equal weight to each side of the debate. The Sages have in such a case a strong constitutive power to determine and shape the law out of many equal options. In contrast, the Ran argues that although God revealed the Torah with different opposing options, from God's own perspective there is a right answer. Such a right answer may be intuited by a prophet or expressed directly by God through a *bat kol*, a heavenly voice. The Ran argues innovatively that although there is a right answer from God's point of view, and although the Sages may be aware of that right answer, they have to follow their own understanding since "Torah is not in heaven." The Ran's position is clearly stated in his explanation of the famous story of "Tanuro shel Achnai," in which the Sages refused to follow the heavenly voice which ruled in favor of their opponent, R. Eliezer:

> They all saw that R. Eliezer follows the truth more than them, and his miracles were all true and right, and it was ruled from heaven according to his [R. Eliezer's] opinion, nevertheless they acted according to their ruling. Since their reason tended to declare [the oven] impure, even

though they knew that they rule against the truth, they did not want
to purify, because if they ruled [the oven] pure they would have trans-
gressed the words of the Torah. This is the case because their reason
tended to [rule the oven as] impure and the ruling was granted to the
Sages of the generation—whatever they decide it is what God commanded.

Even though the Sages knew God's contrary opinion on the matter,
voiced through R. Eliezer, they still followed their own understanding.
The rule that the "Torah is not in heaven" grants the Sages the privilege of constituting the truth of the matter from the human point of
view and following human reasoning, even against God's opinion. Thus
the Ran differs from Ritba in understanding the constitutive privilege
of the Sages as formulated by Nachmanides (both use Nachmanides'
own terminology). Ritba grants a greater constitutive power to the
Sages, since they shape the truth of the matter out of a completely
open-ended revelation. According to the Ran, however, although the
Sages' constitutive power is more limited in its scope, it is more daring
in its application and autonomy, since they constitute halakhic answers
even against what they know to be God's view of the matter. Yet despite
their differences the Ritba and the Ran share the general Nachmanidean
approach. Both describe controversy as rooted in revelation itself, and
both assume a constitutive power of the Sages.[42] In that respect their
conceptions differ deeply from the retrieval and the cumulative models
of Ibn Daud and Maimonides.

In another version of the constitutive model, revelation is not open-
ended. God had a clear-cut intention in revelation but nevertheless
granted the future Sages the authority to interpret the text as they
understood it and to overrule his original intention. Thus not all rabbinic opinions have their heavenly counterpart; they can in principle
diverge from the original, clear-cut intention. The aim of interpretation in the second type of constitutive model is not to discover an intention (for, unlike the previous constitutive approach, this understanding
does not deny the very existence of original intent), but rather to constitute the meaning of the text through the Sages' reasoning even if it
differs from the original intention of God. This view also bases itself
on the argument that the Torah is not in heaven, and it was expressed
by one of the most prominent figures of Halakhah in this century, R.
Moshe Feinstein: "In a dispute, the Sages should follow the majority
even when its ruling is far from the truth and is not as God intended

it. The Holy One, blessed be He, gave the Torah to Israel . . . and God will no longer interpret and decide concerning the rulings of the Torah as 'it is not in heaven' and He has retroactively agreed to the understanding and interpretation of the Sages." In Feinstein's statement the constitutive approach also serves as the ground for the authority of the Sages of later generations, who, in comparison to earlier generations are considered to be of lesser wisdom:

> The Sages of later generations are allowed and obligated to rule although they would have not been considered as worthy of ruling in the generations of the talmudic Sages, and although we can certainly fear that they would not rule according to the true law as it is true in heaven. But it is already said that the truth in ruling is not in heaven but [the law] is as it seems to the Sage. After the Sage has properly investigated the Talmud and the *poskim* . . . and it seems to him that his conclusion is the true ruling, he is obligated to rule according to his conclusion even if it is clear in heaven that his ruling is wrong.[43]

This version of the constitutive approach, which has deep roots within midrashic and talmudic material, has far-reaching theological implications. As David Hartman has pointed out, such bold interpretative approach redefines the relationship between God and humans as, through the interpretative process, they become participants in constituting the commandments themselves.[44]

After the Middle Ages, each of these three models acquired a history of halakhic interpretations which deserves further exploration. Among them is a fascinating responsum of R. Yair Bakhrakh, a seventeenth-century halakhist. In this responsum, which appears in Bakhrakh's *Havot Yair*, all three models are juxtaposed. In his attempt to find his own way among the different alternatives, Bakhrakh sheds light on the internal problems inherent in each model, and his discussion is of great value for further explication of what is at stake.

In the first part of his argument Bakhrakh marshals impressive counterevidence to Maimonides' view that there is no controversy regarding the laws given to Moses at Sinai and shows that the Talmud is full of controversies concerning these laws. Among the interesting texts Bakhrakh uses, in addition to the actual talmudic controversies on "*halakhot* given to Moses on Mount Sinai," are the haggadic material attesting to the pervasiveness of forgetfulness. Three thousand *halakhot* were forgotten after Moses' death, and even Moses himself forgot some that were given to him at Sinai. Forgetfulness is inherent in the very moment of reception, and tradition can only erode further at each subsequent stage of transmission. Bakhrakh's explanation for the rise of controversy is thus similar to Ibn Daud's, and the motif of forgetting is present throughout his responsum. He concludes: "It is clear that forgetfulness and controversy are present in Halakhah le-Moshe me-Sinai."[45]

After refuting Maimonides' position, Bakhrakh presents a wonderful formulation of what is at stake in this debate:

> Behold, the Rav [Maimonides] built a fortified wall around the Oral Law—in writing that concerning [the received traditions from Moses] forgetfulness never exists. Would that we could strengthen and rebuild such a wall! Which in my [Bakhrakh's] opinion is impossible. Indeed, all that was gained [in Maimonides' position that there are no controversies concerning the norms Moses received] was lost through his declaration that the remainder of the Sages' controversies—which constitute most of the Oral Torah and almost all of the Mishnah—are not from Sinai.

Bakhrakh points out that the price Maimonides pays for his position, which strengthens the credibility of tradition by ruling out the possibility of controversy, is to exclude most of the Oral Torah, replete as it is with controversies, from its divine source at Sinai. Supported by massive evidence from the Talmud itself, Bakhrakh opts for a counter-Maimonidean history of Halakhah, which roots the Oral Law in revelation. He thus arrives at a position very similar to that of Ibn Daud's.

In the heat of his debate with Maimonides, however, Bakhrakh distanced himself from the retrieval model on an important point. As noted, this model typically minimizes controversy. Bakhrakh's affirmation that the Mishnah and the Oral Torah are replete with controversies—central to his argument against Maimonides—departs from the retrieval model. This argument, used so skillfully against Maimonides, seems in fact to undermine Bakhrakh's own position. If his two contradictory propositions are correct—that all of the Oral Law was given at Sinai and that the Mishnah consists almost entirely of debates—it follows that most of the Oral Law has been forgotten. It makes sense to base the authority and meaning of the Oral Law in the revelation at Sinai if we minimize controversy, as Ibn Daud and Nieto had done. Yet if most of the Oral Law has indeed been forgotten, not much is gained by claiming that it was all given at Sinai.

Under the pressure of this dilemma, Bakhrakh explores the constitutive approach—that all of the Oral Law, including controversies, was given at Sinai:

> And concerning the statement in the first chapter of Tractate *Berakhot*, that the Mishnah and Talmud were given to Moses from Sinai, there is yet a vital issue that demands investigation: does that mean that all the opinions mentioned in the Mishnah and Talmud and their counterparts were revealed to Moses? As it is said in the Tractate *Hagigah*, the verse "all were given by one Shepherd" refers to the opinions of those who defile and those who purify, those who disqualify and those who approve, those who prohibit and those who permit, those who obligate and those who acquit. And the Ritba said that the expression "These and these are the words of the living God" means that God told Moses that the ruling of the Halakhah should be handed over to the Sages of the generation.

His examination of this view shows that it, too, entails internal contradictions:

> This is questionable, since what advantage could come from the Sages' decision that something is pure if it is truly impure and that [a truly impure thing] has the power to arouse the *kelippah* ["the shell"] and defilement and the *sitra akhra* [literally, "the other side," the force of evil]? Of what good is a physician's contention that poison is the elixir of life? We could content ourselves with what, in truth, is an unsatisfactory explanation, saying that impurity and the evil husks do not gain strength with every instance of [prohibited] contact or eating or intercourse or any loathsome act, but only because certain acts are evil and despicable in the eyes of God; and if God were to say that the court can decide the matter as they wish, no harm would be done.

Bakhrakh's discussion of the constitutive model links the history of Halakhah with the problem of the meaning and effect of the commandments. To his mind the claim that the Torah was open-ended when it was given and was left to the Sages' future decisions is incompatible with a strict ontological conception of the commandments. According to such a conception, halakhic categories such as purity and impurity are no mere legal constructs. They are, rather, causally connected to the very nature of reality. The proper analogy to impurity is poison.

   This view of halakhic categories defines a strict criterion of truth in
the legal process. Something is impure if it affects reality in a negative manner and pure if it has a positive effect on reality. Categories
with such a causal impact are thus completely independent of human
decisions. Just as a physician's pronouncement that poison is curative
is nonsense, so too the Sages' ruling that something truly impure is
pure has no meaning.[46] The constitutive approach is thus incompatible
with a strict ontological conception of the commandments. The
problem of the place of human creativity in Halakhah, as reflected in
opposing accounts of its history, is thus connected to the deeper issue
of the ontological status of halakhic legal categories.

   Bakhrakh, who adheres to the ontological view, attempts to reconcile it with the constitutive approach. In his reformulation reconciling
the two, the ontological impact of halakhic categories ought to be mediated through God's will. Nothing in the nature of impurity as such
affects reality. Rather, impurity has a negative impact on reality because
it is despicable in God's eyes. Therefore, if God grants the court the
privilege of determining what is pure and impure, this, in turn, will
have a causal impact on reality. Hence nothing is "truly" impure as
such, but only through God's will.

   Bakhrakh's discussion of the constitutive view introduces tension
between the ontological qualities he attributes to halakhic categories
and the open-endedness of revelation, which envisages future decisions
by humans. Although he formulates an ontology that seems to solve
the problem, Bakhrakh is dissatisfied with the solution. In the continuation of the responsum he again explores Ritba's formulation and
rejects it:

> Concerning what is written in the first chapter of *Erubin*, "These and
> these are the words of the living God," and in the fourth chapter of
> *Hagigah*, "all of them [conflicting opinions] were spoken by one God":
> the Ritba wrote that God gave Moses forty-nine arguments for [a ruling
> of] impure, and forty-nine for [a ruling of] pure, and that the final deci-
> sion should be left to the Sages of Israel. . . . How very strange it is to
> say that God did not express His true opinion and will concerning the
> Halakhah and the interpretation of Scripture. In fact, the opposite is
> more reasonable—that in apprehension of controversy God should have
> clarified the norms and made His will known. . . . Therefore, on what
> basis can one fabricate the contention that God pronounced a mistaken
> opinion along with the true opinion? Perhaps He spoke only the truth
> but it was forgotten.

Bakhrakh's criticism of Ritba's constitutive approach is very similar in pattern to his criticism of Maimonides' cumulative history of Halakhah. He notes that the Ritba's attempt to ground all of the Oral Law, including contradictions, in open-ended revelation undermines the element of truth in revelation.

It is interesting that Bakhrakh faces a tension inherent in his background as a kabbalist. On the one hand, the theology of Kabbalah, which pictures God as a multidimensional organic being, allows for a conception of an open-ended revelation filled with many contrary opinions mirroring God's own inner multiplicity; and indeed many formulations of an open-ended pluralistic revelation are cast in kabbalistic terminology.[47] On the other hand, the ontological view is at the center of kabbalistic conceptions of Halakhah. Bakhrakh opts for the strict ontological view and the claim that open-ended conceptions of revelation undermine the ontological causal effect of Halakhah. This dilemma forces Bakhrakh to return to the retrieval model: truth was given in complete and definitive form at Sinai, but it was forgotten afterwards.

By juxtaposing all three models, Bakhrakh's fascinating discussion reveals the internal tensions inherent in them. Do we have to safeguard tradition at the cost of excluding debates from revelation, debates which make up most of the Mishnah? Must we include controversies in the open-ended revelation and thus forgo the very idea of halakhic truth and the ontological force of legal categories? The alternative to the cumulative and constitutive models—the retrieval model—is what Bakhrakh chooses. Yet we are left with the undeniable impression that the necessity of forgetfulness in the retrieval model troubles Bakhrakh throughout the responsum. At times, like a juggler, he seems to want to keep all three models in the air at the same time.

Through its version of the history of Halakhah, each of the three models structures the basic conceptions of the Law in its own way. These are the role of legal reasoning, the emergence and explanation of controversy, and notions of authority.[48] In addition, essential to each model is a specific understanding of truth in Halakhah. Ibn Daud's retrieval model assumes a correspondence theory, Maimonides' cumulative model implies a coherence notion, and the constitutive model as presented by the Ritba undermines the very idea of an a priori criterion for examining such an issue. Bakhrakh introduces a fourth conception of halakhic truth, that of ontological causal effect on the state of the world. The idea of the open-endedness of text and the constitutive role of the interpreter are the boldest options produced, both theologically and hermeneutically, by an internal rabbinic reflection on the canonization of controversy.

❧ FROM A FLEXIBLE CANON TO A CLOSED CODE

While the Mishnah is a flexible code, the Talmud seems to be even farther away from being a code of any sort. The Babylonian Talmud is a compendium of statements and discussions conducted by the Amoraim (talmudic Sages) from the first half of the second century until the end of the fifth century. Elaborated around the Mishnah and following its order, the Talmud has as its primary concern the interpretation of the Mishnah, but its discussions are not dominated by the subject matter of the Mishnah. By way of associations, loose connections, and indirect allusions, the talmudic *sugiya* (a unit of discussion) drifts away from the Mishnah to a variety of subjects ranging from profound theological observations to trivial folk tales and from intricate legal discourse to magic, science, and demonology. The text is edited as a multigenerational discussion, layer upon layer, and most talmudic discussions do not reach definite legal opinions concerning the previous controversies. Rather, they preserve and clarify the wealth and multiplicity of approaches to the problem at hand. In many talmudic discussions the *sugiya* does not proceed by way of selection aimed at approaching or approximating the right answer. Astonishingly, many of these discussions manifest the opposite tendency as they progress dialectically. Instead of refuting and thereby favoring one of two or more opposing interpretations, the *sugiyot* attempt to maintain the validity of opposing interpretations against potential challenges, challenges which are raised and refuted in turn. The talmudic *sugiya* manifests an interesting feature of canonization. While defending an Amoraic opinion against an earlier Mishnaic source, the *sugiya* reinterprets this source in a radical manner in order to adapt it to the Amoraic view. The commitment of the Talmud not to debate the Mishnah is not a blind adherence to the Mishnah; often it entails a commitment to reinterpret it and to transform its meaning. In this manner, through refutation of challenges, the talmudic discussion advances to multiple understandings of the Mishnah instead of narrowing those interpretative options as far as possible. Within this dialectical process, of course, those opinions are reinterpreted, sometimes rephrased or articulated within a new context, and therefore perceived in a novel light. The use of the Talmud as a source of legal and behavioral norms is thus secondary to its editorial policy. With the help of meta-rules such as "the law is like Samuel in monetary matters and like Rav in ritual matters," norms can be deduced from the variety of controversies in the Talmud, but it is not the primary aim of the text to reach the single definite norm.

The canonization of the Talmud meant that no Sage could propose a norm contradictory to the opinions expressed there; any future norm could be justified only as an interpretation of the existing text. Nevertheless, a process of selection is necessary in order to reach a conclusive norm from the talmudic material, since the Talmud is by no means a code. The Talmud became a source of authoritative norms of the Halakhah through the influence of the Geonim after it was edited and sealed.[49] Yet neither the Mishnah nor the Talmud are closed codes. The canonization of those texts does not determine a fixed judicial norm but rather sets a range of opinions among which future generations can choose, though they may not deviate from them. In the case of the Mishnah, an Amora (a talmudic Sage) cannot argue with a Tana (mishnaic Sage) unless he has support from another Tana.[50] The same rule was applied to the canonization of the Talmud: a medieval scholar cannot argue with an Amora unless he has support from another Amora. Both texts can therefore be defined as relatively open canons.

A major change in the form of authoritative texts appeared with the rise of monumental halakhic codes, the most prominent of which were Maimonides' *Mishneh Torah* (Repetition of the Law) in the twelfth century, and Rabbi Joseph Karo's *Shulchan Arukh* (Set Table) in the sixteenth century. Unlike the Mishnah, these codes present straightforward norms, and, unlike the Talmud, they omit the argumentation that led to variant rulings. The process of codification and the reactions to the codes have been treated extensively and thoroughly by Chaim Tchernowitz and Menachem Elon.[51] Based on their work, this section will attempt to conceptualize the responses to the movement from flexible canon to closed codes.

Maimonides apparently viewed his code as a comprehensive and self-sufficient summary of all Halakhah, so that it can serve as an authoritative text in and of itself. The attempt to replace the Talmud with a code, and the divergence from the traditional form of authoritative texts that are both reasoned and more open, encountered serious objections. Indeed, attempts to codify the Halakhah had been made prior to Maimonides' code, but those attempts were either limited to a specific topic or, like Alfasi's important eleventh-century code, were written in conjunction with the Talmud and continually referred to the talmudic sources. The novelty of Maimonides' code lay in its all-encompassing ambition and in its authoritative, straightforward style, a novelty that immediately aroused criticism.

Maimonides' critics also objected to the issuing of rulings directly from the code. Many of them maintained that a code can never replace the intricate discussions of the Talmud, because ruling from a code without knowledge of the argumentation in the Talmud is deficient and inadequate. They argued that knowledge of the Talmud's reasoning is essential in arriving at a ruling, for it may affect the scope and future application of that ruling. R. Asher ben Yechiel, known as the Rosh, a leading talmudic authority in the late thirteenth and early fourteenth centuries, objected to the practice of ruling directly from the *Mishneh Torah* and, therefore, to the very idea of replacing the Talmud with a code:

> All those who rule from the words of Maimonides and are not versed in the Talmud and unable to distinguish the sources on which his ruling is based, may well make mistakes, permitting what is prohibited and prohibiting what is permitted. For he [Maimonides] did not do as all other authors, who brought proofs for their statements and demonstrated their derivation from the Talmud, thus enabling the reader to grasp the essence and the truth. But he [Maimonides] wrote his book as if prophesying from the mouth of the Almighty with no reasoning nor proof, and anyone who reads him presumes that he understands, which is not the case, for if he is not an expert in Talmud he can have no true understanding of the matter and will fail in the law and in ruling. Therefore a person should not depend on his reading in the *Mishneh Torah* to rule on the Halakhah unless he has found its source in the Talmud. (Responsa 31:9)[52]

The same criticism was raised against R. Joseph Karo's work,[53] though Karo himself seems to have been less ambitious than Maimonides, never making the bold claim that no other book would be necessary after his. Moreover, before the *Shulchan Arukh* appeared, Karo had written his great *Beit Yosef*, in which he issued authoritative norms only after long deliberations based on sources and arguments. Yet it seems that Karo

did not object to ruling from the *Shulchan Arukh*, and in the intro-
duction to his running commentary on the *Mishneh Torah*, the *Kesef
Mishneh*, he defended the practice of ruling directly from the *Mishneh
Torah* against Maimonides' critics.

Anticipating these objections, Maimonides based his own code on
the precedent of the Mishnah, as he says in several places. Unlike the
Talmud, the Mishnah states its norms without argumentation, and the
same is done in the *Mishneh Torah*. In Maimonides' own words, the
Mishneh Torah is not a *perush*, meaning a commentary like the Talmud;
it is rather a *hibur*, a compilation like the Mishnah:

> The method of *hibur* [compilation] is to mention only correct statements
> without questions or answers and with no proof, as our saintly Rabbi
> [Yehudah the Prince] did in the compilation of the Mishnah. And the
> method of *perush* [commentary] is to mention both the correct state-
> ments and other statements that contradict them and questions and
> answers on each statement and proof that one statement is true and
> another false or that one is appropriate and another inappropriate. The
> latter is the method of the Talmud since the Talmud is a commentary
> on the Mishnah. And I [Maimonides] did not write a *perush* [commen-
> tary] but a *hibur* [compilation], following the method of the Mishnah.[54]

Maimonides argues that issuing norms without deliberation has its precedent in the Mishnah; consequently he rejects his critics' claim that his
authoritative code violates the basic form of canonization in Halakhah.

Moreover, as Isadore Twersky pointed out, Maimonides raised an
even deeper issue—the connection between crisis and codification.[55]
The Mishnah was compiled despite the prohibition of putting the Oral
Law into written form because of a sense of acute crisis. At the time
it was described as a response to the historical upheavals of the second
century. The Torah was being forgotten, and a document like the
Mishnah was desperately needed. Alluding to the precedent of the
Mishnah, Maimonides describes his code in the same way, as a response
to the historical condition of exile and to the fear that, because of the
dispersion of the Jews, the Torah will become splintered:

> In our days severe vicissitudes prevail, and all feel the pressure of hard
> times. The wisdom of our wise men has disappeared; the understanding
> of our prudent men is hidden . . . On these grounds I . . . intently studied
> all these works with the view of putting together the results obtained

from them in regard to what is forbidden or permitted . . . in plain language and terse style, so that thus the entire Oral Law might become
systematically known to all, without . . . one person saying so and another
something else . . . so that no other work should be needed for ascer-
taining any of the laws of Israel but this work might serve as a compendium of the entire Oral Law.

In his introduction to *Beit Yosef* and the *Shulchan Arukh*, Karo voices
the same fear. Echoing Maimonides' words, he writes:

As the days passed and we were poured from one vessel into another . . .
and troubles came upon us until, because of our sins, the prophecy was
fulfilled, and the wisdom of his Sages shall be lost, and the Torah and
her students are powerless, for the Torah is now not like two laws but
rather like many laws because of the many books explaining its rules
and ordinances. Everyone writes a book for himself repeating what
someone else had written before or ruling the opposite of what his colleagues have written.[56]

Karo's own experience of the expulsion of the Jews from Spain at the
end of the fifteenth century and its aftermath lay behind his sense of
the urgent need to codify the Halakhah in the sixteenth century.
Another point he raised,the proliferation of books offering contradictory norms, was most likely an effect of the flourishing art of printing.[57]
Codification is a response to an overabundance of opinions and their
too facile dissemination; the code serves to stanch the flow of legal
opinions at a moment when the authority of the law is threatened.
Crisis and codification thus go hand in hand.

But Maimonides' reliance on the precedent of the Mishnah is insufficient. True, the Mishnah is not a reasoned commentary like the
Talmud, but it does mention minority opinions and is brimming with
controversies.[58] In the same letter Maimonides attempts to account for
his divergence from the Mishnah and introduces an interesting view of
the canonical nature of the Mishnah and the Talmud:

It is quite clear therefore, that only decided rules should be mentioned.
However, at the time, [of the Mishnah] there were people who accepted
controversial opinions, cases in which some followed the opinion of one
authority and others that of another, for this reason they all had to be
mentioned. Since I chose to model my work on the Mishnah, and every

law has already been decided by the Talmud, either on its own merits or as a general principle following from the rules of decision-making there postulated, such parallel modes of conduct are no longer possible.

Maimonides views the Mishnah as a flexible code not out of choice but out of necessity: its editor left norms open-ended only when he could not decide the ruling or when he could not force a decision upon the community. For himself, Maimonides claims to be in a better position, since the Talmud decided matters that were left open in the Mishnah. Therefore in his own code there is no need to mention rejected halakhic opinions. He presents the Talmud as a text that aims at closure, clarifying and deciding doubts in the Mishnah. Yet he realizes that many readers of the Talmud have an opposite impression of its aim. Rather than fixing the norm, the Talmud adds more controversies that arise from diverse interpretations of the Mishnah, and seems to preserve the plurality of such views rather than rule among them. Despite his appeal to the precedent of the Mishnah, Maimonides established a new and unprecedented form of canonization: a completely closed code, different from all that came before it in its unanimity and lack of argumentation. Hence it gave rise to certain objections to the very project of codification. I will focus on four issues connected with the notion of a closed code as an authoritative halakhic text. These issues were raised in full force by Ashkenazi halakhists who responded to the *Shulchan Arukh* during the sixteenth century.

First, a uniform code denied the validity of diverse local traditions and practices. The need to respect such a plurality was also one of the objections raised against Karo's code.[59] Second, closed codes replace the authority of the rabbi with the authority of the text. The Talmud and the vast number of varied commentaries accumulated around it allowed varieties of interpretation, leaving room for the authority of the individual rabbi and his own understanding of the Halakhah derived from the previous canon. The absence of a fixed code and the flexible canonization of tradition allowed the rabbi to respond to a particular situation with his view of the needs of the hour. After the appearance of the *Mishneh Torah* and the *Shulchan Arukh* as authoritative texts, the authority of the rabbi and the validation of his individual understanding of the sources was seriously threatened.

This predicament was raised as an argument against codification by the founding fathers of Polish halakhic and talmudic learning, R. Jacob

Polak and R. Shalom Shachne, even before the appearance of the
Shulchan Arukh. Both of them rejected their students' attempts to convince them to write a code.

> I know [that if I write a code] rabbis would rule only according to me
> because [in case of a disagreement between an earlier and later authority]
> the Halakhah follows the later and I do not want "the world" to rely
> upon me. For example, when there is a disagreement between rabbinic
> authorities, a rabbi should decide or entertain his own opinion since "the
> judge should only follow that which he sees with his own eyes." Everyone,
> therefore, should rule according to the needs of the hour as his heart
> decrees.[60]

The rabbi can exercise his prerogative to rule according to his understanding and contemporary circumstances only as long as the relatively
open canon of the Talmud and its many interpreters is maintained. R.
Shalom Shachne's argument in favor of the authority of the rabbi and
against the authority of a code was later used by Shachne's students
against the *Shulchan Arukh*.[61] Moreover, a fixed code might lead to
power struggles, since the code is accessible to the layman and can provide a vantage point from which expert rulings are criticized. Indeed,
one of the *Mishneh Torah*'s defenders, a figure from outside of the rabbinic establishment, claimed that criticism of Maimonides' code was
motivated by rabbis' fears that their power would be diminished as a
result of the popularity and accessibility of the *Mishneh Torah*, and that
through the code their shortcomings would be exposed by lay people.[62]
A bitter confrontation between a layman and a rabbi concerning Karo's
code is reported by an Italian rabbi, Yehudah Arieh of Modena. A Jew
ignorant of Halakhah told him: "Now, after the printing of the *Shulchan
Arukh*, I have it under my hands and have no need of any of you
rabbis."[63]

The third argument against codification was to question the assumption that a code would serve as a self-sufficient text and would end once
and for all the ongoing debates and doubts concerning the Halakhah.
One of the most beautiful formulations of this criticism against a completely authoritative text was expressed in the sixteenth century by R.
Shlomoh Luria, known as the Maharshal. In his view, no text can exist
without lacunae; the Torah was deliberately composed in a terse style
to engender the need for supplement it with oral tradition and discussion.

It is impossible to produce books concerning this [the Halakhah] for there is no end to the matter. Were all the heavens above scrolls and all the oceans ink, they would not suffice to expound even one passage and all the doubts arising from it and all the innovations emerging from it. . . . Moreover, supposing He [God] wrote all that in the Torah, there would necessarily be vast, unending quantities of additional interpretations. In other words, I mean to say, additions upon the additions. It is impossible that doubts, changes and profundities would not arouse upon the first addition so that when it reaches the second addition there will tens of thousands like it. Thus, the wise one has informed us that it is unreal and impossible to explain all the doubts arising from the Torah without an infinity of distinctions which are beyond human reach. For that reason it was necessary that the Torah be given to the wise men seen in each generation, each and every one of them in accordance with his understanding, hewed from the source of his intellect in the upper world.

The history of Jewish canonization, according to Maharshal, thus manifests a paradoxical pattern. He denied not only the possibility of a final, complete text but made yet a stronger claim: the attempt to produce texts that seek to clarify doubts and fill the gaps left by previous texts will necessarily give rise to further texts, and instead of reducing the need for interpretation they accelerate its production. According to Maharshal, this logic governs the halakhic interpretative tradition. The Mishnah was an attempt to record the Oral Law and in fact produced a text greater than itself—the Talmud, composed to clarify problems produced by the Mishnah. The Talmud, in turn, produced medieval commentaries, among them the works of the Tosafists of the twelfth and thirteenth centuries, whose aim was to clarify and give coherence to talmudic discussions. Those commentaries produced the need for further texts, and Maimonides' own ambitious code added more fuel to the flame of textual interpretation. The more monumental and more extensive the text, the more doubts and gaps it produces. In addition, Maharshal raises serious objections to Karo's strategy of basing rulings on majority opinions voiced by the three great halakhists of the medieval period: R. Yitzhak Alfasi, Maimonides, and R. Asher ben Yechiel. In Maharshal's view the sole authoritative text is the Talmud; none of the medieval interpreters has a privileged position unless he offers what seems to be a superior interpretation of the Talmud.[64] A complete and finite code is, therefore, both a conceptual mistake and also a violation of the authority of the Talmud.

4

The fourth basic objection to closed codification was raised by
another sixteenth-century Ashkenazi authority and student of R.
Shalom Shachne, R. Chaim ben Bezalel (brother of the famous Maharal
of Prague). His criticisms were directed against R. Moshe Isserlis, the
great Ashkenazi halakhist known as Rama, who produced a code titled
Torat Hatat. Rama had justified his code by pointing to the inadequacy
of the previous halakhic material in Ashkenaz, mainly its central text,
Sharei Dura. Chaim ben Bezalel saw Rama's attempt as a betrayal of
Ashkenazic tradition, which was always against codification, and he
responded with a most brilliant and sharp criticism of codification. He
argued that Rama made a categorical mistake. If the previous normative material in Ashkenaz was perceived as attempts at codification,
Rama was indeed correct in claiming that it had been insufficient. But
the whole point was that the previous authors in Ashkenaz resisted that
genre altogether, so that to argue that their attempts had failed was to
miss the point altogether. In his description of the literary nature of
halakhic texts in Ashkenaz, R. Chaim provides an important boundary
between the canonical and noncanonical. Previous texts in Ashkenaz
were produced for private consumption, written in a semi-esoteric,
unsystematic terse style, and more important, these texts were unscaled,
and new rabbis added their own glosses to the text. In R. Chaim's
opinion, the author of the (inadequate) *Sharei Dura* must have thought
that "a person should not live exclusively by his book but rather rely
on other books as well." Codification is, after all, an act of censorship
dooming the vast previous literature to oblivion. Rama's predecessors
in Ashkenaz, writing in their noncodifying style, were careful to preserve the diverse traditions of the past. R. Chaim argued that the
halakhic situation that prevailed until the rise of various codes is not
mere accident or failure to reach consensus; rather, it reflects what is
both essential and valuable in Halakhah, its open-endedness:

> This was the traditional procedure in Israel: any matter in need of deci-
> sion would come before a wise man who had reached maturity of ruling,
> which is to say that he has reached forty, the age of wisdom. He would
> then open all the books of rulings in which he would read the positions
> of those who prohibit and those who permit, and he would study them
> trembling with awe and fear. If the matter tended to prohibition he
> would immediately incline to stringency, and if there was a custom to
> leniency he would follow it as well. If it were possible, he would con-
> vene all the wise men of his city and they would argue the matter until
> they reached agreement. If a similar matter arose again he would follow

the same ruling but cautiously, because the minutest difference could overturn the matter, as I have already written. A man's opinion, moreover, is not stable over time, and he might not tend to rule today as he did yesterday. This does not imply change or deficiency, that is, suggesting that the one Torah is rendered as two God forbid; on the contrary, this is the very path of Torah, "for both these and those are the words of the living God." It follows, therefore, that the Rabbi's [Moshe Isserlis'] codification, whereby all matters of ruling in ritual matters are displayed openly and publicly to all readers, is improper.

This is a vivid description of the process of ruling in the absence of a fixed code. The various sources the rabbi consults do not provide him with an unequivocal answer to the problem; thus he relies on his own judgment and rules between those conflicting opinions. As in the previous criticism of the codes, the emphasis here is on the authority of the rabbi rather than the authority of the closed code. With no code at hand, the rabbi is not even committed to be absolutely consistent. He may revise his ruling because some of the contours of the case at hand are different then his previous case or simply because he has changed his mind. This fluidity of ruling, which was a major motivation for the creation of a fixed code and was mentioned by Karo explicitly—that the Torah not split into two or more—is to R. Chaim essential to the nature of Halakhah as the path of Torah: "For both these and those are the words of God."

The change in the form of authoritative texts from flexible canon to closed codes provoked deep tensions[65] in the complicated relations between the authority of the text and the authority of the rabbi and between a unified norm and the relative, plural understandings of the tradition. Both issues are interconnected in Rabbi Chaim's reaction to codification. The open-endedness of the tradition validated the authority of the rabbi and the court as well as the multiple understandings of the Halakhah. This tension between text and institution leads us to consider the basis of the court's authority in its relation to the text.

☙ THE INSTITUTION AND THE CANON

One of the options concerning canonization was the idea that the canon is handed to an institution which will preserve the text and produce the authorized reading of it. Such an institution could be the Supreme

Court, the Church, the Sanhedrin, and so forth. The relationship between the institution that safeguards the text and the text itself is complex. In what sense does the institution own the text? What is the source of its privilege in reading the text?

Before discussing the general question of that source, it will be useful to examine tensions within rabbinic literature regarding the extent of institutional monopoly over the canon's interpretation. Can an individual issue a legitimate reading of the canon that will diverge from the court's position? Under what circumstances is this possible, if at all?

The discussion as it developed from the Middle Ages onward stemmed from presumably contradictory interpretations in the Talmud of the verse in Deuteronomy (17:11) obligating one to follow the rulings of the court: "Thou shalt not depart from the word which they shall tell thee to the right nor to the left." The *Sifrei* (A Tannaitic *midrash* on Deuteronomy) reads the verse as stating an absolute command: "Even if they show you before your own eyes that right is left and that left is right—obey them."[66] This reading developed in the context of the law of the rebellious elder who refuses to accept the Sanhedrin's ruling. According to the Mishnah, such an elder deserves capital punishment. "If he [the elder who is a member of a lower court] returned to his town and taught again as heretofore, he is not liable. But if he gave a practical decision, he is guilty, for it is written 'and the man that will do so presumptuously,' shewing that he is liable only for a practical ruling" (Sanhedrin 10:3). An opposing reading appears in the Jerusalem Talmud, as follows: "Only if the court rules that right is right and left is left should you obey the court."[67] In this version an individual is obligated to follow the court as long as it rules properly. The context of this reading is a ruling in the Mishnah that asserts:

> If the court ruled that any one of the commandments mentioned in the Torah may be transgressed, and an individual proceeded and acted through error in accordance with their ruling . . . he is exempt because he relied on the court. [If however] the court issued [an erroneous ruling], and one of them, who knew that they had erred, or a disciple who was himself capable of deciding matters of law, proceeded and acted in accordance with their ruling . . . he is liable. (*Horayot* 1:1)

This Mishnah implies that an individual is obligated to diverge from the court's ruling if he is capable of ruling himself and has good reason to think that the court erred. Even more sharply, both the Babylonian Talmud and the Jerusalem Talmud in *Horayot* argue that such a scholar is obligated to bring a sin offering, since he erred in thinking that he had to submit completely to the authority of the court. While the Mishnah in *Sanhedrin* argues that if a scholar follows his own ruling against the court he is liable to capital punishment, the Mishnah in *Horayot* claims that if such a scholar avoids following his own ruling, he needs to atone. The attempts of subsequent commentators to harmonize these opposing readings part from different views concerning the extent of the institutional monopoly of the canon.

One way to resolve the opposition was to qualify the statement of the *Sifrei*. The qualification was based on an understanding of the phrase "before your own eyes" to mean "when it seems to you." Thus when it only *seems* to you that the court is wrong, you ought to obey the court, but when you are confident that the court erred, you ought to disobey it, as ruled in *Horayot*.[68] This way of harmonizing the conflicting opinions implies that the institution does not have an absolute monopoly in reading the canon. The canon is not completely mediated through what the court says, and its proper reading is in principle independent of the court's reading.

Another way of harmonizing the sources was to qualify the statement in *Horayot*. This applies only to a case in which the arguments of a person who disagrees with the court were not yet heard in the court; when these arguments were voiced and considered by the court, that person must obey any ruling of the court, even if he is confident that the court erred.[69] After considering the objections, the court has absolute control of interpreting the canon.

I think that the most plausible reconstruction of the Mishnah's view on the court's authority and individual dissent is through reading the Mishnah *Sanhedrin* not in the context of obedience and uniformity but in relation to sectarianism. The text does not prohibit the elder from practicing what he believes to be the truth. Nor does it prohibit a scholar from teaching against the court's ruling, as it explicitly states: "If he returned to his town and taught again as heretofore, he is not liable." What the scholar is prohibited from doing is issuing his own public ruling. The monopoly of the court is on ruling, not on truth; therefore a scholar is allowed to teach against the court's ruling, and, according to the Mishnah *Horayot*, he is obligated personally to act against what the court ruled. In such a view, the court can in principle be wrong, and obedience to the court is not demanded. The case of the rebellious elder attempts to establish the court monopoly over ruling itself, and to avoid a sectarian situation in which unresolved controversies result in the establishment of competing institutions of ruling. A scholar is not allowed to challenge that monopoly, but he is obligated to follow his own views.

The different views concerning the right or obligation of a scholar to disagree with the court's ruling are deeply connected to views of the source of institutional authority. The relationship between institution and canon can be constructed in three different ways. According to the first, a certain kind of institution is endowed with a privileged access to the true meaning of the text. The Church believed it was guided by Divine Providence and thus correct in its readings of the text. One of Nachmanides' rationalizations for control by the institution and the obligation to obey the court even if its ruling seems to contradict your clear conviction was as follows: "And surely you are obligated to think that what they say is 'right' truly is right, because God's spirit is upon the ministers of His Sanctuary and He forsaketh not His saints; they are preserved forever from error and stumbling."[70] The Great Court in Jerusalem had a God-given privileged access to truth; the institution was thus uniquely qualified to represent the authorized version of the canon. Two centuries before Nachmanides this same idea was expressed by R. Yehudah ha-Levi in his *Kuzari.*[71]

The second possible relationship between institution and text—the procedural—is radically different. In the procedural version, the institution does not have unique access to the true meaning of the canonized text; rather, someone must decide, and a particular institution is authorized to make that decision. The directive to follow the rulings of this institution is one of the laws of the canon. The institution must be obeyed because it has a procedural priority.[72] A medieval author expresses a variant of the same procedural approach: "Even if they [the Sages] erred in some rule, we ought not disagree with them and we should act according to their mistake. It is preferable to endure one mistake and to have everyone submit to their usually good opinion and not that every one should do according to his will. Since in such a case religion will be destroyed, the heart of the people divided, and the nation will be completely ruined."[73]

In ordinary usage we refer to two different conceptions of authority. We say "she is the authority on Russian literature," and by this we mean a special capability, endowment, or achievement that justifies that state of being "an authority" on the subject. In the second use we say "he now has the authority," which means that he was appointed or gained his authority by a legitimate procedure, without appealing to any of his unique qualities. The question regarding institution and text is whether the institution is the authority on the text because it claims a special endowment, or whether it holds the authority regarding the text.[74]

The third possible relationship between the institution and the text is the constitutive. According to this approach, the institution constitutes the meaning of the text. It is not endowed with unique access to the meaning of the text, for that meaning does not exist before it is constituted by the institution that reads it. As Nachmanides put it: "Scripture, therefore, defined the law that we must obey the Great Court . . . For it was subject to their judgment that He gave them the Torah, even if it appears to you to exchange right for left."[75] In this explanation there is no a priori right and left; rather, the court defines what is right and what is left. The court cannot be mistaken about the meaning of the canonical text because it has the privilege, given by the Author, to constitute that meaning. Both views—that the court is endowed with special access to the truth, and that the court constitutes the truth—assume that the institution is never wrong. Such views will therefore attempt to minimize the possibility of dissent and will limit the reading of the Mishnah in *Horayot*. The procedural account of the authority of the institution is the only reading that will allow for restricting the scope of the rule against the rebellious elder.

The same constitutive argument regarding constitutional theory is made by legal realists. According to that school of thought, when we make a statement about the law we are actually trying to predict the decision of the court. This position was articulated by Oliver Wendell Holmes, Jr.: "The prophecies of what the courts will do in fact and nothing more pretentious, are what I mean by the law."[76] The law is what the judge will decide and nothing more. When interpretation is merely tactical, a prediction of judiciary behavior, the difference between legislator and judge evaporates. Ruling in court and voting in Congress become two different procedures for the same act, legislating, and there is no longer any separation of powers.

Critics have serious doubts about the validity of this account of the interpretative practice of judges and lawyers. If we say that a court was mistaken, is this solely a political judgment? Do judges try to create coherence between their verdicts and the written canonized text[77] or is this impression of coherence arbitrary? I am certainly not the first to raise these questions, nor is this the proper context in which to clarify them. What is important for our purpose is not the correctness of the statement about the law but the pattern revealed in the relationship between institution and text.

One of the main earlier sources of the different approaches to the relationship between institution and canon as presented by medieval and later authors is the story told in the Mishnah about a clash over the Jewish calendar. It is quoted by Nachmanides in his commentary on Deuteronomy and by many other authors as well. This interesting controversy arose in the second century, when the beginning of every month was still decided according to testimony of witnesses who saw the new moon. There was no fixed calendar yet, and no way to know whether a given month was twenty-nine or thirty days. A special court would hear from witnesses who claimed to have seen the new moon, and it declared when the new month had begun. Determining the first day of the month was crucial, because each holiday occurs on a particular date and could be properly observed only on that date. Agreement about the calendar is therefore vital in preserving communal unity and homogeneity.

The clash described in the Mishnah occurred as a result of a controversial decision made by Rabban Gamaliel. R. Gamaliel, who was head of the court at Yavneh, accepted the testimony of two witnesses who claimed they had seen the new moon. On the basis of their evidence, he declared the beginning of a new month on that same day. During the following night the moon did not appear, which seemed to prove they were false witnesses. Rabbi Dossa B. Harkinas in fact did not accept the decision made by Rabban Gamaliel: "They are false witnesses. How can men testify that a woman has given birth to a child when on the new day we see her belly still swollen?"[78] Rabbi Yehoshua, another member of the court, accepted this refutation and put Rabban Gamaliel's ruling in doubt. When Gamaliel heard of this controversy he sent Yehoshua a severe order bidding him to desecrate the day which, according to R. Yehoshua's calculation, would be the Day of Atonement. Obedience would force R. Yehoshua publicly to acknowledge the authority of the head of the court through the "desecration" of that most holy day. R. Yehoshua found himself in grievous predicament until R. Akiva came to his aid. Akiva wished to release him from torment, so he gave Yehoshua a reason why he should follow the court's rule even if he was convinced the court had been wrong, and that to follow the court's order would cause the desecration of a sacred day. R. Akiva's argument affirmed the constitutive power of the institution. He said: "I can bring proof [from Scripture] that whatever Rabban Gamaliel has done is valid, because it says, 'These are the appointed seasons of the Lord holy convocations, which ye shall proclaim in their appointed seasons.' [This means that] whether they are proclaimed at their proper time or not at their proper time, I have no appointed seasons save these." Akiva emphasized the last part of the verse, "which ye shall proclaim," as giving the court constitutive power to define the appointed seasons. The court therefore constitutes the calendar. Time is not an objective state but something which is socially dependent. In this instance it is the constitutive privilege of the court. Time is solely what the court claims it to be. R. Yehoshua then went to R. Dossa to convince him to follow the court and made another argument which is procedural in its very nature: "If we call in question [the decisions of] the Beth Din [court] of Rabban Gamaliel, we must call in question the decisions of every Beth Din which has existed since the days of Moses up to the present time."

Rabbi Yehoshua followed his point with another procedural argument: "For it says: 'They went up, Moses and Aaron, Nadab and Abihu and seventy of the elders of Israel.' Why were the names of the elders not mentioned? To show that every group of three which has acted as a Beth Din over Israel is on a even standard with the Bet Din of Moses." The names of the members of Moses' court were not mentioned in the Torah because the authority of the court does not rest upon the unique qualities of its members.

When Rabbi Yehoshua arrived and desecrated his holy day before Rabban Gamaliel, the latter's response was remarkable, further reinforcing the procedural quality of the institutions's authority: "Rabban Gamaliel rose and kissed him on his head and said to him: Come in peace my teacher and my disciple—my teacher in wisdom and my disciple because you have accepted my decision." By calling Yehoshua "my teacher in wisdom" Rabban Gamaliel recognized him as the superior scholar; he made clear that his own privilege was by no means the privilege of unique endowment, but the procedural privilege of being the official. Rabbi Yehoshua is indeed the authority on Halakhah;

Rabban Gamaliel is in authority. This account of the conflict between the two and its resolution embodies two views on the privilege of the court. On the one hand, it is not possible that the court could ever be mistaken, because the court constitutes meanings rather than discovering them. On the other hand, it is not possible to question the authority of the court even if it could be mistaken, because of the procedural priority of the institution.

The procedural and constitutive approaches manifest a complex attitude to the issue of truth in interpretation. The constitutive approach questions the very idea that such truth can be uncovered, either because it pictures revelation as open-ended with no fixed meaning, or because it grants the interpreter the privilege of defining the text regardless of the original intent. The procedural approach does not deny the existence of a correct, fixed meaning about which the court might be mistaken, but it questions the criterion of rightness as the sole operative principle.

Not surprisingly, thinkers who were concerned mainly with "getting it right" rejected the second approach, especially when they attributed an ontological effect to commandments. In this view the mistaken ruling of a court that permitted forbidden, impure food is not merely a legal error which can be overruled in due course. For to adhere to the court's mistaken ruling would cause "spiritual damage" to the soul of the person who consumes the food. Truth, according to the ontological understanding, does not consist of a fixed meaning that can be overridden for the sake of the court's authority. Truth is defined by correspondence with an unalterable reality which will operate even if a mistake is legitimized.

This is the basis for Isaac Abravanel's rejection, in his commentary on Deuteronomy, of the procedural argument which accepts the possibility that the court could be mistaken. Abravanel argues that it is an error to take literally the verse " that right is left and that left is right." This does not mean that the court ruled mistakenly, but rather that the ruling is regarded as erroneous by the losing contender. Thus, Abravanel argues, the addition of the phrase "before your own eyes" in the *Sifrei* is crucial.[79] He proceeds to criticize the attempt to harmonize between concern for the ontological effect of the commandments and the procedural deference to the court's authority. According to Abravanel, the harmonizers believe that the ontological damage caused by the court's mistake is counterbalanced by the benefit that results from the very act of submitting to the court. The medical analogy for such a balance would be that a person's belief that he is consuming something beneficial—while in reality it is damaging—could neutralize the noxious effects of that substance. Abravanel refuses to accept such a view:

> It is improper to believe that either in many or few [cases] something evil might result from the divine commandments. Heaven forbid that our rabbis blessed their memory, intended such a thing. And the Torah would not rely upon the operation of the imagination of the commandment's observer, that he should think of the impure as pure, of the prohibited as allowed and of the damaging as beneficial. Since God's Torah pursues justice and God is true and his Torah true.

The debate whether procedural authority can be accommodated with an ontological picture of norms reveals the intricate ways in which conceptions of authority are related to notions of normative truth, which are in turn related to competing ideas about controversy. The starting point in this cross-generational meta-controversy was the emergence of a flexible code, that is, the canonization of controversy itself in the Mishnah. Continuing reflection on this unique canonical mode initiated a controversy over controversy that involved opposing understandings of tradition, interpretation, and authority, and a deep debate over the possibility of codification.

Canon and Curriculum

ॐ FORMATIVE TEXT

The previous discussion of the normative canon focused on the text as a source of behavioral norms, examining the complex notions of authority that are attached to the normative function of the text in the Jewish canon. Taking this discussion one step further, the formative canon is not only obeyed but also serves other functions: it is studied, taught, transmitted, rehearsed, performed, and reflected upon. It affects and influences many domains, including attitudes, beliefs, judgments, sensitivities, aspirations, ideals, language, self-identity, and so on. Among the various domains the most fundamental formative level is the one that contains beliefs, attitudes, and narratives that shape the framework for future discourse within a community and constitute its terms. Borrowing Wittgenstein's concept of framework, this fundamental text will be called the "framework text."

Wittgenstein developed the idea of framework while examining some assertions that have the power of generality and certainty, such as "the world existed before I was born," or "there is an external world." He claimed that although these sentences sound like empirical propositions, they actually have a constitutive role in language. If they are verified at all, they are not verified the way we verify empirical propositions, and if taught, they are not taught in the same manner. The relationship between these statements and other statements and practices is complicated. On the one hand, the assertion that the world existed before us is an intrinsic condition of much of our discourse and practice. On the other hand, this belief, which appears to be a condition for much of our discourse, is supported by that very discourse itself. Though we are never taught that there is an external world, our language, practices, and way of living continuously exhibit and support such an assertion. For Wittgenstein, taking these framework propositions to be straightforward empirical propositions engenders deep confusion, which lies at the heart of many philosophical pseudo-problems such as skepticism.[1] (When someone is asked: "How do you know that there is a chair in the room?" he can answer: "I was told so by someone I trust," or "I saw the chair an hour ago." Unlike doubt regarding knowledge of the presence of a chair, doubt concerning the framework leads us to question the very means available for verifying anything. Such a doubt appears to have no meaning, since it is not clear what type of answer is expected.) The epistemological role of framework assertions is not our subject. The idea of a matrix that serves as the constitutive framework of a discourse may be useful, however, in elucidating the fundamental role of certain texts.

In text-centered societies the framework shared by a community is intimately connected to a canonical text, which in its turn may be a framework narrative, one that members of a society identify as their own. Framework narratives usually concern the events that constituted the community, and their protagonists are founding fathers, characters larger then life who shaped the society when things were still fluid, like the gods in creation myths who formed the cosmos out of chaos. The American Revolution, the French Revolution, the Exodus from Egypt are but three examples of framework narratives. However, these narratives are not tied to a single canonical text unless the society itself is text-centered. The story of the American Revolution is not connected to any canonical text; it is an event that is taught, told, and commemorated through a variety of texts (though a canonical history of the American Revolution may exist within academic circles). In text-centered societies, by contrast, the framework narrative is intimately connected to a specific text. Allegiance and identity with a narrative are mediated through allegiance to a text. Belief in the Exodus and belief in the Book of Exodus are basically indistinguishable. In effect, belief in the Torah and belief in what is reported in the Torah are so nearly identical that it would be difficult to describe their relationship as mutually dependent. In oral traditions the founding narrative is typically connected not to a text but to a version of the narrative memorized, cherished, and revered by members of the community. The Homeric epics, for instance, are described by certain scholars as the tribal encyclopedia of the Greeks which played an all-encompassing didactic role. These oral narratives informed people of public and private law, taught them the basic skills of life, such as navigating and hunting, and constituted the ethical guidelines.[2] The function of the Homeric texts in shaping Greek values is similar. These values are conveyed by a cherished text (or to put it more precisely, a cherished, transmitted version of the oral poetry), and the text is cherished both for itself and also because it embodies values that are cherished independently.[3]

The dominant mode of intellectual creativity in a text-centered community is interpretative. This is true of many aspects of Jewish culture. Much of Kabbalah and talmudic learning takes the form of interpretation of underlying canonical texts. Even achievements in philosophy are interpretative, though one might expect philosophy to be discussed in a conceptual, noninterpretative mode. Maimonides' *Guide of the Perplexed* is mainly an interpretation of the Torah, and the same is true of other philosophically oriented texts. Interpretation is not only a mode of representation; it reflects and shapes a way of thinking with antisystematic tendencies. The Talmud, an interpretative text, does not discuss questions such as "What is justice?" and search for a definition. The talmudic concept of justice (if there is one) is articulated through intricate interpretations of the Mishnah and presented through distinctions among cases.

Another aspect of text-centeredness is that intimate knowledge of shared texts exists at least among the learned, and references to them are used as a medium of exchange. The language of the letters written by medieval rabbis is saturated with the formative texts, so that the untrained reader needs a complicated apparatus of references to explain the textual allusions. In modern Hebrew literature S. Agnon is the last of the text-centered writers in this sense. His work makes constant reference to earlier texts, and although one can understand the plot without knowledge of these texts, much of the subtle meaning is lost. By contrast, the works of Amos Oz do not require such intimate knowledge of earlier canonical texts. In this sense, Oz and most contemporary Israeli writers illustrate the loss of the shared former text. Intimate knowledge of a chain of formative texts can no longer be taken for granted.

This is not, of course, to claim that a text can be all-pervasive in shaping every corner of human life and thought of a text-centered society. Local customs certainly develop independently of the central text;[4] ideas external to the text often influence world views; and the text is situated in the midst of changing historical circumstances far beyond its control. All these factors affect even the most text-centered community imaginable, weakening the formative role of the text. But in text-centered societies, even if the text is neither a direct nor an indirect source of customs and ideas, they become linked to it to a varying degree. Some are validated directly through the text; others have a less immediate connection to it but are articulated in terms of the text and accommodate to its language. In any event, these ideas or practices must enter into a relationship of exchange with the text. Moreover, much of their success will depend on their ability to shed new light on the formative texts and to infuse them with new energies.

This notion of formative texts may be expressed in a yet more paradoxical manner. If the new ideas or customs are not criticized or compromised while confronting the formative text, they will eventually change the way the text is read and perceived. Rather than being modified to accommodate to the text, they come to modify the interpretation of the text so that it will accommodate them. In any case, in the text-centered community domains initially independent of texts are destined to enter into a dialectical relationship with them.

On occasion, ideas that originated outside and were later articulated in terms of the existing formative text themselves become part of the formative stock of the culture. Among Jewish formative texts the Zohar is an example of this phenomenon. Written at the end of the thirteenth century as an interpretation of the Torah, it subsequently became an integral part of the canon for many Jews. After almost two hundred years in which the Zohar was known only to an exclusive group of kabbalists, it became the canonic text of Kabbalah. Its influence and prestige grew when it acquired a normative status, and in the sixteenth century R. Joseph Karo in his *Beit Yosef* used it as an authoritative book for halakhic ruling. The Zohar became a formative text in the sense we described above, for in large measure further developments in Kabbalah originated as interpretation of that sacred book.[5]

In a text-centered culture, outside ideas are either articulated in terms of the canonical text or change the way the text is read. If those ideas are powerful enough, the internal logic of text-centeredness will soon make them part of the formative texts. Now a *formative* text must be distinguished from a *central* text. While the latter might affect the direction, knowledge, and future shape of a given field of inquiry, a formative text is one in which progress in the field is made through interpretation of the text itself. A text-centered culture that has formative texts proceeds in that mode; its achievements are interpretative. In a text-centered culture the choice of texts that become objects of constant reflection and interpretation, and the extent of their self-containment and self-sufficiency are of great consequence. Let us turn now to the discussion of this problem in the Jewish curriculum.

?◦ THE CONCEPT OF TORAH IN "TALMUD TORAH" (TORAH LEARNING)

The transformation of the study of Torah into a major religious ideal is one of the distinct innovations of the rabbinic period. In the Bible itself the study of Torah serves a primarily didactic role: to guarantee the continuity of memory and tradition. Scholars are not presented as ideal biblical figures, and the study of Torah is not central to religious life as a spiritual mode of achieving intimacy with God. In the rabbinic period, in contrast, the Torah becomes an object of ongoing reflection, and the ideal of learning comes to be considered a major religious obligation, equal if not superior to other religious obligations such as the practice of the *mitzvot* and prayer.[6] The Talmud states: "The study of Torah is greater than the daily sacrifices of the Temple."[7] Elsewhere Raba maintains that "anyone who studies Torah needs neither the burnt offering nor the atonement sacrifice nor the guilt offering."[8] Along with the shift of authority from priest and prophet to scholar, a change essential in the formation of a text-centered community, the Torah came to be portrayed as the locus of God's presence. "Even for one who studies the Torah alone, the Shechinah is with him."[9] Study of the Torah is thus conceived as an intimate form of communication with God.

Schematically, we could describe three approaches to the sacred; that of the priest, the prophet, and the scholar. In the priestly conception of the sacred, God is manifest in a sacred geography; He has a territorial presence in the Temple. For the prophet, history serves as the stage for the divine drama, and God is revealed in sacred events. The scholar conceives the text as the medium for the sacred; it is in the Torah itself that God is found. This triad of space, history, and text is a schematic representation because the positions overlap, and in reality they do not form mutually exclusive clusters. Ezekiel was a priest-prophet and the rabbis revered sacred events as well. But despite all reservations and the necessary caution against generalizations of this kind, a new weight and emphasis undeniably appears in relation to the text as the center of divine presence. Bereft of sacred territory after the destruction of the Second Temple and alienated from divine history in their exile, Jews found comfort in the Torah, their portable temple.[10] The brilliance of this religious ideal is owed, in part, to the infinite possibilities it opens. New layers discovered in the text and the multiplicity of its interpretations are potentially identical with the infinity of divine presence. No wonder then that Jewish scholars entered every possible fissure in the text, followed every subtle allusion within it, and probed its depth with so many imaginative interpretative strategies.

The rise of this intellectual-religious ideal generated conflicts that became central from the Tannaitic period onward. Action and learning clashed on two levels. First, the obligation of constant Torah study was difficult to reconcile with the burden of earning a living. Does the ideal of Talmud Torah presuppose a miraculous order in which scholars who are totally devoted to the study of Torah are freed from the burdens of ordinary life and supported by the help of heaven? Or, to rephrase the question: do scholars, like priests, form a distinct class which must be supported by the rest of the community or must they rely on their own means? This issue was debated continually from the early rabbinic period until the Middle Ages and even later.[11] The second level of the conflict between study and action was more internal, involving the relationship between study and other religious obligations, among them prayer and other commandments such as charity. Is study only a means for learning correct practices, and if more than that, should it take precedence over other religious obligations? The Talmud proposes a variety of rules to settle such points, but the tensions between spiritual fulfillment through intellectual endeavor and other kinds of religious excellence were never resolved in principle within the Jewish tradition. Those tensions provoked later developments critical of the culture of study, such as the hasidic movement beginning in the eighteenth century, and the Musar movement of the nineteenth century.[12]

Attention will be focused here on the second level of tensions, those that are internal to the ideal of study. To begin with there is the question of precisely what ought to be studied in the Torah. In the context of Jewish curriculum the criterion for choice is not aesthetic superiority or educational merit but the type of reflection that enhances the religious perfection of the soul. The issue of what should be learned is central both because of the primary role of learning intrinsic to the ideal of Talmud Torah and also because the selection of texts and subject matter reflects the deepest religious sensitivities. The question of which texts are religiously worthy of intellectual endeavor became acute in response to the tendency to regard the Talmud as the exclusive, all-consuming object of reflection. But before entering the debate, let us consider the Talmud and its place in the curriculum.

Following its sealing the Talmud, through the work of the Geonim, had become commonly accepted as canonical, the normative text from which Halakhah can be prescribed.[13] Although the Talmud was not originally composed as a source of the law but rather as record of innumerable discussions and debates, it is possible to infer halakhic rulings from it, guided by certain principles (for example, in all disagreements between Rav and Samuel concerning monetary matters the law is in accordance with Samuel). In time the Talmud became central not only in the normative realm, to reach halakhic decisions, but also as the major text to be studied, in the sense that learning is its own reward. Talmudic learning and scholarship in the period immediately after the formation of the Babylonian Talmud was not widespread. Expertise in Talmud was concentrated among the Geonim and their yeshivot in Babylon. The dynastic structure of the yeshiva at that time gave a de facto monopoly on the study of the Talmud to a few families that served as legal authorities for the rest of the community, for which it was a normative text but not yet a formative one. During this period learned Jews who were not affiliated with the yeshiva saw the Talmud as a subject for legal experts and not as a formative canon for the learned. There was a clear division of labor between the yeshivot of Babylon and the community at large.[14]

Talmudism in the full sense flourished later, after the Geonic period, with the emergence of centers of study in Germany and France from the eleventh century onward. Rabbi Shlomo Yitzkhaki, known by the acronym Rashi, was a product of these schools and produced a running commentary on the Talmud which is both subtle and clear. Its clarity made the text available to a wider audience and contributed to the spread of Talmud, and its subtlety was a source of ongoing discussion that marked the work of the next generations of Franco-German scholars known as the Tosafists. As Chaim Soloveitchik described it, the Tosafists problematized every line in the Talmud and engaged in an overall project of talmudic dialectics that aimed at discovering contradictions between one section and another and then reconciling them by making distinctions between the cases. The work of the Tosafists was the culmination of the burst of talmudism in France and Germany, both in scope and depth.[15]

In Spain the situation was somewhat different. Although we know of important figures of talmudic learning in Spain such as Isaac Alfasi and Joseph Ibn Migash, talmudic study in the eleventh and twelfth centuries was not as widespread as in France and Germany.[16] Maimonides, a product of the Spanish school, painted a gloomy picture of talmudic study in Spain, a situation that served as one impetus for his codification of the Talmud in the *Mishneh Torah.*[17] Through the second half of the thirteenth century in Spain talmudic study and creativity flourished around the school of Nachmanides and his disciple R. Shlomo Ibn Adret, known as Rashba. The Spanish school integrated some of the Tosafists' achievements but emphasized conceptual work rather than the harmonizing dialectics of the Tosafists. In addition to France and Spain a thriving school of talmudic learning developed in Provence, and toward the end of the twelfth century Provence was considered by Maimonides the future center of talmudic learning.[18]

Thus it was between the eleventh and the thirteenth centuries, not immediately after its production, that the Talmud was fashioned into what we know of it today: a text to struggle with, a fountain of originality and subtlety that has captured countless minds for generations. The emergence of the Talmud in the early Middle Ages as a text of study and reflection, and the interpretations that were produced in Spain, Provence, France, Italy, and Germany from the eleventh century onward were achievements at least equal if not superior in importance to those the kabbalists and the philosophers reached in the same period.

NB

A major consequence of the rise of Talmud and its predominant role especially in Ashkenaz is the subordinate status of the study of Bible in the curriculum. The Talmud itself recommends dividing the time of study into three: one third Bible, one third Mishnah, and one third Talmud.[19] (The "Talmud" recommended here does not refer to the text

of the Talmud, but, as many medieval commentators understood, it
means gaining understanding and reasoning about the Mishnah and
the ability to deduce laws from the previous material. "Talmud" therefore includes various types of legal reasoning.)[20] The Talmud's own balanced definition of "Talmud Torah," or Torah-learning, combines all
the elements of study: the written Law, the Mishnah, and the Talmud.
The reaction of Rabbi Jacob ben Meir (Tam), the greatest Tosafist, to
this talmudic statement reflects a situation in which the Talmud was
studied predominantly, while the Bible and Mishnah were relegated
to a marginal position in the curriculum. R. Tam defended the practice of studying Talmud exclusively by claiming that the Babylonian
Talmud in fact includes all three components. According to R. Jacob
ben Meir, the name Talmud Babli [Babylonian Talmud] derives from
the Hebrew root *balal* (mixed), and that means that it contains both
the text of the Mishnah and passages from the Bible.[21] Consequently,
there is no need for independent study of the Bible and the Mishnah
outside of the Talmud. According to this view, the Talmud becomes
a full mediator for the other elements and, most remarkably, for the
Bible itself.[22]

The history of Bible study in the Jewish curriculum is complicated
and fraught with tension. What follows is merely a general sketch of
the role of Bible in the curriculum, concentrating on statements relevant to our line of inquiry. The medieval tendency to marginalize the
study of the Bible was condemned by various writers and scholars. In
the late fifteenth century, for example, Isaac Abravanel commented on
the mishnaic Tractate *Avot*'s prescription to study the Bible until age
five as follows: "He [the author of the Mishnah] did not say that until
age five one should study Bible and no more, the way the Ashkenazim
are practicing today."[23] Abravanel condemns the Ashkenazi practice
because he believes that age five is the appropriate time for beginning
study of the Bible, not ending it and neglecting Bible study from then
on. Abravanel's comment on "the Ashkenazim" points to a difference
in the place of Bible study between the curriculum in France and Germany and that of Spain. The situation described by Abravanel had its
roots in the difference between Ashkenaz and the Spanish tradition
three centuries earlier. In Ashkenaz, the rise of talmudic study and the
impact of the Tosafists caused a decline in Bible studies. Yehudah, the
son of the Rosh, who grew up in Germany and moved to Spain with
his father at the beginning of the fourteenth century, wrote to his sons

in his will: "Make regular times to study the verses [of the Bible] with precision and commentary. Since I did not study the verse [Scripture] in my childhood because they are not used to study the verses in Ashkenaz, I could not study it here [in Spain]."[24] In the late fourteenth century Isaac Profirat Duran the Efodi was sharply critical of Ashkenazic practice: "and they [in Ashkenaz] consider a fool one who spends his time in Bible study, because the Talmud is [considered by them] the principal thing *{ikar}*. This malady is very strong in France and Ashkenaz."[25] This practice continued into the sixteenth and seventeenth centuries, however, although an impressive attempt at an overall reform of the curriculum, including a return to Bible studies, did take place, initiated by R. Yehudah ben Bezalel (the Maharal) and his circle in the sixteenth century, but it met with little success.[26]

While these descriptions may be somewhat exaggerated, we do find explicit disparagement of Bible study. A sixteenth-century rabbi, Aharon Land, said: "No Jew should learn anything but the Talmud. All other books, including 'Meiras books' and even the twenty-four books [the Bible, which consists of twenty-four books]—no Jew has to learn much of it."[27] The Bible is mentioned among texts superfluous to the curriculum in the same breath as the "books of Meiras," a traditional reference to heretical works. A more elaborate and fascinating justification for this policy appears in another opinion expressed in the sixteenth century: "The coming redemption will happen only because the merit of the study of the Talmud, which is not the case with the study of other subjects, even Bible. Bible study does not cause anyone to be pious, because we cannot understand the foundations of our sacred Torah which is the written Torah, except through the oral Torah which is its interpretation. And even a little Talmud is enough to bring more fear of God than much learning of other subjects."[28] Since direct access to the foundational text does not enhance piety, it is better to read the Talmud exclusively.

This sixteenth-century attitude toward Bible studies echoes earlier and astonishing interpretations of the talmudic injunction to "prevent your sons from the *higayon*."[29] Zemach ben Paltoy, one of the Geonim, understood "higayon" to mean Bible study and said: "prevent your sons from reflecting upon the biblical verses that lean towards heresy."[30] According to this interpretation, the Talmud itself warns against unmediated study of the Bible. The need to guard the canon because of its subversive potential is manifest in the design of a curriculum that emphasizes the study of interpretation and minimizes the study of the canonical text itself. An unmediated reading of the Bible might lead to problematic conclusions, hence it is better not to study the Bible but rather to study its traditional commentaries. In this school of thought the centrality of the Talmud in the curriculum is not at all accidental. It results both from the distance between the foundational text and the actual tradition and from the potential danger of unmediated access to the sacred text.

Once the Talmud became the principal formative text in Jewish life, it came to determine not only what people should do but how to think, how to see the world, and what objects to choose to meditate upon. The Talmud thus exerted a tremendous influence on Jewish life. In the Middle Ages it was surrounded by creative interpreters whose work itself became part of the Talmud, endowing the text with prestige and depth and offering a variety of approaches to it. This development did not pass unchallenged.

?⟡ THE CHALLENGERS OF TALMUDISM

A distinction may be drawn within the category of the formative canon between weak and strong canon. By "strong" canon I mean that the canonical text becomes the sole text to be studied. In certain halakhic schools, before the Talmud was completed, the Torah acquired the status of the exclusive canonical text allowed as the subject of study. That is, not only was "Talmud Torah" an obligation, but the study of all other texts not part of Torah was forbidden. In the Babylonian Talmud's Tractate *Menachot* the following story is recounted:

> Ben Damah, the son of R. Ishmael's sister, once asked R. Ishmael, "May one such as I, who have studied the whole of the Torah, learn Greek wisdom?" He thereupon read to him the following verse: " 'This book of the law shall not depart out of thy mouth but thou shall meditate therein day and night' (Jos. 1:8). Go then and find a time that is neither day nor night, and learn then Greek wisdom."[31]

In other words, the study of sources other than the Torah is not allowed. The exclusive canonization of the Torah as the sole text worthy of study, along with the prohibition of everything external to it, represents a crucial decision in the spiritual history of the traditional Jewish community. Had the spiritual energy and intellectual effort expended in the Talmud been directed to another text, that would have created a completely different tradition.

A more moderate view has always coexisted with the view that perceived the Torah as the exclusive text of study. To the moderates the canonization of the Torah marked it as a text demanding study, yet this obligation did not forbid study of other texts. In opposition to the position cited above, it was maintained that the recitation of the Shema in the morning and evening could be thought of as "meditating therein day and night" and was thus a fulfillment of the obligation of Talmud Torah.[32] The question of the Torah's canonical status did not concern it in the normative sense, for both factions agreed on its normative role; it concerned the Torah in the sense of a text demanding study and whether that study must be exclusive. This question has been among the important issues debated by the generations to this day.

Beyond this debate another, more acute and radical dispute was waged within the traditional camp over the Talmud's canonical status in the curriculum. This is one of the most interesting and important debates in the history of canonization in Jewish tradition, and in investigating it I will build upon Isadore Twersky's view that challenges to exclusive talmudism came from two directions: Jewish philosophers and Jewish mystics.[33] The most extreme and least common position goes so far as to question whether the Talmud is a text worthy of reflection, to be part of the formative program of Jewish studies, or is simply a normative text, a legal tract. Joseph Ibn Kaspi and others were critical of the function of the Talmud even in its weaker formative version. In their view, the Talmud should not be supplemented but rather replaced in the curriculum. They tried to restrict Talmud study to legal specialists alone and challenged the spiritual value of learning the Talmud.[34] Another Provençal Jew and one of the most prominent Maimonideans of the thirteenth century, Jacob Anatoli, reported a hostile encounter with a talmudist. This unusual story reveals the way the Talmud (and also the Kabbalah) were perceived by some philosophical circles, and it is worth quoting:

> It is clear that our rabbis were versed in the study of wisdoms [meaning science and metaphysics]. They said that "the least among the eighty students of Hillel did not leave out anything that he did not study, neither a great thing nor a small thing." The Sages explained that Ma'aseh Merkabah is the great thing, and that all wisdoms are directed towards

it and are introductions to it. Because only in it is there a great and perfect advantage, since through it a man can approach the King. The Sages
say of the discussions of Abaye and Raba [the Talmud] that they are a
small thing. This is because the Mishnah and the rest of the codified
rules of Halakhah are sufficient for those seeking wisdom; this is the
opinion of our Rabbis of blessed memory. However, a "great thing"
today—in the eyes of our scholars the talmudists—is the study of the
deliberations of Talmud. Not the study of the actual rulings that are
derived from them [the rules of Halakhah], but the study of the questions and answers [talmudic deliberations]. The "small thing" in their
eyes is Ma'aseh Merkabah, which is the science of the Divine. It is not
a small thing among the good things, in their eyes, but an evil and bitter
one. The condemnation of this wisdom (philosophy) caused them to go
astray and call Ma'aseh Merkabah the empty names which they invented
in their heart—those heartless people. God will forgive this since it is
the opinion of most of our scholars, the rabbis. In accordance with this
mistaken opinion, it happened to me—Jacob the son of Rabbi Aba Mari
the son of Rabbi Shimon the son of Rabbi Anatoli—that one of the
rabbis of my generation reproached me a number of times for occasionally studying in Arabic bits of Hokhmah Limudit [preparatory sciences]
under the great scholar my father-in-law, Rabbi Shmuel the son of the
scholar Rabbi Yehudah Ibn-Tibon. And when he disturbed me with his
ongoing reproach and compelled me against my wish, I answered him
by the same token: do not treat my study as you would treat someone
taking a walk or playing the dice. (Introduction to *Malmad ha-Talmidim*)

The Talmud itself mentions Ma'aseh Merkabah as the "great thing"
and, following the Maimonidean tradition, this subject was identified
by Jacob Anatoli as metaphysics. Talmudic deliberations, in contrast,
are described by the Talmud itself as a "small thing." Moreover, in
Jacob Anatoli's view, for those who seek wisdom it is enough to study
the Mishnah and the rulings derived from the Talmud, and it is unnecessary to study talmudic deliberations. The study of Talmud is not a
worthy aim in itself, and the rabbis of his generation erred gravely in
attributing so much importance to the study of the discussions of Abaye
and Raba. While Ibn Kaspi wanted to limit talmudic study to legal
experts alone, Jacob Anatoli sought to restrict it to the derivation of
the Halakhah and as an introduction to the study of wisdom.[35] It is
clear that these philosophers challenge the exclusive canonization of
the Talmud as a formative text. Other, more influential and moderate
critics were also critical of the Talmud in the stronger version of its

formative function. They wished to supplement talmudic learning with additional texts, either in philosophy or Kabbalah. Although these men did recognize the value of talmudic study, they were disturbed by the Talmud's exclusive role in the curriculum and wished to add to it without, however, replacing it. These critics propose various formulations of the internal hierarchy between the Talmud and other material. Some saw the supplements as superior in value while others saw them as equal to the Talmud, but all insisted that the Talmud should not be the only subject of study.

This sort of moderate criticism was the position of many kabbalists and philosophers who had credentials as talmudists and wished to combine other intellectual interests with Talmud study. The formulation of their criticism is supported by Talmud's own references to the esoteric subject matter of Ma'aseh Merkabah, and, following Maimonides, the critics will usually identify the necessary companion to the Talmud as Ma'aseh Merkabah. The esoteric tradition does not serve only as an important supplement, however; it supplies the key to the understanding of the Talmud itself. Without the background of Ma'aseh Merkabah, the secrets within the Talmud cannot be uncovered.

It is important to stress again that neither moderate and radical critics ever challenged the normative status of the Talmud. They agreed that the Talmud is canonical in regard to norms; at issue was how formative the Talmud should be. Typically, these critics did not try to weaken the strong sense of the canonicity of the Torah so to allow study of secular matters or non-Torah texts. Rather, both kabbalists and philosophers strove to enlarge the concept of Torah so to include other matters and texts far beyond and more important than the Talmud.

It is not possible here to go into the fascinating history of Jewish curriculum, an endeavor that would be far beyond the scope of this work. Rather, I will present examples from each camp—philosophers and kabbalists—and discuss their approaches to the problem of Jewish formative texts. Through them I hope to examine what is involved in the concept of formative canon.

?❧ CODIFICATION AND DECANONIZATION

Maimonides, one of the greatest talmudists of all time, codified the discussions and compiled them in volumes of decisions arranged by subject. The thick forest of talmudic debates, many of which are conducted through association and intertwined in a complicated series of negotiations, was clearly and definitively reformulated in Maimonides' impressive work, the *Mishneh Torah*. In his introduction Maimonides writes: "And therefore I called this book *Mishneh Torah* since a person reads the written Torah first and then reads this book; and knows from it the whole of the Oral Torah and needs no other book besides them." This statement can be understood in two ways. The first and the more radical reading is that since Maimonides' work was meant to be an exhaustive summary of all the laws decided in the Talmud, he had produced a code that would replace the Talmud as an object of study. It would still have the status of a normative and binding text, for it dictated Maimonides' presentation of the law, but the clear organization and comprehensible language of *Mishneh Torah* rendered direct study of the Talmud itself unnecessary.

Maimonides' codification of the Talmud casts a potentially sophisticated effect upon the canon. It has the power to alter the canonical status of the Talmud; formerly both a normative text and the object of continual study, the Talmud could now revert to being just a normative text again. Paradoxically, anchoring the Talmud with an orderly and decisive code like the *Mishneh Torah* opens the way for its decline as a text to be studied.

Another, more moderate interpretation is that Maimonides did not in fact wish to replace the study of Talmud with the study of his code; rather, he aimed to summarize the Talmud for those who were incapable of studying the primary text.[36] Maimonides' own explicit statements about his intentions are contradictory. In a letter to Pinchas ha-Dayan, who criticized Maimonides for aiming to replace the Talmud, Maimonides denies such intentions, claiming that he meant to facilitate the study of Talmud and not to replace it.[37] But on other, less defensive occasions, he seems to take another position. To one of his students he recommends a thorough study of the *Mishneh Torah*, since "The aims of the Talmud and the like were fulfilled with the *Mishneh Torah*." And after this statements he condemns those who see talmudic dialectics as a goal in and of itself.[38] When *Mishneh Torah* arrived in Baghdad and was criticized by the local rabbis, one of Maimonides' students wrote to him with a great deal of anxiety. In a comforting response, Maimonides predicts that after the jealousy of other scholars fades, "all the Sons of Israel will be satisfied with the *Mishneh Torah* alone, and every other book will be surely abandoned."[39] In the same letter he claims not only that his work is a successful and comprehensive summary of the Talmud, but that the study of Talmud after his work is a waste of time: "And if you spend your time in interpretation and the interpretation of the Talmud's dialectics, and those matters to which we gave rest from their labor [by writing the *Mishneh Torah*], this will be a waste of time and of very little use."[40]

Even if Maimonides did not intend to create a full replacement for the Talmud with the *Mishneh Torah*, it is clear that he did aim to reduce the need for extensive talmudic dialectics.[41] He believed that canonization, which made the Talmud the only text worthy of study, was a serious spiritual error. Any investment of time and thought in the Talmud for ends other than knowledge of Halakhah was an effort unjustifiable in a spiritual sense. Maimonides believed that physics and metaphysics were the most suitable objects of study as a path to understanding God, which is the highest aspiration of intellectual religious effort. The Talmud, of course, does not deal systematically with metaphysics or theology; it is full of legal arguments on issues of partnership, damages, laws of evidence, contracts, and transactions but quite lacking in natural and supernatural science. The codification of the Talmud, which facilitated the halakhic decision-making process by sparing its students the work of untangling talmudic discussions, freed them to spend more time on other subjects worthy of reflection. Maimonides' opinion of people who ignored philosophy and studied only Talmud is clearly expressed in the parable of the palace in the *Guide of the Perplexed*. He compares the degrees of intimacy between various spiritual groups and God to the intimacy that various subjects share with the king in his palace. Some have never even seen the walls of the palace courtyard; those who have only studied Talmud without philosophy have reached the courtyard but have never entered the palace itself.[42] Maimonides did not conceal his preference for the study of physics and metaphysics over Talmud study, and he codified his view in the *Mishneh Torah* in a passage that aroused the anger of some of his expositors. It comes after four chapters at the beginning of the "Laws Concerning the Basic Principles of the Torah," in which Maimonides presents the essence of Aristotelian physics and metaphysics:

> The topics connected with these five precepts, treated in the above four
> chapters, are what our wise men called "Pardes," as in the passage "Four

went into Pardes" (T.B., *Hagigah* 14). And although these four were
great men of Israel and great sages, they did not all possess the capacity
to know and grasp these subjects clearly. Therefore, I say that it is not
proper to dally in Pardes until one has first filled oneself with bread and
meat, by which I mean knowledge of what is permitted and what forbidden, and similar distinctions in other classes of precepts. Although
these subjects were called by the sages "a small thing" (when they say
"A great thing Ma'aseh Merkabah; a small thing the discussion of Abaye
and Raba"), still this should have precedence. For the knowledge of these
things gives primarily composure to the mind. They are the precious
boon bestowed by God to promote social well-being on earth, and enable
men to obtain bliss in the life hereafter. Moreover, the knowledge of
them is within the reach of all, young and old, men and women; those
gifted with great intellectual capacity as well as those whose intelligence
is limited.[43]

Though the Talmud prescribes the acts of divine service in minute
detail, it never describes the object of worship—God Himself. Perhaps
for that reason, Maimonides thought, many halakhic experts had some
mistaken impressions, for instance, that God was corporeal. Their worship was thus defective despite their extensive knowledge and attention to every detail of the Talmud. The most important object of study
in the long run is He who must be served. Compared to metaphysical
ideas, traditional Talmud Torah is seen as "a small thing," even though
it should be approached before metaphysics. According to this reading,
one of the implications of codification was to demote the canonical
status of the Talmud from a text that is studied as a formative canon
to a text whose main role is normative. Such a change is central to the
philosophical culture Maimonides wished to cultivate, at least among
the elite.

Four Maimonideans in thirteenth- and fourteenth-century Spain and
Provence, Jacob Anatoli, Shem Tov ben Joseph Falaquera, Yehudah
ben Shmuel Ibn Abass, and Joseph Ibn Kaspi, all share the philosophical
attitude to Talmud study and express that view explicitly. In the words
of Falaquera,

> At first one should study the written law and then its interpretation, the
> oral law. Nowadays it is sufficient for a man to read the *halakhot* of Rabbi
> Alfasi of blessed memory, and along with them the books of our Rabbi
> Moses of blessed memory, which are called *Mishneh Torah*, for they are

truthful. [Maimonides'] commentary to the Mishnah is also a very useful book and sufficient for whoever wishes to comprehend the halakhic norm. And should he have leisure, it is good to study Mishnah and its commentary the Gemara, so as to exercise the mind and sharpen it for this is necessary for study . . . But I will tell you something [namely], that one ought not spend all one's days in problems and refutations as many do who tire themselves all night in comprehending one *halakhah* and in the morning, if asked anything about it, have no answer.[44]

Yehudah ben Shmuel Ibn Abass outlined a curriculum with a heavy philosophical program in which he suggested that the student should avoid studying the Tosafists,

since their discussions are a waste of man's time. They are futilities, a pursuit of wind, superfluous and of no value for the goal that is intended by the Talmud: the interpretation of the *mitzvot* and the rulings of Halakhah. One should make the effort to study so as to acquire the knowledge which would enable one to derive the Halakhah independently and correctly . . . One should always have before him those books which follow forth from the Talmud, specifically the book *Mishneh Torah*, authored by the great light, the genius of the exile of Ariel, the powerful hammer, whose name is greater than any rabbi, the Rambam blessed be his memory, who will not be valued by gold and crystal . . . It is the choicest of books written on the Talmud from the days of the Tannaites, i.e., the time of our holy rabbi [Yehudah the Prince], up to and including today.

These statements reveal a shared outlook concerning the aim and value of Talmud study. The first point is that Talmud study is mainly instrumental to the derivation of the law and is not an aim in itself with intrinsic religious significance. As Ibn Abass put it, "the goal intended by the Talmud [is] the interpretation of the *mitzvot* and the ruling of Halakhah." Falaquera recommends the study of halakhic codes, and Anatoli claims that "the Mishnah and the rest of the codified rules of Halakhah are sufficient for those who seek wisdom!" Second, Talmud study is inferior—a "small thing"—in comparison to the study of metaphysics, Ma'aseh Merkabah—the "big thing." Thus Talmud study or, more correctly, the derivation of norms is a preparatory stage for the study of wisdom. Third, talmudic scholars are in great spiritual error when they regard the probing of talmudic intri-

cacies as the highest spiritual achievement. Ibn Abass attacked those
who deal with talmudic deliberations for their own sake and described
the work of Tosafists—the crown of talmudic subtlety—as pursuit of
wind and superfluous. Anatoli dismisses those who study talmudic
deliberations and consider them to be a "big thing." Falaquera warns
against indulging oneself in talmudic problems and refutations, and
Ibn Kaspi asks rhetorically: "Is not the faculty of expounding the existence and unity of God as important as familiarity with the rule concerning a small milk spoon?" Fourth, a natural conclusion from these
three assumptions is that the *Mishneh Torah* ought to play the major
role in talmudic curriculum. In one way or another all four reach this
conclusion. This shared though differently nuanced outlook echoed
something deep in Maimonides' own intellectual program, which was
expressed in his *Mishneh Torah*.

Although a school of Maimonideans was active in the thirteenth century, Maimonides' campaign to decanonize the *Mishneh Torah* did not
meet with success. In fact, the cunning of history caused the reverse of
his wishes to be realized: rather than diminishing traditional Jewish
involvement in Talmud and its commentators, Maimonides' work
served to increase it. His own book became the focus of endless dialectics and debates over halakhic problems—on what sources Maimonides
based his decision, on how he interpreted a *sugiya*, whether he interpreted it correctly, and so on. Immediately after the work appeared it
was annotated by one of the generation's greatest scholars, Rabad of
Provence, and drew various expositors who offered challenges and
responses. Indeed, Maimonides was so successful in his codification of
talmudic law that his book became a fundamental instrument of
halakhic decision-making. However, most scholars of his generation
and the next did not consider it the sole text worthy of study on these
issues but thought it was an important text, itself a sort of commentary on the Talmud. Hence it was not seen as a substitute for the
Talmud and its commentators. Thus Maimonides, who wanted his codification to put out the age-old fires of debate over minute details of
Halakhah, merely poured oil on the flames.

For Maimonides, philosophy had a central religious role in the curriculum since it is a means to knowledge of God, which is equated
with the love of God. "A person does not love God but with the knowledge that he knows of Him, and according to his knowledge will there
be love, if little then little and if much then much. Therefore, one must

dedicate himself to understanding and comprehending the wisdoms that teach him about his creator as much as man is capable of understanding and comprehending"[45] (*Teshubah* 10:6). Philosophy is also crucial in creating the appropriate image of God in the worshiper's eyes; it is the safeguard against anthropomorphism, which is worse than idolatry. The perception of God that is shaped solely by the Bible and the Talmud might lead to this sort of idolatrous belief. Thus a talmudic education, which provides all the information about the proper way to worship God yet lacks rigorous philosophical training, does not convey the proper image of the God who must be worshiped.[46] Philosophy also provides the code by which the apparent anthropomorphism of Scripture may be surmounted; it directs the reader to the hidden meaning of Scripture. Philosophy is not an added corrective to the traditional texts, but it probes the innermost meaning of the tradition itself. Maimonides, moreover, equates the eternity of the soul with the acquisition of eternal truths. What remains in the afterlife is the impersonal body of knowledge a person gained in his life on earth; in Aristotelian terminology, what remains is the person's active intellect.[47] The radical consequence of such an approach is that the traditional talmudist has no afterlife.

Weighty issues are therefore at stake in the problem of curriculum and the role of philosophy in curriculum, among them the proper nonanthropomorphic conception of God, the notion of the afterlife, and the network of concepts that provide the interpretive key to the Torah's true meaning.[48] This Maimonidean curriculum and its supporters came under attack in one of the most interesting debates on curriculum in Jewish history, which took place in the early fourteenth century in Provence. The story deserves some detail because of its intricacies and its importance in determining the formative canon and the exclusive place of the Talmud within it.

ESOTERICISM AND CENSORSHIP

Among the three main centers of Jewish learning in the late thirteenth century—France-Germany, Spain and Provence—the Andalusian tradition of studying philosophy as a major part of the curriculum was kept alive mainly in Provence. In the late twelfth and early thirteenth centuries Provençal Jewry was rapidly affected by Maimonidean philosophy, and the northern and southern parts of France became culturally more and more differentiated. The Jews of Provence identified with the Andalusian tradition and distinguished themselves from their northern neighbors, the "Tsarfatim," or French Jews. R. Shlomo of Lunel, a typical representative of Provençal Jewish culture in the early fourteenth century, described the French Jews in this terms: "Our brethren in France, those whose soul hates the wisdom of nature and philosophy and loves the Torah alone."[49]

While the influence of philosophical culture throughout the thirteenth century accelerated in Provence, in Spain itself the tradition of philosophy was on the decline. One of the opponents of philosophy and a great talmudic authority of the first half of the fourteenth century, Asher ben Yehiel, known as the Rosh, spent time in the three principal centers of study. He was educated in Germany, and early on became an authoritative figure there. He then moved southward to Provence, where he encountered the philosophical culture of the Provençal Jews, describing his experience as follows:

> I entered the land of Provence and I saw a good land, and the people in that land according to what I saw were people of excellent virtues, fluent in language, with clear minds, and possessed of wisdom. And I gave praise to the Lord of my life who had brought me there. But when I entered the chambers of their hearts expecting to find them white, I found them black, and I found only two or three people whose hearts God had touched to strengthen in His Torah and separate themselves from the multitude who stray after lies.[50]

The Rosh then moved to Spain and served as the Rabbi of Toledo, which was described by another opponent of philosophy as "the city that was once full of the wisdom of nature and philosophy and now, thank God, has become fine flour."[51]

The rise of Maimonidean influence in Provence did not pass unchallenged. In the fourth decade of the thirteenth century a debate about Maimonides' writings erupted there, rapidly turning from a local argument into an intercommunal one.[52] The opponents of Maimonides turned to the French rabbis for support, and his disciples appealed to the Spanish side. The inability of the Provençals to enlist total support among the Spanish elite for their Maimonidean position evinces the cultural shift that began in the first decades of the thirteenth century.

Provence had become the Maimonides bastion while Spanish Jewry moved away from the Maimonidean trend. After the bitter struggle ended, a relative equilibrium was achieved. A policy of noninterference was accepted, and in Provence the Maimonidean culture retained the upper hand. Seventy years later the peace was shattered, and at the beginning of the fourteenth century the place of philosophy in the curriculum became the central issue of a heated debate between Spanish and Provençal Jewry.

A Provençal rabbi from Montpelier, Aba Mari, was struck by the radical allegorization of Scripture practiced in the region and alarmed that this mode of interpretation had penetrated the public sermons in the synagogue. In the collection of letters entitled *Minhat Kenaot* (offering of jealousy) he gathered as a record of his struggle, Aba Mari mentions a wedding at which he himself was present, where the speaker claimed that Abraham and Sarah were allegories of form and matter.[53] This instance was one of many in which allegory, a tool permissible in dealing with difficult talmudic passages and accepted by Aba Mari himself, became a component of scriptural interpretation and was applied to narratives from Genesis.[54] In the process the figures of the biblical narrative lost their historicity and were seen as representing Aristotelian concepts. The four kings (Gen. 14:1) represented the four elements, the twelve tribes, the twelve stars of the zodiac, and so on.[55]

Shocked by this phenomenon, the rabbi began a campaign against such public sermons. After a short time, realizing that support for philosophical culture in Provence was overwhelming, Aba Mari and his sympathizers turned to an outside authority to intervene in what had hitherto been an internal regional matter. This authority, R. Shlomo Ibn Adret from Barcelona (Rashba), was the most important figure of Spanish Jewry at the time. Aba Mari assumed that with the support of the Rashba, who was respected in Provence as the greatest rabbinic authority of the generation, the opposition would collapse. The Rashba gave his full support to Aba Mari, condemning the allegorical interpretations and forcefully attacking the extensive philosophical teaching of the youth. The antinomian potential of allegorical interpretation was stressed in a polemical letter Rashba sent from Barcelona. If allegorization of the biblical narrative was thought to be necessary to elevate the meaningless, trivial, and particular details of the Genesis narrative to the conceptual and universal realm, the same logic would apply to the commandments. "Their [the allegorists] true intention is clear. They want to say that the commandments have no literal meaning, because what does God care if an animal is [correctly] slaughtered or not?"[56]

The line between allegorizing the biblical narrative and allegorizing the commandments is a fine one, and the allegorizers were accused of harboring a secret intention to cross that line. Greek wisdom was denounced as the alien concubine who leads Jewish youth astray from the legitimate Israelite wife, the Torah. Heretical potential was attributed to Aristotelianism given its denial of the possibility of Creation, Providence, and miracles. Who can guarantee that a young person will be able to distinguish between what is worthy and what is dangerous in Aristotelianism? In addition to its heretical potential, philosophy was thought to be dangerously seductive, like the Moabite women who seduced Israel to the sin of idolatry in the Shitim. After tasting the charms of philosophy, no young man will be willing to return and devote himself to the minutiae of the Talmud.

The community of Montpelier was called upon to prohibit the study of philosophy and to excommunicate allegorizers. A striking analogy was drawn between what should be done in the Jewish community of Montpelier and the contemporary persecution of heretics by the Christians: "All the Gentiles punish them like heretics, even about minor things that they have written in their books, and what about someone who says: 'Abraham and Sarah are form and matter,' would not they surround them with bushes and burn them?! All of the nations view themselves as descendants of Abraham and Sarah and they [the allegorists] claim that Abraham and Sarah are just allegories."[57]

The irony was that by elevating the concrete particular to the universal and the conceptual through allegory, the philosophers undermined not only the importance of the particulars in the biblical narrative but also the very idea of the particularity of the People of Israel. Sarah and Abraham, their flesh-and-blood forefathers, received the status of mere allegories. At this point the interpretative assimilation of the Torah to the Aristotelian realm becomes an act of assimilating the concrete people of Israel into the universal realm. No wonder that, among the many proposed allegorical readings of Genesis, this one was the most offensive to Aba Mari and his allies in Barcelona.

The harsh condemnation elicited a countermove. Aba Mari failed to achieve a consensus regarding the ban and to impose it in Montpelier.[58] The philosophical circles, including previous supporters of Aba

Mari, realized that their Provençal Jewish culture had been called into question by the Rashba's overall attack against philosophical culture, and that the matter extended far beyond the few public incidents of allegorization in preaching. Some Provençal figures, among them Jacob ben Machir, a relative of the Tibonite family who was most responsible for the success of philosophical culture in Provence, appealed to the Rashba. They questioned the legitimacy of his intervention. Alluding to the figure of Maimonides, they implied that the Rashba stood in opposition to a great and loyal tradition and to its champion, Maimonides.[59] The opponents of Aba Mari assumed that by portraying the debate as one about the essential way of life of Provençal Jewry and its vibrant philosophical tradition, they could get the Rashba and the Barcelona community to back off. The Rashba, who might have been mislead by Aba Mari's reports that his opposition came from marginal members of the community, recognized the strength and prominence of the opposition and announced his withdrawal, with the intention of leaving the matter to local authorities.

Later the Rashba realized that his opponents in Provence emphasized philosophy far in excess of the Maimonidean tradition with which he had hoped to avoid conflict. They advocated teaching philosophy to the young,[60] whereas Maimonides himself had warned against exposing the unprepared to philosophy. Moreover, all the traditional barriers of esotericism concerning divine matters were violated in Provence. While the Rashba was willing to tolerate philosophical learning among the few, he feared the effects of Aristotelian philosophy upon the many.[61] With the encouragement of Aba Mari, the Barcelonian community decided upon the following strategy: they would pronounce a ban upon those who teach philosophy to people younger than twenty-five and upon those who publicly offer allegorical interpretation of Scripture of the sort that proclaims Abraham is form and Sarah matter. The whole of Spanish Jewry would honor the ban and, with the assured support of the French Jewish community, the Provençal Jews would be isolated and thus forced to honor it as well.

The ban was formulated so as to avoid direct conflict with the Provençal tradition yet to undermine its philosophical culture and its widespread effects. There was no move to prohibit the study of philosophy as such but only to delay it to more mature age in order to shield the young from the dangerous effects of Aristotelianism, for even devotees of Aristotelian philosophy were aware of the great dangers it poses for the pious. The postponement of philosophical study could also be justified within the Provençal tradition itself. If, following Maimonides, philosophy were defined as Pardes or Ma'aseh Merkabah, the tradition itself manifestly warned against widespread exposure to such wisdom and its obvious dangers. Had Maimonides himself not warned against the teaching of philosophy to the uninitiated?[62]

Rashba's ban was therefore presented not as a direct attack on philosophy but as a pedagogical move to protect the young from its dangerous effects. First let them immerse themselves in Talmud, so that later they can safely overcome the dangers of philosophy. To restrict the study of philosophy, which the Rashba and his allies considered totally heretical and alien, they made subtle use of the traditional constraints regarding the teaching of esoteric matters. To avoid the appearance of attacking the Provençal tradition and its legacy, the ban explicitly exempts the writings of Maimonides. The Rashba's allies did that also for another reason: because they feared an analogy would be drawn between their struggle against philosophy and the failed, traumatic, and unsuccessful campaign against Maimonides' writings that had taken place in Provence seventy years earlier. Thus, while they spoke with little respect for philosophy, they expressed great veneration for Maimonides, an attitude which the Rashba went out of his way to demonstrate.[63] Further, contemporary masters of philosophical learning in Provence such as Jacob Anatoli or Ibn Tibon were never explicitly attacked. The complaints were usually lodged against two or three anonymous figures who had dared indulge in philosophical allegory in public or denied the possibility of miracles.

In Provence the ban was understood as an outright assault on the local tradition and its prominent figures.[64] In retaliation they promulgated a countervailing ban ostracizing those who would not teach their sons philosophy. In public defiance of the original ban, the Provençal community in Montpelier gathered in the synagogue on the Sabbath and studied Anatoli's philosophically oriented text, *Malmad ha-Talmidim*. Aba Mari's circle immediately issued a ban against that group, and the community became embroiled in a painful barrage of bans and counterbans.

The majority of the Provençal elite regarded Aba Mari's appeal to the Spanish community as an act of betrayal. In their view, by illegitimately inviting outside intervention, Aba Mari had put their entire tradition under the cloud of suspected heresy. Menahem ha-Meiri, one of the principal representatives of the Maimonidean tradition in Provence (Perpignan) and an important talmudic authority, expressed the philosophers' attitude in a powerful and bitter letter personally addressed to Aba Mari. The letter was stolen from the addressee and fell into the hands of his opponents in Montpelier. Seeking to inflict a painful blow to Aba Mari's party by using Meiri's prestige, they did everything in their power to publicize the letter. It was quickly copied and widely distributed in the city and was read in the synagogue on the Sabbath.[65] "With all due respect to the Rashba," wrote Meiri to Aba Mari, "were you unaware of the deep division between us and the Barcelonians concerning philosophy? They [in Barcelona] follow the Kabbalah and consider philosophy harmful!"[66]

As long as Aba Mari was only conducting a local campaign against making extravagant philosophical allegories in public, he apparently enjoyed Meiri's support. But the appeal to the Rashba changed the nature and the scope of the issue, for it was understood by Meiri as a violation of the Provençal cultural autonomy and an attack on basic spiritual convictions. If the whole issue were public allegorical sermons, he asked, why should we ban the teaching of philosophy? If one person errs, does that mean that the gates of Pardes should be barred to the whole community? Is philosophy not essential for establishing proof of God's incorporeality and unity? Are those who know God intellectually not preferable to mere believers? How can the opposition claim that philosophy corrupts piety when in Provence there were pious figures who combined Talmud and philosophy, and even those philosophers who were not talmudists were known for their piety?[67]

To expose the real attack masked by the compromising language of the ban, the Meiri pointed out the inconsistency of prohibiting the study of philosophy while allowing the study of the *Guide of the Perplexed.* How can anyone understand the *Guide* without vast philosophical training? Although the ban specifically excluded Maimonides from the prohibition, the Meiri drew an analogy with the debate over Maimonides' writings of seventy years earlier. From the Meiri's perspective the similarity between the two debates was undeniable, and Aba Mari's attempt to distinguish between them seemed totally artificial. Then as now, the cultural autonomy of Provence was being violated by external interference that had been illegitimately summoned. The failure of the first campaign and its traumatic effects should have taught Aba Mari a lesson.[68] The fight was over the value of wisdom itself, not over the mere restriction of its study based on the admitted dangers inherent in the subject matter. The attack on the marginal figures who had allegorized the Genesis stories publicly was understood by the Meiri and others as casting the shadow of heresy over the entire Provençal tradition. Under cover of guarding against certain dangers of philosophy, the aim of the Rashba and Aba Mari was "to abolish wisdom and to expel her completely from dwelling in our land."[69]

Most of the material documenting the struggle over philosophy and its place in the curriculum has reached us from Aba Mari and his circle rather than from the proponents of philosophy. Similarly, the Meiri's letter is known only from quotations in *Hoshen Mishpat*, a long polemical epistle addressed to the Meiri in reply to his allegations against Aba Mari. *Hoshen Mishpat* was written by one of Aba Mari's supporters and students, Shimon Ben Yosef, who was probably a former student of the Meiri and therefore a natural candidate to respond to his allegations, and it offers us an inkling of the way the circle around Aba Mari understood the problem.

Three claims were raised in response to the Meiri's accusations. First, expressing great praise for wisdom, Shimon ben Yosef argued that the ban was not against philosophy per se but against its popular misuse. Thus the true aim of the ban was to reestablish philosophy as an esoteric tradition.[70] Second, the people under attack were not the representatives of Provençal Jewry. Shimon ben Yosef went to great lengths to honor even the members of the Tibonite family, who were not notable talmudists. The attack was directed against the extreme allegorizers (a fascinating account of the nature of their allegories follows in this response to the Meiri).[71] Third, this campaign is radically different from the former struggle against Maimonides in Provence. Instead of opposing Maimonidism the campaign sought to restore the self-imposed restraints of Maimonidean culture in Provence.[72] In sum, according to Shimon ben Yosef, the Meiri had been deceived by the opposition. Aba Mari's struggle was in full accord with Provençal mainstream culture, and the Meiri should have joined the ranks of the ban's supporters instead of praising the opposition. He should have identified Aba Mari's party as the true heir of the Provençal tradition; by misjudging them, he had done them much harm.

Were these arguments a result of self-deception, or, even worse, a conscious deception? Probably not. These were the genuine feelings and claims of Aba Mari and his Provençal circle, though the Meiri did not take them to be so, especially after the matter mushroomed into an intercommunal controversy.[73] The Rosh, who lived in Toledo, more distant from Provence than Barcelona and thus free from the constraints of proximity, told Aba Mari in his letter: "You know that I signed your ban against my will. How should I sign that students should not study philosophy till twenty-five, implying that I allow the study of philosophy after twenty-five?! In my view, in this generation, the study of philosophy is prohibited throughout one's whole life."[74] To avoid the appearance of attacking Maimonides directly, the Rosh qualifies his statement with the words "in this generation." His reaction allows us to understand why the French rabbis were not invited to join the ban against philosophy, as they had in the first debate over Maimonides' writings. The Tosafists, who were independent of the Spanish tradition, acknowledge no obligation to Maimonides, not even the slight deference shown by the Rosh and certainly not the respect that the rabbis of Barcelona had for the philosopher. Had the issue been placed before them, open war would have been declared, and Provençal Jews would have reacted with even greater extremism in the defense of their culture. Aba Mari thought the Rashba was close enough to be a legitimate partner in this internal debate. But, as often happens in political maneuvers, the Rashba was searching for a center, amenable to compromise, that did not exist. The French Tosafists would not accept the implied permission to study philosophy after the age of twenty-five, and the Provençal Jews would not agree to limit the study of philosophy only from twenty-five onwards. An effort was made to reach a compromise between these two extremes by applying the restrictions of esotericism to the study of philosophy, thus avoiding the denunciation of philosophy while diminishing its influence, but this was a failure. For its extreme opponents, philosophy was a heresy that did not deserve the status of Pardes—the esoteric teaching of Judaism. Provençal Jewry, however, regarded it as a basic component of the education of their youth and would not allow it to be stifled behind the veil of esotericism.

The ban was therefore understood in three different ways by the three parties involved. For the Meiri and the Provençal opponents of the ban, it meant an overall assault on their culture. Aba Mari's circle, however, understood the ban as restoring the esoteric status of philosophy, a move which was in agreement with the mainstream of Provençal tradition. The Rashba, who resented philosophy in any case, intended the ban as a way of repressing such studies by again restricting philosophy to the esoteric realm.

The different understandings of the ban and its purpose reveal deep tensions in the relations between esotericism and canon. On the one hand, widespread access is not necessarily to be identified with importance. With esoteric texts there is often an inverse relation between access and importance. Since the text is too important to be easily accessible, restrictions are imposed on study. Preparation and initiation are demanded before approaching the text. The more remote the canon, the more potent and sacred it becomes. However, esotericism may also be a form of censorship, usually for texts which cannot be completely rejected. Restrictions are imposed mainly during the formative years of education in order to minimize the impact of the text. Thus two different and opposing agendas can converge in the demand for esotericism.

A similar paradoxical convergence occurred in a totally different historical context, during the debate over the printing of the Zohar in sixteenth-century Italy. Opposition to printing the Zohar came from two different camps: one considered the Zohar to be a heretical text presenting a mythical and antimonotheistic conception of God; the other perceived it as a sacred text which ought to be accessible only to the elite. Printing it would devaluate its canonical status, as the printed text would fall in the hands of those who have no understanding or appreciation of its importance or true meaning.[75] Interestingly, with this kind of convergence, what one group considers heretical and dangerous and the other regards as the most important and revered religious knowledge is subject to the same treatment.

Although the Meiri called the Rashba's circle "kabbalists," throughout the entire debate the Rashba avoided the mention of the Kabbalah as the true Pardes and the substitute for philosophy. Loyal to the strictly esoteric tradition of Nachmanides' school of Kabbalah, the Rashba did not recommend the study of Kabbalah as supplement to talmudic studies. From his perspective, it would be sufficient to adhere to the curriculum of Talmud study alone, following the pious Rashi and Rabeinu Tam of Ashkenaz.[76] The debate concerned the coexistence of Talmud and philosophy and not of Kabbalah and philosophy. The Rashba urged one of his admirers in Provence, Samuel ha-Salmi, to shun any further study of philosophy. Arguing against Maimonides' claim that philosophy is a condition for meriting life in the hereafter, the Rashba asked Samuel: "Are the pious men of Israel without philosophy not worthy of an afterlife?"[77] The Rashba posed the controversy in terms of exclusive talmudism and the arrogant challenge of philosophy. Kabbalah is an esoteric matter, and he did not promulgate the study of Kabbalah. Had the philosophers of Provence been as strictly esoteric about philosophy as was the Rashba about Kabbalah, the crisis might have been avoided. The open challenge of Kabbalah to the exclusive role of the Talmud in the curriculum came from other kabbalists, who were less strict than Nachmanides' school in their esotericism.

❧ KABBALISTS AND THE TALMUDIC CURRICULUM

The battle over the formative canonical status of the Talmud was not waged by Maimonides and the philosophical school alone. Criticism of exclusive study of the Talmud was also voiced by the kabbalists. After the publication of the Zohar near the end of the thirteen century, the restraints of kabbalistic esotericism were relaxed, and we find its adherents calling for supplementing the study of Talmud with Kabbalah. Significant differences exist among kabbalists regarding both the value they ascribe to the unsupplemented study of Talmud and the recommended balance between the study of Kabbalah and of Talmud. Some extremists declared that the study of Talmud without the knowledge of Kabbalah was empty, because only Kabbalah provided access to the inner meaning of the Talmud. The anonymous author of *Sefer ha-Kannah ve ha-Plia'ah* held such a view. Another sixteenth-century kabbalist, Meir Ibn Gabai, wrote: "He who deals only with the garment and the body of Torah and claims that there is nothing but these, expels the soul and denies the essence of the Torah . . . and it would have been better for him had he never been created."[78] The author of *Rahayah Meimanah* used metaphors drawn from Israel's enslavement to Egypt to describe the heavy burden of the exclusive study of Talmud.[79] More moderate kabbalists recommended the study of Kabbalah only to those who were well-versed in Talmud and insisted on continuing Talmud study while studying Kabbalah.[80] Jacob Katz has mapped the different approaches to the tension among kabbalists, and I shall attempt to clarify some of the issues involved in the debate over the curriculum.[81]

A review of the two main trends in Kabbalah described by Moshe

Idel—the ecstatic and the theurgic—will clarify the type of criticism that was raised against exclusive talmudism.[82] According to Idel's phenomenological account, for the ecstatic school the goal of the mystical life is to achieve *devekut*, a state of unity with God, through mystical techniques such as breathing exercises, visualizing colors, and so on. Talmud study could not help one attain the mystical goal of *devekut*, for the demand for constant attention to intellectual detail conflicts with self-negation. If a person aspires to negate his own ego and immerse himself in God, how can he achieve such a state when his mind is troubled with the legal distinction between a harmless bull and a gorer? Moreover, with his subtle dialectics the talmudist is also adding ever more distinctions and debates to the Torah, contrary to the mystic's innermost aspiration. Rather than elevating the particularized Torah to its origins in the undifferentiated realm of God, the talmudist augments the Torah's particularization. In neo-Platonic terminology, the talmudist is on the way down while he should be on the way up. These objections were also raised by spokesmen of hasidism, who agreed with the view of *devekut* as the prime moment of religious life. Rabbi Dov Baer of Mezirech, an outstanding figure of the first generation of hasidim, advised the scholar to cease his learning periodically in order to engage in *devekut*. The story is told that when the Ba'al Shem Tov, the founding father of eighteenth-century hasidism, studied Talmud, he learned the white space between the letters rather than the black print.[83]

The criticism voiced by the ecstatic stream of Kabbalah was at times radical in tone because, as Idel points out, some of the practitioners of ecstatic Kabbalah came from outside the rabbinic establishment and lacked credentials as talmudists. Abraham Abulafia, a thirteenth-century kabbalist and mystic, himself not versed as a talmudist, distinguished three groups with specific views concerning curriculum.[84] The first, the talmudists, he called incurable because they find no spiritual excellence beyond the fulfillment of the Halakhah and the study of Talmud. Therefore they reject any possible supplement which, in Abulafia's view, is necessary to perfection. The second group, the philosophers, are desperately ill but still curable since, like the true mystics, they understand that something beyond Talmud is necessary for spiritual perfection. Philosophers and kabbalists share the idea that in order to achieve spiritual perfection the Talmud must be supplemented; hence the philosopher is in a better position than the talmudist. The third group is the kabbalists, who have deserted philosophy but have not yet achieved full knowledge of God's Name and its functions. They are easily curable because, like the philosophers, they are unsatisfied with the exclusivity of the Talmud, yet unlike them they are on the right track in their search for the supplement within mystical tradition. Abulafia promises to provide the unwritten secret of spiritual perfection, which is the achievement of mystical perfection through the knowledge and use of the divine Name. This subject, of course, has little to do with the concerns of the talmudists.[85]

The second trend in Kabbalah, in Idel's terminology, is the theurgic. According to this school the divine realm is not a "simple unity" but a complex organism with many aspects—the *sefirot*. The *sefirot*, which emanate from within the Godhead, form a delicate hierarchy of balance and tension, such as between *Din*, which is the principle of judgment and limit, and *Hesed*, which is the principle of abundance and love. This structure is always in danger of disintegrating, and man's task is to secure the unity of the divine realm through the performance of the commandments, which affect the Godhead. The role of the mystic is primarily theurgic. In fulfilling the law he preserves God's internal cohesion, thus maintaining the divine abundance both within the Godhead itself and within the world. The theurgic mystics' criticism of exclusive Talmud study usually concerned the talmudists' ignorance of the esoteric and inherently more important meaning of the Halakhah. Unaware of the secrets of the divine world and the cosmic effect of the fulfillment of Torah commandments, the exclusive talmudists are blind to the essence of being. The theurgic school invested the minutiae of the law with great cosmic and symbolic significance: every act makes a cosmic difference. Paradoxically, the talmudists, although masters of the legal minutiae, are indifferent to this great effect.

According to the theurgic branch of Kabbalah, the divinity is self-emanated, and the Torah serves as one of the major symbols of its emanation. Like the Godhead, the Torah and its different strata are also a product of the process of emanation, a process finalized in the articulation of the Torah's final and exoteric form.[86] The inner meaning of the Torah uncovered by the mystics is therefore connected to an ontology in the Godhead superior to the talmudists' exoteric reading, since it correlates with a higher realm in the process of emanation. This view of the Torah as a product of emanation anchors the importance of the study of Kabbalah, over and above any other subject matter, in the very essence of the divine realm. The most extreme formulation stemming from this hierarchical view is expressed by the *Tikunei Zohar:*

> Alas for those fools whose minds are closed and whose eyes are shut, of whom it is said (Psalm 115:5) "They have eyes but they do not see" the light of the Torah. They are animals, who do not see or know anything except the straw of the Torah, which is the outer husk or the chaff, of which it is said: "Chaff and straw are exempt from the tithe." The sages of the Torah, the mystics, throw away the straw and chaff which are without, and eat the wheat of Torah which is within.

In most cases, the hierarchical view of Torah was presented in a less extreme manner. The external meaning of the text was included in a continuum with the internal meaning and not contrasted to it. But even in those more moderate and ordinary approaches, the superiority of the study of Kabbalah was anchored in the ontology of the divine realm.

Since the achievement of the theurgic effect depends on the fulfillment of Halakhah and the study of Torah and not on the performance of mystical techniques common in the ecstatic school, many kabbalists of the theurgic school, including Nachmanides, the Rashba, and many others, were in fact great talmudists as well. But another and more important difference between the theurgic and ecstatic branches came up during one of the most interesting debates on talmudism in the nineteenth century, that between the formidable talmudist Rabbi Chaim of Volozhin and the critics of strict talmudism among the Hasidim. As noted, the rise of the ideal of *devekut* in Hasidism conflicted directly with the traditional value of Talmud Torah. R. Chaim of Volozhin, the guardian of the intellectual Lithuanian tradition of Talmud Torah, wrote a book called *Nefesh ha-Hayim* in defense of the value of talmudic dialectic against its spiritual critics. He defended talmudism without rejecting the outlook of the Kabbalah and reiterating that nothing should be added to the Talmud. Instead, he used the theurgic ideal of Kabbalah to support his position, which enabled him to integrate his own background as a kabbalist and his loyalty to the highest value of Lithuanian culture, Talmud Torah.

According to R. Chaim, the importance of Talmud study lies in its theurgic effect on the Godhead, but this effect can be engendered through the traditional forms of learning. That is because the subtle dialectics of the yeshivah is of cosmic importance, talmudic studies are actually grounded in the kabbalistic outlook, and the theurgic effect can thus be achieved even without detailed knowledge of the causal chain provided by the Kabbalah.[87] A talmudist not versed in esoterica achieves those effects by his complete devotion to study as well as the kabbalist who claims to understand divine secrets. According to this view, nothing should be added or deleted from the talmudic curriculum. The Kabbalah serves not to revolutionize the curriculum but to imbue it with enormous importance. Although R. Chaim emphasizes the theurgic effect of the study of Torah in *Nefesh ha-Hayim*, he mentions *devekut* as well. He attempts to integrate that ideal with the study of Torah without changing the scholar's consciousness while he learns. Since God and the Torah are one, "while studying and reflecting on the Torah it is clear that there is no need for the matter of the *devekut* at all, since with contemplation and study alone he cleaves to God's will and speech, for God, His will and His speech, are one."[88]

Interestingly, a very similar version of *devekut* was recommended in the sixteenth century by R. Joseph Karo, a great halakhist and mystic. In his *Magid Mesharim* he equates *devekut* with the scholarly study of Torah. The mystical moment is therefore not opposed to the traditional way of meditating on the Law. In fact, to interrupt the study of the Law is to fall away from the mystical state: "Be careful not to interrupt the *dibbuq* [*devekut*] between you and your Creator . . . for the study of Torah strengthens the communion, and grace is infused into him from heaven to strengthen the communion further."[89] Such a sophisticated defense is unacceptable to mystics, who claim that mystical achievement is a personal experience of self-negation and *devekut*. To achieve this state a different mindset is needed. The mode of intellectual specification in talmudic legal argumentation must be overcome. One common hasidic technique for achieving this state was through cleaving to the essence of the letters of the Torah. In an act of inner concentration, the mystic penetrates the materiality of the letter, attaching himself to its divine essence, and through that meditative activity achieves a state of *devekut* with God. In such a state, the letters of the texts no longer convey linguistic meaning; they become material carriers of divine essence, and their ordinary linguistic function is annihilated. Such a technique, placing emphasis on the mystical power of pronunciation of the letters, is described by the great Magid: "The Blessed One concentrated Himself into the Torah; there-

fore, when someone speaks on issues of Torah or prayer, let him do it
with all his power, since by it he unites himself with Him may He be
blessed, since all his power is in the pronounced letter, and He, may
He be blessed, dwells in the pronounced letter."[90] This technique conflicts directly with the talmudist's mindset and threatens its ideals. As
a theurgic kabbalist, Rabbi Chaim allowed the preservation of the talmudic mindset and endowed it with magnificent weight. The hasidim,
with their strong inclination toward ecstatic Kabbalah, rejected such
harmonization. A different orientation was needed for the achievement
of their mystical ideal. In more radical hasidic formulations, the traditional talmudism defended by R. Chaim was seen as representing yet
another step away from God.[91]

Neither camp—kabbalist or philosopher—was content with merely
supplementing the curriculum or, in more extreme versions, replacing
it. They claimed that the supplement they proposed affected the reading
of the shared textual material; that it was the hidden meaning of the
traditional text, its allegorical interpretation, or its profound symbolic
layer. This attitude expands the scope of the issue, for now it concerns
not only the question of what, if anything, should supplement the
Talmud, but also how to read the Talmud itself. Are the homiletic passages of the Talmud treasures of mystical hidden allusions, to be read
according to esoteric allegorical codes? Or should they be understood
straightforwardly the way the talmudists read them? The debate
between talmudists and philosophers also raises the question whether
a shared "rational" cultural discourse can exist between Jews and non-
Jews.

⁊ STRONG CANONICITY AND SHARED DISCOURSE

Strong canonization of the Talmud may be expected to have an impact
on the relationship between the Jewish and the surrounding Gentile
cultures. "Strong canonization" implies that the Talmud is not merely
the most important text in the curriculum but the only one. The study
of other texts is prohibited either because of the danger they pose to
the tradition (they are denounced as "Greek wisdom"), or because of
the pervasive obligation of uninterrupted reflection on the Torah. A
wall is thus erected between the Torah community and the non-Torah
community, influencing not only practice but also modes of thought

and the objects of reflection. The second aspect of the exclusivity of the canon is the prohibition of teaching Torah to Gentiles. The Talmud states that a Gentile who studies the Torah deserves death. The metaphor used to explain this rigorous prohibition is illuminating. The Torah is likened to Israel's wife; the non-Jew who studies Torah is compared to a man committing adultery. This simile is grounded on a play on the words of a verse in Deuteronomy, which describes the Torah as Israel's *morasha*—inheritance. The Talmud revises the verse: "Do not read '*morasha*' but '*meorasa*,' " meaning betrothed. The Torah, according to this reading, is more than Israel's inheritance; it is Israel's bride.[92] The Torah is claimed to be Israel's exclusively and, as in marriage, it cannot be shared. It is "cultural capital" available only to members of the community. Following the same line of exclusivity, another *midrash* asks why God gave two Torahs to Israel—the Oral and the Written. The answer is that since the Gentiles will translate the Torah and claim it for their own, God gave Israel an unwritten Torah as Israel's own hidden treasure.[93] The translation of the Written Torah into Greek and Latin made it a common property of Gentiles and Jews. The possession of a secret and unwritten Torah which is never shared guarantees Israel's exclusivity.

This double prohibition of denying Jews access to non-Jewish texts and also denying Gentiles access to Jewish texts creates two communities that share no common discourse. The interdiction against teaching Torah to non-Jews and the midrashic response to translation have their roots in the Jewish polemic against Christianity. In the context of the Church's claim of being the new Israel, disinheriting the Jews, the translation of the Bible was perceived by them as an act of appropriation rather than an act of communication. The problem of translation is acute because ownership of the canon is one of the signs of being elect. Thus the notion of the exclusivity of the Oral Torah developed as a response to the Christian act of appropriation.[94]

When the argument is presented in these terms, it is hard to imagine a space where shared discourse could occur. Thus the Jews who supported supplementing talmudic studies with the study of philosophy did more than add to an existing curriculum. They broke a barrier by creating a shared space in which discourse between Jews and the world could occur. This would not mean anything like the notion of a Judeo-Christian culture or a Judeo-Islamic culture, for such cultural constructs were unknown to medieval thinkers. Rather, philosophers appealed to

a shared discourse of rationality that has its roots in Aristotelian philosophy.

The philosophers offered an interesting justification from the tradition. It is based upon a verse in Deuteronomy (4:6) that describes the
Torah and its laws as Israel's wisdom in the eyes of the nations. The
Torah itself thus states explicitly that it shares a basis for rational discourse with the world and can be recognized as a wise legal system
even by outsiders who are not committed to the internal premises of
the tradition. It comes as no surprise that this verse is quoted by Maimonides in the *Guide of the Perplexed* in support of the claim that the
laws of the Torah are founded on a rational basis. The Meiri quotes the
same verse in defense of Provençal philosophical culture.[95] For the Maimonidean tradition, this domain of shared discourse is not a marginal
aspect of spiritual life but the very heart of Ma'aseh Merkabah and the
proper notion of God. It is the process by which intimacy with God
is achieved through knowledge, and it provides the active intellect with
the content that defies death.

The debate between talmudists and philosophers over the curriculum
therefore revolves around the major question of how self-contained is
the tradition. Or, to rephrase it, the argument is about the extent to
which the tradition might be exposed, interpreted, and justified in
terms of a discourse beyond itself. The debate concerns not only whether
the curriculum should consist of any text which is not the Talmud or
an interpretation of the Talmud, but also whether any text which is
not the Talmud or the interpretation of the Talmud may be instrumental in understanding the Talmud. The opponents of philosophy in
the curriculum maintained that tradition is self-contained, and they
rejected the view that philosophy may have an essential role in understanding the tradition. For example, in fourteenth-century Toledo the
Rosh wrote a responsum condemning the use of philosophy in halakhic
ruling:

> For the wisdom of philosophy and the wisdom of Torah are not of the
> same mode. The wisdom of the Torah is a tradition from Moses at Sinai,
> and the wise will interpret the Torah using rules with which the Torah
> can be interpreted, and will make an analogy between case and case.
> Even if those legal inferences are not according to the wisdom of nature
> we rule according to tradition . . . and do not think of comparing these
> two, Torah and Philosophy, and of bringing a proof from one to another

because that will pervert judgment. Since they [Torah and Philosophy] are two opposites, they are mutual enemies and will not dwell in one place.[96]

No outside forms of reasoning should be involved in talmudic interpretation. The Talmud contains rules of interpretation and derivation; it supplies the code for its own evolution. The shared space of discourse created by the curriculum of the philosophers is both dangerous and unnecessary. Against the attempt to create a common discourse, the Rosh raised the claim of total incommensurability.

Three central problems of curriculum emerge from the debates on the strong canonization of the Talmud as an object of constant reflection. The first is the relationship between the tradition and the foundational text. In some formulations and practices concerning the curriculum, strong canonization of the Talmud minimized Bible study. The critics of that position condemned it as alienating the community from its sacred text. Scholars well versed in every intricacy of talmudic discussion were accused of ignorance of God's own word. The defenders of exclusive talmudism, on the other hand, pointed to the danger of an unmediated approach to the sacred text. They contended that the Bible approached without the aid of the Oral Law had subversive potential. Thus tension prevails between the need to anchor the authority of the Bible through study and the danger of exposing the foundational text to direct scrutiny unmediated by the prism of traditional interpretation. This tension is at the heart of the debate about the strong formative canonicity of the Talmud vis à vis the Bible, a debate, it must be stressed, that concerns the place of the Talmud in the curriculum and not its normative authority. Hence we can describe this debate as taking place within a single tradition in which both sides agree about the normative role of the Talmud.

The second important point concerns the relations between Talmud, Kabbalah, and philosophy, and the implications of that triangle on the problem of values. The kabbalists and philosophers reexamined the text of the Talmud within a new context of metaphysical outlook and spiritual ideals. The Aristotelians among the Jews conceived of human perfection as the attainment of the knowledge of God; to that end, the study of metaphysics seemed more useful than talmudic learning. The kabbalists introduced the ideal of *devekut*—the cleaving of the self to God. The mindset of the mystic in contemplation, on the path toward self-negation, stands in conflict with the acute analytical awareness of the scholar. The exclusive value of the study of Talmud was therefore also threatened by this ideal. The theurgic trend of Kabbalah introduced the esoteric cosmic meaning of the Law and its theurgic effects. Higher wisdom became identified with the secrets of the divine realm and with laying bare the strata hidden in the depths of the text, far beneath the surface scratched by the talmudist.

These new approaches modified the role of the Talmud as the exclusive item in the curriculum to varying degrees. In most cases the Talmud was supplemented, and in some instances it was replaced. The value of a text is related to its place in the greater picture. In the case of the Talmud, its value was relative to metaphysical outlooks and ideals of perfection. The worth of the text as an object of reflection is not derived solely from its internal quality, for evaluations of this feature may differ according to the function of those judging it and their general outlook.

The third important point of the debate on the exclusive role of Talmud concerns the problem of self-containment or shared discourse. A curriculum can be designed to create a self-sufficient internal discourse. In this version of the text-centered community, the text marks the exclusive boundaries of reflection. Every text which is not canonical is prohibited. The debate between talmudists and philosophers specifically concerned the issue of the exclusivity defined by the text and its realm.

Conclusion

The movement toward text-centeredness has been conceptualized as the primary feature of rabbinic innovation and self-perception. Three changes characterize this movement: (1) the scholar rises to become the main authority figure, thereby linking authority to textual expertise; (2) the Torah becomes the object of ongoing reflection and a locus of religious presence and experience; and (3) the boundaries of the community are shaped in relation to loyalty to a shared canon. Such a text-centered community can only evolve through reinterpretation of the canonical text. Major shifts within the tradition were accompanied by the emergence of new and bold conceptions of Torah and language; they provided hermeneutical strategies which integrated radically different world views into the tradition. The emergence of both Kabbalah and philosophy as esoteric readings of the canon in the Middle Ages became possible through innovative conceptions of the canon and its language. In turn, the possibility of redescribing the canon made it open to reading with greater flexibility. Further, the legitimation of controversy between certain rabbinic schools through the detachment of authoritative meaning from authorial intention gave rise to new interpretative possibilities, portraying the text as open-ended and the interpreter as constituting its meaning.

Despite upheavals and changes in Jewish life, the rabbinic revolution lasted until the eighteenth century and succeeded in making the

Jewish community a text-centered community. One important consequence of the emergence of modern national identity among Jews is
that text-centeredness has been displaced by other features of commonality.[1] Loyalty to a shared text no longer marks the boundaries of
the modern-day Jewish community, for the assumption that the values
and norms of the community should be justified in reference to a shared
text has lost its validity. The formative role of the common text—the
idea that the culture advances through interpretation of the canonical
texts and that its achievements are interpretative—has also lost its
power. Powerful new ideologies no longer represent themselves as interpretations of the Torah or Talmud but question the very authority of
the text as the source of norms and values. As a natural consequence
of this movement, the authority of the scholar has been diminished and
leadership models have changed radically.

What made disparate world views "Jewish" despite their diversity
was their shared interpretative commitment to canonical texts. With
the decline in text-centeredness, Jewish thought and creativity can no
longer be defined simply in those terms. The modern conception of
noninterpretative Jewish creativity and thought, which is considered
Jewish only because it is produced by Jews, is symptomatic of the crisis
in Jewish life. Although freed from the burden of the text and the limitations that are supposedly imposed by the interpretative process,
modern Jewish creativity has not yet flourished, for it appears to have
lost its language and its main mode of development.

The rise of Jewish national identity not only loosened the bonds of
text-centeredness but also affected the nature of the curriculum. In the
official curriculum of Israel's secular state schools, the Bible rather than
the Talmud is regarded as the central Jewish text. Although, strictly
speaking, this development extends beyond the limits of our subject,
it sheds interesting light upon it. Until the eighteenth century, Jewish
education consisted mainly of Talmud study. At the preliminary stage,
in the *heder*, the boys studied the weekly portions of the Pentateuch
read in the synagogue, as well as the short sections from the prophets,
the *haftarot*, which are associated with the weekly readings. While the
study of the Bible was connected to the liturgical practices of the community and aimed at integrating students into the life of the synagogue, the rest of the Bible—the books of the prophets and the writings themselves (aside from those included in the *haftarot*)—were not
studied. In Europe Jewish boys were taught to read the Torah, trans-

late it into Yiddish, and base its interpretation on Rashi's commentary, that is, on rabbinic interpretation, since Rashi's commentary is heavily based on rabbinic sources. The student soon progressed to Talmud study, which from then on dominated the curriculum of the *heder* and more advanced institutions of learning. The Hebrew language was not an independent subject but was part of the study of the Bible and Talmud. Hence the Talmud occupied a far more central place than the Bible in the curriculum.

At the end of the eighteenth century, the Haskalah (Jewish Enlightenment) offered another approach that diminished the formative role of the Talmud. The spokesmen of the Jewish Enlightenment (Maskilim) called for a return to the Bible. This shift in the canon was tied to their new conception of Jewish identity called forth by the promise of emancipation, already articulated by Moses Mendelssohn.[2] Jewishness, according to this view, is a layer of particularism built upon a more fundamental universal layer of humanity, and this universal dimension, shared by Jews and non-Jews alike, ensures civil equality and the participation of both parties in the same political unit. The Jews were called upon by the Maskilim to stress and develop their universal dimension and, surprisingly, the movement back to the Bible played a major role in this scheme.

One proponent of the new conception was Naphtali Herz Wessely, a poet and educator who addressed a letter entitled "Divrei Shalom ve-Emet" (Words of Truth and Peace) to the Jewish communities in the Austro-Hungarian Empire, encouraging them to accept reforms in the educational system. These had been proposed by the government as a measure for alleviating certain discriminatory measures against the Jews. Among other changes, Wessely urged return to the Bible as an optimal bridge to the life of citizenship. Since it is a book common to Christians and Jews, stressing its formative role would be more conducive to the goals of Enlightenment than was talmudic learning. The exclusive study of the Talmud was identified by the Maskilim with ghetto life. According to Wessely, it addressed only the particular dimension of the Jew. He also advocated abandoning the Yiddish translation of the Bible in favor of Mendelssohn's German translation and stressed the aesthetic, literary qualities of the Bible, which has yet another advantage over the Talmud: it offers a model of complete political and economic life, dealing with agriculture, war, and government, and is therefore a better introduction to citizenship.[3]

With the rise of Jewish nationalism, the relation of many Jews to the Bible and the Talmud took another turn. The Zionists preferred the Bible to the Talmud as the national literature, for the Bible tells a heroic story of the national drama whose focus is the Land of Israel. While they objected to the Haskalah politics of emancipation, Zionist thinkers also stressed the role of the Bible, but they thought of it as an element in building a particular national consciousness rather than as the basis of a shared Judeo-Christian heritage enabling the integration of Jews in Europe.[4] Unlike the Talmud, they held, the Bible had the potential to become a national epic. Its drama unfolded in the hills of Judea, and it connected the national claim to the land with a historical past. Nothing in the Talmud, in contrast, appealed to the romanticism vital to national movements. It does not tell the glorious story of a nation; it has no warriors and heroes; no geography which arouses longing in the reader or a sense of connection to an ancient home.

Written in Aramaic on the shores of the "rivers of Babylon," the Talmud also had little to offer toward the revival of Hebrew as the national language. For some Zionist thinkers the Talmud was an emblem of Diaspora, the past they sought to reject. They maintained that the minutiae of talmudic discourse and its restrained style represented Diaspora qualities—timidity and small-mindedness. In their attempt to change the Jewish ideal type, some Zionist educators and leaders chose different role models: King David rather than Rabbi Akiva, for the courageous warrior was preferable to the pale Yeshiva boy. In 1910, Ben Zion Mossinson, an educator and the first Bible teacher in the Hebrew Gymnasium at Jaffa, wrote: "Let it [the Bible] be laid as the foundation of our children's education, and then our youth will not turn their backs to their people; and a new generation will arise sound and strong, a generation striving toward renaissance, a generation loving its people and its land—a Hebrew generation!"[5]

Some early Zionists objected strongly to this approach. The distinction between "Jews" and "Hebrews" seemed too radical, and the attempt to return to the Bible, overlooking the rich Diaspora creativity in order to forge the Hebrew identity, seemed to be a denial of something constitutive to Jewish identity. After his visit to Mossinson's school, Ahad Ha'am wrote: "If you remove the middle links from the chain of history, then its beginning and end will never fit together. The Jewish child of our time, in Eretz Israel as well, is the fruit of the historical life of all generations; and in order for him to know himself and his people, he ought to know our national riches—including the Bible—not only in their alleged original form but in all the forms in which it was clothed over the generation, becoming a living force in the lives of the people."[6] This tension between Mossinson's formulation and Ahad Ha'am's accompanies Israeli culture to this day.[7] Nevertheless, a major shift has occurred in the conception of the formative canon.

In 1953, David Ben-Gurion, then Israel's prime minister, responded critically to Avraham Kariv, a writer who claimed that the Bible should be read through the lens of the Midrash and the Talmud. "The Bible," wrote Ben Gurion, "existed before there was a Midrash and is not dependant on the Midrash. We should not understand the Bible through the Midrash but *in and of itself*. . . . I reject with all my moral and Jewish force the statements of Kariv that 'every verse in the Bible began to live its universal and eternal life only in the epoch after the Bible.' If I [Ben Gurion] did not know who Kariv was I would say that his words are blasphemy."[8] The return to the Bible was regarded as a sort of national Reformation, and Ben Gurion linked that tendency to the return from Diaspora: "In two thousand years of Diaspora our creativity did not completely disappear, but the light of the Bible was dimmed in the Diaspora, since the light of the people of Israel was dimmed. Only with the renewal of Hebrew independence we can understand the true and full light of the Bible." In his next lines Ben Gurion addresses educators: "Rashi's interpretation to the Bible is very important but it is Rashi's interpretation alone. The Bible shines in his own light, and this light should be exposed to the eyes of the young generation. This is the task for educators, teachers, writers, scholars, poets and artists— to envelop our people, in the Land of Israel and the Diaspora, with the dazzling light of the book of books in a manner that our redeemed generation can see it."[9] The otherworldliness and rootlessness of Jewish existence in the Diaspora did not suit the earthly quality of the Bible. Zionism, a movement of return to the Land, exemplifies the return of the Jews to the body. Only once back in the Land can Jews rediscover the true nature of the Bible and its deepest meanings.

Two important issues are at stake in the modern-day return to the Bible as national literature and the concomitant decanonization of the Talmud. The first concerns the shift in Jewish identity, from a group defined by its adherence to Halakhah and the Talmud as its normative canon, to a definition based on characteristics typical of national groups such as shared history, language, and territory. The second issue is related to the effect of Jewish nationalism on the characterization of an ideal type. This ideal type was founded, as were those of many other nineteenth-century national movements, on the tales of the ancient epics. In the Jewish case, the reversal of the curriculum from Talmud to Bible represents a major shift in political awareness and identity, alongside the weakening of the text-centered nature of the community. We recall that in the Middle Ages there was an attempt to decanonize the Talmud as a formative text while keeping its normative authority intact. For many modern Jews, the situation is reversed. The Talmud has lost its normative status; the question now is whether it can still serve a formative role and become an integral part of the language, associations, concerns, and mode of thought of present-day Jewish culture.

Appendix: The Sovereign and the Canon

Although contemporary interest in the *Leviathan*[1] ignores Hobbes's use of biblical interpretation in his treatment of politics, in fact he devoted major parts of the treatise to this subject. So did Spinoza; though he wrote only two works on politics—the *Political Theological Treatise*, and *A Political Treatise*—he dedicated most of the former to an ambitious attempt to develop a general interpretative methodology and exegesis of the Bible. These works are essentially political polemics, and their arguments are marshaled in reference to the authoritative text of the canon. The point relevant to our discussion is their views on the authority of the canon and the authoritative interpreter.

Both Hobbes and Spinoza reach the same conclusion: the authoritative interpreter of Scripture is the civil sovereign. This appears to be somewhat unlikely claim, for nothing seems to qualify the sovereign to interpret a sacred text. He is neither a prophet nor a scholar, nor does he have any other unique qualifications as an interpreter. Hobbes and Spinoza's attempt to prove to their readers that Scripture itself advocates their view makes the argument even more interesting: direct appeal is made to Scripture to undermine its own independent authority and to subordinate it to the civil sovereign.

Both philosophers are concerned with the biblical threat to their political program, and their extensive interpretative campaign is designed to neutralize that threat. Hobbes's concern is that political use of the Bible might split the sovereignty of the state between king and priest. Spinoza's agenda is tolerance, freedom of thought and speech. Through biblical exegesis Spinoza strives to prove that the state has no interest in legislating true beliefs or a specific uniform religious way of life. Only a minimum of religious belief, in Providence and divine retribution, for example, is necessary for maintaining social order. The rest should be left to the free reflection of the philosopher. Both Hobbes and Spinoza try to contain the political claim of the canon, but in the service of two radically different political programs. Hobbes writes in the service of the Leviathan, the absolute unified sovereign, while Spinoza does so in the service of a relatively pluralistic state, where issues of truth and falsehood are divorced from the state's coercive powers.

Hobbes addresses the problem of the canon as a political one. In his view, authority is the main political issue, and that category is the axis of his discussion on Scripture. He raises two questions: what is the source of the authority of the canon? and who is the authoritative interpreter of the canon? Before embarking upon a long stretch of biblical exegesis, Hobbes phrases the problem with utmost clarity. In the section entitled "The Question of the Authority of the Scriptures Stated," Hobbes rejects other formulations of the problem. The first to be rejected is "from whence the Scriptures derive their Authority," and the second is "how we know them to be the Word of God or why we believe them to be so." Hobbes claims that only those who heard the words of God directly are obligated by them; since none of the others had a direct experience of revelation, they cannot be certain of the existence of such revelation and therefore have no obligation to follow it. People believe in Scripture without direct evidence, but belief, Hobbes claims, is dependent on subjective feelings and therefore cannot provide the proper foundation. Hobbes redefines the question in this manner: "By what authority they [Scripture] are made Law." He then asks who is the authoritative interpreter of Scripture as Law. Hobbes's answer to both questions is decisive and absolute: it is the Civic Sovereign of the State. Scripture cannot be made law by someone's claim that it is revealed by God. For those who did not personally witness the revelation, such a claim cannot be a source of obligation. Each individual must decide whether the so-called revelation originated from a true prophet or a false one. Nobody can justifiably be coerced to obey the canon until the sovereign makes Scripture the law of the state. According to Hobbes, the sovereign has absolute control of the canon. It is he who endows Scripture with authority, and he is the only legitimate interpreter of the canon. The sovereign has the power granted him by the Bible to distinguish between a false prophet and a true one. Hobbes argues that those two aspects of control are internally connected: "For, whosoever hath a lawful power over any Writing, to make it Law, hath the power also to approve or disapprove the interpretation of the same."[2] In Hobbes's view, the modern separation of powers—between the legislator who authorizes the law and the courts which are its authorized interpreters—seems to break the unity of the sovereign's control of the canon.

Hobbes's approach is fascinating because he argues his point from Scripture itself, making the canon admit that its authority is entirely derived from the sovereignty of the Leviathan. To sharpen the totally derivative nature of the canon's authority, Hobbes introduces a distinction between two kinds of canon:

> There be two senses, wherein a Writing may be said to be Canonical; for Canon, signifieth a Rule; and a Rule is a Precept, by which a man is guided and directed in any action whatsoever. Such precepts, though given by a Teacher to his Disciple or a Counsellor to his friend without power to compel him to observe them are nevertheless canons; because they are Rules: but when they are given by one who he that receiveth them is bound to obey them are those Canons, not onely Rules but Laws: The question therfore here, is of the Power to make the Scriptures (which are the Rules of Christian Faith) Laws.

Hobbes thus distinguishes between canonical rules that are offered as advice or guidance, and a canon of rules which are enforced by the sovereign. Only the latter can properly be called law. Prior to the authorization of the Scripture by the sovereign of a state, its status is merely advisory. The teachings of Saint Paul, for instance, were not considered by Paul himself to be laws, nor did their author consider himself an authorized interpreter of Scripture. Like Paul, the clergy has no authority regarding Scripture; rather, they are teachers who try to offer convincing interpretations that will be authorized by the sovereign. "For to Interpret the Laws, is part of the Administration of a present Kingdome; which the Apostles had not."[3]

The laws of the Old Testament became canonical only when Israel accepted Moses as the sovereign of the commonwealth and not when the Scriptures were announced as God's revelation. "But Moses and Aaron, and the succeeding High Priests were the Civill Soveraigns. Therefore hitherto the Canonizing, or making of the Scripture Law, belonged to the Civill Soveraigne."[4] And again: "Therefore hitherto the Power of making Scripture Canonicall, was in the Civill Soveraign."[5] As with Moses, so with Abraham: Abraham's descendants were obligated to keep the commandments, which were revealed only to him, because he was the civil sovereign. As such, Abraham is the exclusive judge and interpreter of the divine word.[6]

The sole basis of the authority to command, claims Hobbes, rests on the social pact according to which people transfer their rights to the sovereign. Hobbes attempts to reduce the authority of the canon to this conception of political authority. In contrast to the view that the authority of Scripture is independent of the political authority of the sovereign, Hobbes introduces an intermediary between the people and their obligation to the canon: the civil sovereign who canonizes Scripture as law. The reduction is as follows: Moses and Abraham received the commandments from God, but that is not sufficient justification for imposing the authority of Scripture upon the people. As mere prophets, they could not claim anyone's allegiance. It was the contract between the people and Moses or Abraham and his followers that gave them authority as civil sovereigns, and as such they authorized Scripture. The people are obligated to follow Scripture only because they were subject to Moses' and Abraham's rule independently of Scripture. The authority of the canon is derived from social contracts and therefore rests upon the political conception of the sovereign's authority.

Nowhere in the text of the Scriptures, however, is there mention of a contract between Moses and the people, the contract that ostensibly made Moses the social sovereign. True, Moses is a mediator between two contracting sides—Israel and God—but when was he made the civil sovereign by the people through an independent pact which, according to Hobbes, is the source of the canon's authority? We do have a covenant between God and Abraham, but nothing that designates Abraham a civil sovereign. This is a crucial gap in Hobbes's interpretative project, and the way he forces the text to fit his own scheme of authority reveals the depth of his commitment to his political agenda. Hobbes appeals to direct interpretation of the Scripture in order to undermine its claim for independent authority. In this peculiar reading, Abraham and Moses are made civil sovereigns because, from the Hobbesian perspective, the sovereign monopolizes not only the use of power but also all claims to authority.

Hobbes is a master of subversive reading, circumscribing and appropriating the canon through its supposedly simple meaning. Spinoza follows Hobbes in the art of the political use of interpretation; in his case, the limitation of the canon promotes a different political program. In his *Theological and Political Treatise* Spinoza tries to convince the reader of the desirability of some separation between church and state, so as to create a relatively pluralistic society. Spinoza was convinced that religious groups trying to use the machinery of the state to impose particular beliefs caused much disorder and chaos in politics. He strove to show that the Scriptures have no interest in legislating truth and falsity; rather their concern is solely obedience and piety, simple justice and the love for one's neighbor. The prophets were not philosophers and did not concern themselves with issues of truth; the laws of the Bible are laws for the Hebrew state. These laws do not obligate everyone and do not even obligate the Jews after the destruction of their state.

Spinoza's interpretative slogan is "back to the text." He argues against three conceptions of the authoritative interpreter. The first favors the interpreter who is endowed with supernatural capabilities; the second regards tradition as the source of authoritative interpretation; and the third authorizes the philosopher to interpret the text. Spinoza's conclusion rejects all three:

> For as the highest power of Scriptural interpretation belongs to every man, the rule for such interpretation should be nothing but the natural light of reason which is common to all—not any supernatural light nor any external authority; moreover such a rule ought not to be so difficult that it can only be applied by very skillful philosophers, but should be adapted to the natural and ordinary faculties of mankind.[7]

If the prophets spoke to the common people, then we do not need supernatural capabilities to understand them today. If Scripture reveals the secrets of the universe and the philosopher therefore claims to be its authoritative interpreter, why does it contain so many metaphysical contradictions and errors? Scripture should be interpreted from Scripture itself, by the natural light of reason which is within everyone's reach. Although the court proclaimed Spinoza a heretic dissenter, he never denied the sacredness of the Bible. His interpretative methodology, which is to read the text in its historical and literal contexts, is not intended to undermine its sacredness. Such a denial could have worked against Spinoza's interest, which was to mobilize the prestige and power of the biblical text for his political program. He intended to convince the reader that he is an authentic, unbiased reader of the text. For Spinoza's project as a political propagandist depends on preserving the authority of the canon and then using this authority for his purposes.

In the earlier discussion about charitable reading we contrasted two opposing intuitions, that of Maimonides and that of Yehudah Elfakar. In the Maimonidean approach the canon deserves infinite charity: all its statements are adapted to the highest standard of truth. Yehudah Elfakar thought this approach was outrageous and contended that the meaning of Scripture should guide the reader's conception of truth rather then the opposite. No charity need be granted to Scriptures because they constitute the very terms of charity. The reader should alter his metaphysical views to what he reads in the Scripture rather than reread the Scripture according to his views. Spinoza takes a third approach to the subject, that of compartmentalization. Scripture is not subordinate to reason nor is reason subordinate to Scripture; the two simply deal with separate realms. Both Maimonides and Elfakar, in Spinoza's eyes, are wrong. The issue of truth and falsity should not be determined through the exercise of biblical interpretation:

> We may therefore, put this theory [Elfakar's], as well as that of Maimonides, entirely out of court; and we must take it for indisputable that theology is not bound to serve reason, nor reason theology, but that each has her own domain. The sphere of reason is, as we have said, truth and wisdom; the sphere of theology is piety and obedience. The power of reason does not extend so far as to determine for us that men may be blessed through simple obedience, without understanding. Theology commands nothing save obedience, and has neither the will nor the power to oppose reason.[8]

Because Scripture is self-contained, the clash between reason and piety is avoided. Each is reduced to its own domain, with no need for mutual adaptation.

Spinoza's main target was Maimonides, who in effect serves as a strawman representing all the political ambitions of the Church. Much of Spinoza's technique may be defined as scapegoating, and his scapegoating of the Jews in the *Treatise* has a double effect. First, by attacking the "Pharisees" Spinoza masks a direct attack on the Church, and second, this attack creates a bond between Spinoza and his readers by making clear they share a common enemy. But what was so troubling about Maimonides, a figure to whom Spinoza owed such a great intellectual debt? In Maimonides' account, the prophet has the political skills of the legislator and the theoretical achievements of the philosopher. Thus a prophet legislates perfect law. This law concerns not only social order but the perfection of the soul and true and false beliefs. According to Maimonides, Moses is the perfect legislator, the philosopher king. In a political program that aims to detach the realm of politics from that of the correct conception of the universe, the prophet as Maimonides portrays him is the prime target. Spinoza's Moses, who was a legislator rather than teacher, cannot be a philosopher, whereas Jesus is for Spinoza what Moses is for Maimonides—a perfect philosopher. Jesus is granted perfect knowledge because he is solely a teacher and not a statesman.[9]

The effort to separate prophecy from knowledge is commensurate with the effort to distinguish between the law and the truth. The Scriptures convey the beliefs necessary for the stability of the state, not the true picture of the world. Although Spinoza's quarrels with Maimonides ostensibly concerned the method of biblical exegesis, we should not be misled. The underlying issue remains the status of the canon and its role as a political text. The conclusion Spinoza draws from his so-called scientific investigation of the Bible—that the Bible teaches us simple piety and love of the neighbor and no more—is as far from a simple reading of the text as is Maimonides' Aristotelian reading. At the end of the treatise Spinoza reaches the same conclusion as Hobbes: the sovereign is the authority of biblical interpretation. Since justice and civic order are the sole subject of the Bible, and since what is just and what is necessary for social peace is the concern of the sovereign and his domain of authority, it is up to the sovereign to decide the meaning of Scripture. The long interpretative struggle, the goal of which is to undermine tradition and theology in the name of any person's reasonable reading, ends with the political assertion of the sovereign's dominion over interpretation.

Hobbes and Spinoza share the strategy of free and scientific investigation of the text. The slogan "back to the text" and direct appeals to the canon may serve varied political ends. The Karaites used such a direct appeal to undermine the mediating power of tradition. The Protestants used it to break the institutional control of the Church. Hobbes returned to the text in order to subordinate it to the absolute sovereign, and Spinoza, armed with the aura of scientific reading of the text unbiased by the traditional distortions, tried to contain the political ambitions of the canon.

Notes

Introduction

1. On the concept of book religion and its historical development see J. Leipoldt and S. Morenz, *Heilige Schiften Betrachtungen zur Religions-geschichte der antiken Mittelmeerwelt* (Leipzig: Otto Harrassowitz, 1953); and S. W. Wilford, "Scripture as Form and Concept: Their Emergence for the Western World," in *Rethinking Scripture*, M. Levering, ed. (New York: SUNY Press, 1987).

2. On the radical variety of views concerning the importance of Scripture among different Christian movements see H. Y. Gamble, "Christianity: Scripture and Canon" in *The Holy Book in Comparative Perspective*, F. Denny and R. L. Taylor, eds. (Columbia: University of South Carolina Press, 1985). On the difference between Islam and Christianity concerning the centrality of Scripture see W. C. Smith, "Some Similarities and Differences between Christianity and Islam," in *The World of Islam Studies in Honor of Philip K. Hitti*, James Kritzeck and R. B. Winder, eds. (London: Macmillan, 1959), pp. 56–58.

3. Some of the most important medieval commentators of the Talmud—the Tosafists of the twelfth and thirteenth centuries—took it as a model. As Efraim Urbach pointed out in his work on the Tosafists, their commentary could be inserted in the text without it being noticed, since it follows both the style and the internal logic of the talmudic discussion itself. See E. E. Urbach, *Ba'alei ha-Tosafot* (Jerusalem: Mosad Bialik, 1980), p. 22; see also J. Zusman, "Mifa'lo ha-Mada'i shel Professor Efraim Elimelech Urbach," in *Efraim Elimelech Urbach Bio-Bibliyographia Mechkarit, Musaf Made'i ha-Yahadut* 1 (1993) pp. 18–19.

4. On the canonization of the New Testament and its relationship to Marcion see H. von Campenhausen, *The Formation of the Christian Bible* (London: A and C. Black, 1972) p. 246. For a different opinion see F. F. Bruce, *The Canon of Scripture* (Downers Grove, Ill.: InterVarsity Press, 1988), p. 144. For a general discussion of Marcion and his canon see Campenhausen, pp. 134–144.

For an alternative understanding on the canonization of the New Testament, emphasizing internal developments within the Church, see W. G. Kummel, *Einleitung in das Neue Testament* (Heidelberg: Quelle and Meyer, 1973). For an extensive discussion on the subject see B. M. Metzger, *The Canon of the New Testament: Its Origin, Development, and Significance* (Oxford: Clarendon, 1987). Gedaliahu Stroumsa made an interesting observation concerning the possible connection between the canonization of the Mishnah at the end of the second century and the canonization of the New Testament in the same period. Stroumsa explains this simultaneous occurrence by the historical need of both Jewish and Christian communities to assert their identities in the face of severe crisis and particularly as a result of the struggle between the early Church's interpretation of the Bible and the Jewish interpretation. See G. Stroumsa, "The Body of Truth and Its Measures: New Testament Canonization in Context," in *Gnosis Forschung und Religions-Geschichte: Festschrift Kurt Rudolph*, H. Preissler and H. Seiwert, eds. (Marburg: Diagonal, 1994).

Menachem Haran offered an important distinction between the canonization of the Old Testament and that of the New Testament. According to him, the canonization of the Old Testament did not involve an act of selection between competing texts. Old Testament canonization was not intimately connected to censorship but was rather an attempt to preserve all the material that belonged to a mythical past. See M. Haran, *Ha-Asufah ha-Mikrait* (Jerusalem: Magnes Press, 1996), pp. 23–78. Haran is aware as well that at the end of the gradual process of canonization of the Old Testament, few texts (mainly those from the apocalyptic literature that were ascribed to ancient authors) were rejected from the canon (see pp. 93–102).

5. The close connection between canon and exclusion is manifested in the early use of the term. In its original use *kanon* designates a measuring rule. Irenaeus is the first Christian writer to use this term in his *Adversus Haereses* to mean a rule of faith (*Adv. Haer.* I. 8. 1; in A. Rousseau and L. Doutreleau, trans. and ed. (Paris: Cerf, 1979), vol. 2, pp. 112–17). *Kanon* is thus originally something which measures and fixes boundaries. For a detailed discussion of the term see B. M. Metzger, *The Canon of the New Testament*, pp. 289–93. For an extensive discussion of *kanon* in classical sources see H. Oppel, "Kanon," *Philologus*, suppl. 30 (Leipzig, 1937).

6. H. L. A. Hart, *The Concept of Law* (Oxford: Oxford University Press, 1961).

7. For a similar typology and a fruitful comparison between some of the issues of the canonization of the Constitution and Scripture see S. Levinson, *Constitutional Faith* (Princeton: Princeton University Press, 1988), pp. 9–45.

8. For an example of such restriction of access see the decisions of the

Dominican Council of Toulouse: "Lay people shall not have books of Scripture, except the psalter and the divine office: and they shall not have these books in the vulgar tongue. Moreover we prohibit that lay people should be permitted to have books of the Old or New Testament, except perchance any should wish from devotion to have a psalter, or a breviary for the divine office, or the hours of the blessed Virgin: but we most strictly prohibit their having even the aforesaid books translated into the vulgar tongue" (Canons of Toulouse no. 14; J. D. Mansi, *Sacrorum conciliorum nova et amplissima collectio*, vol. 23 (Venice, 1768).

For a discussion on the connection between literacy and heresy in the eleventh and twelfth century and for an interesting analysis of textual communities see B. Stock, *The Implications of Literacy: Written Language and Models of Interpretation in the Eleventh and Twelfth Centuries* (Princeton: Princeton University Press, 1983), pp. 88–240. See also R. Landes, "Literacy and the Origins of Inquisitorial Christianity: The Exegetical Battle Between Hierarchy and Community in the Christian Empire (300–500 C.E.)," in *Social History and Issues in Human Consciousness: Some Interdisciplinary Connections*, A. E. Banes and P. N. Stearns, eds. (New York: New York University Press, 1989) pp. 137–70. See also n. 7.

9. J. H. Newman, *The Arians of the Fourth Century*, 3d ed. (London: E. Lumley, 1871), pp. 148–49.

10. Benedict Spinoza, *A Theologico-Political Treatise*, trans. R. H. M. Elwes (New York: Dover, 1951), p. 182.

11. See Chapter 1 below, pp. 20–23.

12. For an interesting discussion of linguistic differentiation, the canon, and access to knowledge see J. Guillory, "Canonical and Non-Canonical: A Critique of the Current Debate," *ELH* 54 (Fall 1987), pp. 483–527; P. Bourdieu and C. Passeron, *Reproduction in Education, Society and Culture*, trans. R. Nice (London: Sage, 1977).

13. Deuteronomy 31:10–13.

14. See *Avot de-Rabbi Natan*, first version 1:3 and second version 2:4. (There is a difference between these two versions as to whether wealth was also a criterion for restriction.) See also Babylonian Talmud, *Berakhot* 28a. For a discussion of the social background of the rabbis in first and second centuries and their relationship to the rest of the community see E. E. Urbach, "Ma'amad ve-Hanahagah be-Olamam shel Chachmei Eretz Israel," in *Meolamam shel Chakhamim* (Jerusalem: Magnes Press, 1988), pp. 306–29. See also M. Beer, "Banav shel Moshe be-Agadat Haza'l," *Bar Ilan* 13 (1976), pp. 144–57, and "Banav shel Eli be-Agadat Haza'l," *Bar Ilan* 14–15 (1977–1978), pp. 79–93. The democratic tendency came into conflict with other factors of lineage preference, even among the Sages. See G. Elon, *Mechkarim be-Toldot Israel* II (Tel Aviv: Ha-Kibbutz ha-Meuchad, 1958), pp. 58–72. In the Talmudic period there were differences between the Sages of the Land of Israel and those of Babylonia concerning matters of inheritance. In Israel the sons of Sages played a greater role as Sages themselves and as a privileged class than did their counterparts in Babylonia. See I. Gafni, "Shevet u-Mechokek—al Defusei Manhigut Hadashim be-Tekufat ha-Talmud," in

Kehunah u-Meluchah, I. Gafni and G. Mozkin, eds. (Jerusalem: Zalman Shazar Center, 1987), pp. 62–79. Starting in the eighth century the principle of rabbinic leadership in Babylonia shifts to heredity. See A. Grosman, "Yerushat Avot ba-anhagah ha-Ruchanit shel Kehilot Israel bi-Yemei ha-Benaim ha-Mukdamim," *Zion* 50 (1985), pp. 189 ff. See also Chapter 1 below, nn. 20, 21.

   There were demands for esotericism to regulate highly selective transmission of knowledge of certain divine matters; see Mishnah, *Hagigah* 2:1. For a more extensive discussion on esotericism and curriculum see Chapter 3 below. One other important issue is the set of restrictions imposed by the institutional procedure of authorization. The question is how much the authority of the rabbi was derived from an institutional ordination and how much from his expertise independent of any institutional authorization. A full answer is beyond the scope of this work, but it is clear that the weight of institutional authorization varied from place to place and changed over time. According to the Talmudic sources, *smichah* (ordination) allowed a rabbi to judge in matters that nonordained scholars were not allowed to judge in. This kind of ordination was practiced in Israel, not in Babylonia. Once it was discontinued, rabbinic authority was restricted. While teachers continued to ordain students, ordination meant only that a student was allowed to make rulings during his teacher's lifetime, as without such ordination students were forbidden to rule before their teachers. Ordination therefore became a matter that concerned the relationship between a teacher and a student rather than an official sort of licensing. In fourteenth-century Ashkenaz ordination began to resemble institutional licensing, a development that raised the objections of Sefardic scholars. They claimed that expertise is a sufficient condition to authorize a halakhic ruling; official licensing would add nothing to a qualified individual, and in the case of ordination of an unqualified individual the official licensing would be null and void. For a fuller discussion of the subject and the historical perspective of the problem see J. Katz, "Rabbinic Authority and Authorization in the Middle Ages," in *Studies in Medieval History and Literature*, I. Twersky, ed. (Cambridge, Mass.: Harvard University Press, 1979), pp. 41–59; M. Breuer, "Ha-Smikhah ha-Ashkenazit," *Zion* 33 (1968), pp. 16–46. For a detailed description of the later development and professionalization of the rabbinate in the fifteenth century see J. I. Yuval, *Chakhamim ber-Doram* (Jerusalem: Magnes Press, 1989), pp. 332–428.

   15. On the prohibition of teaching Torah to women see Babylonian Talmud, *Sotah* 20a-b; Maimonides, *Mishneh Torah*, Laws of Talmud Torah 1:13. In modern Halakhah there is a shift and some rabbinic authorities permitted the teaching of Torah to women to a certain extent. See for example Hafetz Hayim, *Likutei Halakhot le-Sotah* (Jerusalem, 1970), pp. 11–12. On the teaching of Torah to Gentiles see below, Chapter 3.

   16. This example was pointed out to me by Yochanan Muffs. See also M. Fishbane, *The Garments of Torah: Essays in Biblical Hermeneutics* (Indianapolis: Indiana University Press, 1989), p. 66.

   17. For a fuller discussion on the Karaites see Chapter 2 below.

18. The earliest emergence of text-centeredness—although not with the full features mentioned above—is dated by Moshe Weinfeld to Josiah's reform, when the cultic worship outside the temple in Jerusalem was destroyed and the reading of the Torah took the place of sacrificial worship. To this phenomenon Weinfeld adds the canonization of Deuteronomy at the same time, which contributed to the emergence of book religion in Israel. See M. Weinfeld, *Me-Yeoshu'a a'd Yoshiyahu* (Jerusalem: Magnes Press, 1992), pp. 173–79. There is a general tendency to make a connection between loosening of Temple worship and strengthening of text-centeredness. The first stage is the prohibition of sacrifice outside the central Temple and the last stage is the destruction of the Temple itself.

1. Canon and Meaning

1. For this distinction see S. M. Gill, "Nonliterate Traditions and Holy Books: Toward a New Model," in F. M. Denny and R. L. Taylor, eds., *The Holy Book in Comparative Perspective* (Columbia, S.C.: University of South Carolina Press, 1985), p. 234.

2. See W. Graham, *Beyond the Written Word: Oral Aspects of Scripture in the History of Religion* (Cambridge: Cambridge University Press, 1987).

3. For a convincing discussion of the comparative phenomenology of Scriptures see M. Levering, "Introduction: Rethinking Scripture," in *Rethinking Scripture*, M. Levering, ed. (Albany: SUNY Press, 1989), pp. 1–17.

4. On the practice of placing the covenant in the Temple see M. Weinfeld, *Deuteronomy and the Deuteronomic School* (Oxford: Clarendon Press, 1972). The location of sacred books in the Temple continues until the end of the Second Temple period. The *Tosefta* mentions a copy of Scripture traditionally believed to be written by Ezra the scribe. See *Tosefta Kelim Bava Metsia* 5:8, and also *Sifrei Deuteronomy*, p. 356.

5. On the problem of literacy in the biblical period see A. Demsky, "On the Extent of Literacy in Ancient Israel," *Biblical Archeology Today, Proceedings of the International Congress on Biblical Archeology* (Jerusalem, 1985), pp. 349–53.

6. On the didactic role of the Torah in Deuteronomy see M. Weinfeld, *Deuteronomy and the Deuteronomic School*, pp. 298–306.

7. On the connection between studying and reminding see Deuteronomy 5:28; 6:1–2; 6:6–9, 12–13, 17, 19, 31, 32, 46.

8. See M. Fishbane, *Biblical Interpretation in Ancient Israel* (Oxford: Clarendon Press, 1985). The author claims (pp.18–19) that rabbinic interpretation had its root in early biblical interpretation. Fishbane's position should be stressed since other historians usually searched for the roots of rabbinic methods of interpretation in the Hellenistic world. See for instance D. Daube, "Rabbinic Methods of Interpretation and Hellenistic Rhetoric," *HUCA* 22 (1949), pp. 239–65, and also S. Lieberman, *Hellenism in Jewish Palestine* (New York: Jewish Theological Seminary, 1962), pp. 56–68.

9. See I. Yadin, *Megilat ha-Mikdash* (Jerusalem: Ha-Heverah le-Hakirat Eretz

Israel ve-Atikoteia, 1977) I, pp. 298–300. On the general concept of interpretation derived from the Dead Sea Scrolls see below, Chapter 2.

10. In the priestly material the term "Torah" designates a particular set of ritual instructions given to priests; see for example Leviticus 6:2. On the different uses of the Torah and the Book of Torah see M. Fishbane, "Torah," in *Enziclopediah Mikrait* (Mosad Bialik, 1982), pp. 469–83.

11. On the verb *li-drosh* see Y. Heineman, "Al Hitpatchut ha-Munachim ha-Mikzoyim le-Peirush ha-Mikra a. Darash," *Leshoneinu* 14 (1946), pp. 182 ff.

12. For the Jain example of fluid canon see K. W. Foldert, "The 'Canons' of 'Scripture,' " in Levering, ed., *Rethinking Scripture*, pp. 170–79. For the Hindu case see T. B. Corbun, "Scripture in India: Towards a Typology of the Word in Hindu Life," ibid., pp. 102–28.

13. The rabbinic discussion arose in the context of debates about whether or not those books defile the hands of those who touch them. Paradoxically, according to the rabbinic ruling, the books of Scripture do defile hands while other books do not. Hence the rabbinic formulation used to describe a book which is not numbered among the sacred books is that it is a book that does not defile the hands of those who touch it. What may explain such a paradoxical ruling is that ritualist purification is needed after touching anything defiling;the ruling would thus prevent unnecessary contact with the book and therefore mark its sacredness. On the paradoxical element of this ruling see Mishnah, *Yadaim* 4:5–6. On the idea of defiling the hands and sacredness see M. Haran, *Ha-Asufah ha Mikrait*, pp. 201–56. Another distinction between canonical and noncanonical books arose in regard to the permission to save books from fire on the Sabbath. See Mishnah, *Shabbat* 16:1, and *Tosefta, Shabbat* 14:4. This is similar to the problem of touching, because in both cases the question of whether a book is sacred or not is discussed in terms of rules of conduct towards such books that sets them apart from other books.

On the debates over the status of Ecclesiastes in the rabbinic sources see Mishnah, *Yadaim* 3:5; *Eduyot* 5:3; *Tosefta, Yadaim* 2: 14; Babylonian Talmud, *Shabbat* 30b; Leviticus *Rabbah*, XVIII, and also *Avot de-Rabbi Natan* 1:4. The only book of the prophets whose status was subject to debate is Ezekiel. See Babylonian Talmud, *Shabbat* 13b. Another debate concerning the book of Esther is mentioned in Babylonian Talmud, *Megillah* 7a.

14. Josephus, *Against Apion* 1:37–43, mentions 22 books because he counts the books of Ruth and Judges as one book and the books of Jeremiah and Lamentations as one book. Some scholars have concluded that the canon was formed and sealed earlier than the rabbinic discussions on the status of books: see S. Leiman, *The Canonization of the Hebrew Scripture: The Talmudic and Midrashic Evidence* (Hamden, Conn.: Archon Books, 1976) and R. Beckwith, *The Old Testament Canon of the New Testament Church* (London: SPCK, 1985); see also J. P. Lewis, "What Do We Mean by Jabneh," *Journal of Bible and Religion* (1964), pp. 125–32. Leiman and Beckwith offer various arguments to explain why the Tannaitic debates in Yavneh should not serve as a proof that the canon was not fixed until this period. Beckwith claims that these are minority opinions which unsuccessfully challenge

an existing fixed canon. Leiman claims that the question whether books defile the hands or not is not identical to whether they have authority or not but is related to the problem of whether they are inspired or not. According to Leiman, even those who believe that books do not defile hands think that they are canonical though not inspired. Among those who claim that the canon was sealed in Yavneh see H. Graetz, *Kohelet oder der Salomonische Prediger* (Leipzig, 1871); G. F. Moore, "The Definition of the Jewish Canon and the Repudiation of Christian Scriptures," in G. F. Moore, ed., *Essays in Modern Theology and Related Subjects as a Testimonial to C. A. Briggs* (New York, 1911), pp. 99–125; J. A. Sanders, *Torah and Canon* (Philadelphia: Fortress Press, 1972), pp. 94–95, and S. Zeitlin, "An Historical Study of the Canonization of the Hebrew Scriptures," *Proceedings of the American Academy for Jewish Research* 3 (1930–31), pp. 121–58. Moore claims that the sealing of the canon at Yavneh is connected to the rise of Christianity, and Sanders connects it to the trauma of the destruction of the Second Temple. For a deep critique of this approach to the formation of the canon at Yavneh, see M. Haran, *Ha-Asufah ha-Mikrait*, pp. 57–63.

Aside from the problem of the sealing of the canon in rabbinic tradition, certain scholars claim that other communities had independent canons of their own. The Hellenistic Jewish community is presumed to have had a large canon of its own that was subsequently coopted by the Church; see, for example, R. Meyer, "Kanonisch und Apokryph," *Theologisches Worterbuch zum Neuen Testament* 3, pp. 979–87. A very convincing argument against the existence of an Alexandrian canon was made by A. C. Sundberg, *The Old Testament of the Early Church* (Cambridge, Mass.: Harvard University Press, 1964). For a similar argument concerning the Judean Desert sect see n. 16.

15. On the connection between inspiration and Scripture see Babylonian Talmud, *Megillah* 7a. For prophecies that did not enter the canon see *Megillah* 14a. Concerning the difficulty of assessing the criteria of exclusion see S. Z. Leiman, "Inspiration and Canonicity: Reflection on the Formation of the Biblical Canon," in *Jewish and Christian Self Definition*, E. P. Sanders, A. I. Baumgarten, and A. Mendelson, eds. (London: SCM Press, 1981), pp. 56–63.

16. See M. Fishbane, "Interpretation of Mikra at Qumran," in *Mikra*, M. J. Mulder, ed. (Philadelphia: Fortress Press, 1988), pp. 362–63. For a position against the existence of an independent canon among the Judean Desert sects see R. Beckwith, *The Old Testament Canon*, pp. 80–81. A convincing argument for the existence of added material in the canon of the Judean Desert sect was made by M. Haran, *Ha-Asufah ha-Mikrait*, pp. 93–102.

17. See *Sifra, Behuqotai* 13; Babylonian Talmud, Tractate *Temurah* 16a. For a general discussion of the relationship between prophecy and Halakhah see E. E. Urbach, "Halakhah u-Nevuah," *Tarbiz* 17 (1941), pp. 1–27.

18. See Maimonides, *Hakdamah le-Perush ha-Mishnah*, Y. Kapach, ed. (Jerusalem: Mossad Ha-Rav Kook, 1963), pp. 3–5, and *Mishneh Torah*, Hilkhot Yesodei ha-Torah 9, 1–2.

19. On the distinction between rabbinic authority and prophetic authority see Jerusalem Talmud, *Sanhedrin* 11:5.

20. D. Weiss Halivni, *Midrash, Mishnah, and Gemara* (Cambridge, Mass.: Harvard University Press, 1986), p. 16.

21. Concerning the use of *bat-kol* in Talmudic material and the reliance on prophetic statements outside the Pentateuch for the purpose of legal decisions, see E. E. Urbach, "Halakhah u-Nevuah." On such use in the Middle Ages and later see A. Y. Heschel, "Al Ruach ha-Kodesh bi-Yemi ha-Benaim," *Sefer ha-Yobel le-Alexander Marx* (New York, 1950), pp. 175–208; see also the vast amount of material gathered by Reuven Margaliyot in his introduction to R. Jacob of Marvege, *Shelot u-Tshubot min ha-Sahmaim*, R. Margaliyot, ed. (Jerusalem: Mosad ha-Rav Kook, 1956), 3.I. Ta-Shma, "Shelot ve-Teshubot min ha-Sahmaim— ha-Kobetz ve-Tosaftav," *Tarbiz* 56 (1988), pp. 51–66.

22. On the relationship between scholars and warriors in the Midrash see I. Heineman, *Darkei ha-Haggadah* (Jerusalem: Magnes Press, 1970), pp. 91–92.

23. On the nature of the Sages' leadership prior to 70 C.E. see E. E. Urbach, *Me-Olaman shel Chakhamim* (Jerusalem: Magnes Press, 1984), pp. 306–29. For the debate concerning the influence of the Sages see G. Alon, *Jews, Judaism, and the Classical World* (Jerusalem, 1977), p. 22, who claims that since the Hasmonean period the Pharisees constituted the majority of the Jewish people. For the opposite position see M. Smith, "Palestinian Judaism in the First Century," in *Israel: Its Role in Civilization*, M. Davis, ed. (New York, 1956), p. 81; see also J. Neusner, "Josephus Pharisees," in *Ex orba religionem: Studia Geo Windengren*, C. J. Bleeker, ed. (Leiden, 1972), pp. 224–44. For a minimalist assessment of the influence of the Sages see also E. Goodenough, *Jewish Symbols in the Greco-Roman Period*, 13 vols. (New York: Pantheon Books, 1953–56), vol. 12, pp. 184–98. For a balanced view on the subject and the institutionalization of the Sages' leadership in the third and fourth centuries C.E. see L. I. Levine, *The Rabbinic Class of Roman Palestine in Late Antiquity* (New York: The Jewish Theological Seminary of America, 1989), pp. 98–195, and also S. D. Fraade, *From Tradition to Commentary* (New York: SUNY Press, 1991), pp. 69–122.

24. See M. D. Herr, "Ha-Rezef shebe Shalshelet Mesiratah shel ha-Torah," *Zion* 44 (1979), pp. 43–56. On the role of priests in leadership after the destruction of the Temple see R. Kiemelmann, "Ha-Oligarchiah ha-Kohanit ve-Talmidei Chakhamim be-Tekufat ha-Talmud," *Zion* 48 (1983), pp. 135–48; D. Ben Hayim Trifon, "Ha-Kohanim le-Achar Churban Bait Sheini" (Ph.D. diss., Tel Aviv University, 1985), and I. Gafni in *Kehunana u-Melucha Yahse Dat u-Medinah be-Israel uba-Amim*, I. Gafni and G. Motzkin, eds. (Jerusalem: Zalman Shazar Center, 1986–87), pp. 79–91.

25. See Mishnah, *Horayot* 3:8. See also Babylonian Talmud, *Yoma* 71a.

26. On Ecclesiastes and its message see H. L. Ginzberg, in *Biblical and Other Studies*, A. Altman, ed. (Cambridge, Mass.: Harvard University Press, 1963), pp. 47–59; E. Bickerman, *Four Strange Books of the Bible* (New York: Schocken, 1967), pp. 139–67. On the canonization of Kohelet see S. Lieberman, "Hearot le-Perek Alef shel Kohelet Rabah," in *Mechkarim be-Torat Eretz Israel* (Jerusalem: Magnes Press, 1991), pp. 53–59.

27. On the Song of Songs and its allegorical interpretation see G. Cohen, "The Song of Songs," in *Samuel Fridland Lectures 1960–1966* (New York: Jewish Publication Society, 1966), pp. 1–21.

28. On the principle of charity see W. V. O. Quine, *Word and Object* (Cambridge, Mass.: MIT Press, 1960), pp. 58–59.

29. See R. Dworkin, *Law's Empire* (Cambridge, Mass.: Harvard University Press, 1985), pp. 53–63.

30. S. Levinson raises this criticism of Dworkin in "Taking Law Seriously: Reflections on Thinking Like a Lawyer," *Stanford Law Review* 30 (1978), pp. 1071–110.

31. Yehudah Elfakar's critique is printed in *Igrot Kenaot, Igrot ha-Rambam* (Lapsia edition, repr. Jerusalem, 1967), pp. 1–2.

32. For Spinoza's approach to the problem see the Appendix.

33. There could be an intermediary position between these alternatives. In response to an improbable statement about the world from a renowned scientist, we might assume she must have meant something else and try to accommodate the statement to the general knowledge. Or, given the prominence of the scientist, we might reexamine our beliefs. We could also accommodate both the statement and the belief by slightly rephrasing and changing each. If the scientist repeatedly makes bizarre statements, at a certain point we would give up the assumption that there must be something to what she said. At this juncture we could assume that she has gone out of her mind, or, more moderately, that she is no longer speaking as a scientist. Hence there are two stages of charity. The first is the assumption that we cannot easily brush aside a particular statement and that we must modify either our understanding of the statement or our beliefs about the world. At the second stage we determine what weight to give to the statement and what weight to our beliefs in the process of accommodating the two.

34. The principle of charity as applied to such canonical texts is not fully exhausted by the idea of giving the text the best possible interpretation. The other important feature of the text is atemporality. F. Kermode emphasizes this feature in his discussion of the classic. What he calls "the imperial view" looks upon the classic as an open and timeless text whose essence is unchangeable. It speaks to us despite great changes that occurred between the age when the classic was written and our own and beyond the voice of the writer and his circumstances; it is a text that is accommodated through complex strategies of allegory and typology. See F. Kermode, *The Classic* (Cambridge, Mass.: Harvard University Press, 1983), pp. 13–45. This text is eternally relevant; it always addresses us. In this respect the classic and sacred texts are similar to legal texts. Legal texts must guide future decisions in questions that have not yet arisen at the time of their composition, and the presumption of relevance is central to the view of the text in legal practice. But in this case that presumption is an outgrowth of an institutional arrangement that commits people to a text as a guarantee of continuity and neutrality. Whether or not the rule of text in the legal practice is a fiction is not the question; it is the commitment to the text that counts.

The relationship between durability and canonicity poses a serious problem. David Hume, in *The Standard of Taste*, viewed durability as an internal property of the work, something that is perfectly and naturally attuned to please us: "durable admiration . . . attends those works that have survived all the caprices of the mode and fashion as the mistakes of ignorance and envy. The same Homer who pleased at Athens and Rome two thousand years ago is still admired at Paris and at London. All the changes of climate, government, religion and language have not been able to obscure his glory . . . It appears then, that amidst all the variety and caprice of taste, there are certain general principles of approbation or blame whose influence a careful eye may trace in all operations of the mind. Some particular forms or qualities from the original structure of the internal fabric are calculated to please and others to displease, and if they fail of their effect in any particular instance, it is from some apparent defect or imperfection in the organ." (*"Of the Standard of Taste" and Other Essays*, J. W. Lenz, ed. (Indianapolis: Bobbs Merrill, 1965), pp. 9–10. A canon, in Hume's description, is something that endures the fluctuations of taste, has a property of pleasing that is inherent in the work, and is attuned to the natural way our organs of taste function, beyond mere convention or social arrangement. If the work happens not to please someone, on Hume's account that is due to a defect or imperfection in the viewer's organ. But the proper and natural function of the organ of literary taste is not readily describable. As Barbara Herrnstein Smith points out, the believers in a canon tend to see it as naturally endowed, not socially contingent and constructed. It is part of the characterization of a book as sacred that one relates to it as an object beyond historical contingency. But durability is not a sign of canonicity; it is what makes a work canonical. There is a complex mechanism of preserving the durability of text, institutions engaged in circulating, preserving, publishing, teaching, and transmitting the text, which are continuously blocking other competitors. Even so, the text that has been preserved and transmitted successfully is no longer the original text. In London and Paris they do not read the same Homer, as Hume thinks they do, and precisely because it is not the same Homer, it endures. The way Homer is read in London and Paris is radically different from the way he was read in Athens and Rome. See B. Herrnstein Smith, *Contingencies of Value* (Cambridge, Mass.: Harvard University Press, 1988), pp. 47–64.

35. For the existence of esoteric layers in the Bible in rabbinic literature see E. E. Urbach, "Ha-Masorot al Torat ha-Sod be-Tkufat ha-Tanaim," *Mechkarim be-Kabbalah ube-Toldot ha-Datot Mugashim le-Gershom Scholem* (Jerusalem: Magnes Press, 1968), pp. 1–28. On the early conceptions of esoteric meaning of the text in the Heikhalot literature see M. Idel, "Tfisat ha-Torah be-Sifrut ha-Heikhalot ve-Gilguleiah ba-Kabbalah," in *Mechkarei Yerushalaim be-Machshevet Israel* (1981), vol. I, pp. 23–49. On the relation of esoteric notions and Midrash see M. Idel, "Midrashic versus Other Forms of Jewish Hermeneutics: Some Comparative Reflections," in *The Midrashic Imagination: Jewish Exegesis, Thought, and History*, M. Fishbane, ed. (New York: SUNY Press, 1993), pp. 45–58.

36. See G. Scholem, *On the Kabbalah and Its Symbolism* (New York: Schocken Press, 1987) pp. 53–61; Idel's "Tfisat ha-Torah be-Sifrut ha-Heikhalot ve-

Gilguleiah ba-Kabbalah"; *Language, Torah, and Hermeneutics in Abraham Abulafia* (New York: SUNY Press, 1989); *Kabbalah: New Perspectives* (New Haven: Yale University Press, 1988), ch. 9; see also the wonderful description of Zoharic hermeneutics in Y. Liebes, *Alpaim* 9 (1994), pp. 87–98.

37. See F. Talmage, "Apples of Gold: The Inner Meaning of Sacred Texts in Medieval Judaism," in *Jewish Spirituality from the Bible through the Middle Ages*, A. Green, ed. (New York, 1986), pp. 315–55. In recent years research on Maimonides has focused more and more on his hermeneutics, both in theory and practice. See, for example, S. Rosenberg, "Parshanut ha-Torah be-Moreh Nevukhim," *Mechkarei Yerushalaim be-Machshevet Israel* (1981), vol. I, pp. 85–158, and especially the works of S. Klein-Breslavy, *Perush ha-Rambam le-Sipur Briat ha-Olam* (Jerusalem: Ha-Chevrah le-Cheker ha-Mikra, 1978), and *Perush ha-Rambam la-Sipurim al Adam be-Parashat Bereshit* (Jerusalem: Reuben Mas, 1987).

38. Introduction to *The Guide of the Perplexed*, trans. S. Pines (Chicago: University of Chicago Press, 1974), vol 1, p. 8. The political argument appears in the preceding paragraph of the introduction. Maimonides claims that by concealing some of the truth in his *Guide* he follows the Torah itself in that matter: "For my purpose is that the truths be glimpsed and then again be concealed, so as not to oppose that divine purpose which one cannot possibly oppose and which has concealed from the vulgar among the people those truths especially requisite for apprehending Him," pp. 6–7.

39. See Maimonides' statement in the *Guide:* "Among the things you have to know and have your attention called to is the dictum: 'And the man gave names and so on.' It informs us that languages are conventional and not natural, as has sometimes been thought" (II, 30).

40. A thirteenth-century Maimonidean, Jacob Anatoli, describes the language of Adam as a language with no equivocal terms, only "separate names." After the tower of Babel, equivocal terms appear in the language along with the rise of the masses. According to Anatoli, equivocation is essential to any political community. See Jacob Anatoli, *Malmad ha-Talmidim* (Lyck, 1866), pp. 9–10.

41. A major problem inherent in the multilayered conception of the canon is how to determine the relative status of the external and internal modes of reading. A moderate position would retain the external meaning and include the internal without undermining the value of the external. For a detailed formulation of this position regarding philosophical allegories and their influence on the external reading see Chapter 3. Concerning this problem in kabbalistic hermeneutics see E. R. Wolfson, "Beautiful Maiden Without Eyes: Peshat and Sod in Zoharic Hermeneutics," in *The Midrashic Imagination*, M. Fishbane, ed., pp. 155 ff. One of the most radical statements of the insignificance of the external meaning relative to the esoteric one appears in Abulafia's writings. See M. Idel, *Language, Torah, and Hermeneutics in Abraham Abulafia*, pp. 75–78.

42. On the conception of language in the Kabbalah and its relation to the Maimonidean tradition see M. Idel, *Language, Torah, and Hermeneutics in Abraham Abulafia*, ch. 1.

43. On this subject see I. Heineman, who claims that the Midrash abounds

with nonconventional modes of interpretation, all based on the assumption that the Torah speaks a different sort of language. See I. Heineman, *Darkhei ha-Aggadah* (Jerusalem: Magnes Press, 1970), pp. 96–136. I doubt that this assumption is shared by all schools of Midrash (seep. 12 n.106) or even those that claim the Torah speaks in the language of humans. On the debate between R. Ishmael and R. Akiva and its general context, see A. J. Heschel, *Torah min ha-Shamaim be-Aspaklaria shel ha-Dorot* (New York: Soncino Press, 1962), vol. I, pp. 3–20; see also J. N. Epstein, *Mevo'ot le-Sifrut ha-Tanaim* (Jerusalem: Magnes Press, 1957), pp. 521–22. For an important discussion concerning the underlying conception of the text in midrashic hermeneutics see D. Boyarin, *Intertextuality and the Reading of Midrash* (Bloomington: Indiana University Press, 1990).

44. For a discussion of Nachmanides' view that Torah includes all knowledge see A. Funkenstein, *Theology and the Scientific Imagination* (Princeton: Princeton University Press, 1988), p. 215.

45. For a detailed analysis of nonconventional aspects of interpretation as they are related to the material form of the text see M. Idel, "Hea'arot Rishoniyot al ha-Parshanut ha-Kabbalit le-Sugeiah," *Sefer ha-Yovel le-Mardekhai Breuer* (Jerusalem: Akademon, 1992), vol. II, pp. 773–784. On the hermeneutics of Hasidei Ashkenaz and their use of letter enumeration see J. Dan, "The Hasidic 'Gates of Wisdom,' " in *Hommages à Georges Vajda*, G. Nahon and C. Touati, eds. (Louvain, 1980), pp. 183–189.

46. The hermeneutical techniques of Abraham Abulafia, analyzed thoroughly by Moshe Idel, are among the most interesting and radical of those that stem from the notion of the Torah's primary and hidden form. Abulafia allows himself not only to change the division of letters into words but also to change the sequence of letters and to create new words. He considers the most elemental divine and canonized aspect of the Torah to be the letter itself. The interpreter deconstructs the text into its pre-formed stage and re-forms it with various interpretative strategies. See M. Idel, *Language, Torah, and Hermeneutics in Abraham Abulafia*, pp. 101–09; 121–24. One interesting consequence of Abulafia's conception is that the border between canonical and noncanonical is completely blurred. Since the atomized letter is the divine element in the canon, any utterance in language can in principle become an object of Abulafia's hermeneutical approach.

47. On the Christian Gnostics see E. Pagels, *The Gnostic Gospels* (New York: Vintage Books, 1979). On Marcion see A. von Harnack, *Marcion: Das Evangelium von Fremden Gott* (Leipzig, 1924), and R. Hoffman, *Marcion: On the Restitution of Christianity* (Chico, Calif.: Scholars Press, 1984).

48. In K. Rudolph, Gnosis: The Nature and History of Gnosticism, trans. R. M. Wilson (San Francisco: Harper and Row, 1987), p. 146.

49. For an a general description of the variety of Gnostic attitudes to the Bible, see B. Pearson, "Use, Authority and Exegesis of Mikra in Gnostic Literature," in *Mikra*, M. J. Mulder, ed. (Philadelphia: Fostress Press, 1988), pp. 635–52. (An extensive bibliography is in note 5.)

50. On the Gnostic creation story and its negative reading of Genesis see K. Rudolph, *Gnosis*, pp. 67–113. On some connections between rabbinic Midrash on the Creation story and Gnostic readings see B. Pearson, "Jewish Haggadic Traditions in the Testimony of Truth from *Nag Hammadi*," in *Religious Syncretism in Antiquity*, B. Pearson, ed. (Missoula, Mont.: Scholars Press, 1975), pp. 205–222; "Some Observations on Gnostic Hermeneutics," in Wendy O'Flaherty, ed., *The Critical Study of Sacred Texts* (Berkeley: Religious Studies Series, 1979), pp. 243–56, and "Jewish Sources in Gnostic Literature," *Compendia* II-2, pp. 443–81.

51. *Bereshit Rabah*, 8.

52. "On the Origins of the World," *The Nag Hammadi Library in English*, J. M. Robinson, ed. (San Francisco: Harper and Row, 1978), pp. 183–85. See also pp. 164–65.

53. *Nag Hammadi*, pp. 367–68 and pp. 215, 282. For a different evaluation see K. Rudolph, *Gnosis: The Nature and History of Gnosticism*, pp. 144–48.

54. *Nag Hammadi*, p. 455.

55. Ibid., p. 112. There is a striking parallel to this problem in the Midrash: if there are no other gods, why is it that God is so jealous? See *Mekhilta de-Rabi Ishmael*, sec. 65.

2. Authority, Controversy, and Tradition

1. The question of whether the Mishnah is an anthology or a code is debated in modern scholarship. H. Albeck, *Mabo la-Mishnah* (Jerusalem: Mosad Bialik, 1960), pp. 270–89, claims that the Mishnah is an anthology of earlier traditions and its editor did not attempt to codify them. A. H. Weiss, *Dor ve-Dorshav* (Vilna ed. 1911), vol. 2, p. 186, is of the same opinion; J. Epstein, in *Mebo'ot le-Sifrut ha-Tanaim* (Jerusalem: Magnes Press, 1957), p. 225, claims that in fact the Mishnah is a code. On the publication and the editing of the Mishnah see S. Lieberman, *Hellenism in Jewish Palestine*, pp. 83–99. According to recent scholarship, the Mishnah was transmitted orally until the sealing of the Talmud in the fifth century. See S. Abramson, "Ktibat ha-Mishnah," *Tarbut ve-Hebrah be-Toldot Israel bi-Yemei ha-Benayim, Kobetz Maamarim le-Zichro shel H. H. Ben Sasson*, R. Bonfil, ed. (Jerusalem: Merkaz Shazar, 1989).

2. Cited in *Karaite Anthology*, trans. L. Nemoy (New Haven: Yale University Press, 1953), pp. 71–82.

3. On intentionalism and the Constitution see J. H. Ely, *Democracy and Distrust: A Theory of Judicial Review* (Cambridge, Mass.: Harvard University Press, 1980), chaps. 1–2. For various discussions and criticisms of the intentionalist view see also *Interpreting Law and Literature*, S. Levinson and S. Mailloux, eds. (Evanston, Ill.: Northwestern University Press, 1988), pp. 37–115. See R. Bork, "Tradition and Morality in Constitutional Law," *Views from the Bench: The Judiciary and Constitutional Politics*, M. Cannon and D. O'Brien, eds. (Chatman, N.J.: Chatman House, 1985), and Bork's "The Constitution, Original Intent and Economic Rights," 23 *San Diego Law Rev.* (1986), p. 823; *The Tempting of America* (New

York: Simon and Schuster, 1990). For criticism of Bork's position see R. Dworkin, "The Bork Nomination," *The New York Review of Books*, August 13, 1987, pp. 3–10.

4. See E. D. Hirsch, *Validity in Interpretation* (New Haven: Yale University Press, 1967).

5. On attacks of the relation between meaning and intention see W. K. Wismat, Jr., and M. C. Beardsley, "The Intentional Fallacy," *Sewanee Review* 54 (July-September, 1946); L. Wittgenstein, *Philosophical Investigations*, trans. G. E. M. Anscombe (New York: Macmillan, 1953); H. G. Gadamer, *Truth and Method*, 2nd ed. (London, 1979), pp. 39–55; S. Cavell, *Must We Mean What We Say?* (Oxford: Oxford University Press, 1969), ch. 8; R. Dworkin, *Law's Empire* (Cambridge, Mass.: Harvard University Press, 1986), pp. 53–68.

6. In some cases the authority of the text rests not on the superior will that produced it but rather on the binding consent of the person who received it. Such a notion of the source of the text's authority provides another sort of connection between the source of the text's authority and its authoritative meaning. In such a consensual notion, the authoritative meaning will not be the meaning intended by the writer but that intended by the party who consented to the text. This is not to say that the consenting party can attach private meanings to the document and claim that his consent was given to this private meaning, and that only his idiosyncratic meaning is binding. The consenting party agreed to follow the document; if he imposes on it an absolutely private meaning, he can no longer be said to be referring to the text. Nevertheless, the consenting party can claim that his own understanding is decisive in selecting between plausible alternatives of the text, since the grounds of the text's authority are derived from his consent. If we have independent evidence regarding the intentions of the consenting party, those intentions rather than the writer's intentions seem to provide the criterion for determining the authoritative meaning of the text. We can avoid such a situation only when there is explicit or implicit evidence that the consenting party bound himself to the meaning of the document as it is understood by the author or by another third party.

The Talmud (*Shebu'ot* 28b) debates about whose intention is crucial in determine the meaning of an oath taken in court. One side argues that the conventional meaning of the terms of the oath is binding and not the private intention of the person who took the oath. Another opinion is that the court has to add explicitly that the oath is binding according to its understanding of the oath, and if this is not done the meaning of the oath is determined by the private understanding of the person who took the oath. (Both sides seem to agree that without the qualification added by the court, the intention of the person who took the oath is decisive when his is a plausible reading of the conventional meaning of the oath.) In order to solve the problem the Talmud brings an interesting proof from Israel's covenant with God concerning the Torah: "Come and hear! And so we find that when Moses adjured the Israelites, he said to them: Know that I do not adjure you according to your own minds, but according to the mind of the

Omnipresent and according to my mind" (Babylonian Talmud, *Shebu'ot* 29a). Since the authority of the Torah rests upon the consent of Israel, without such a qualification to the consent the meaning of the Torah will be determined by Israel's understanding. See also *Tosafot ke-she-Hisbi'a*, and *Hidushei ha Maharsha* on the *Tosafot*. Concerning the motive of consent as the source of the authority of the Torah, see Babylonian Talmud, *Shabbat* 89b.

7. Babylonian Talmud, *Baba Mezia* 59b.

8. I prefer the stronger reading of the story, that is, the claim that intention itself is not the decisive factor, since the text gives no indication that R. Yehoshua questioned the authenticity of the voice as God's voice. The same holds true for the section from Tractate *Temurah* in which God proclaims that He will not intervene in the legal process since the Torah is not in heaven any more. For a different orientation see *Hidushei ha-Ramban, Baba Mezia*, 59b *u-Berchuhu*, and also *Rabeinu Nissim Gaon, Berakhot* 19b. According to both commentators R. Yehoshua knew of a tradition contrary to the statements of R. Eliezer. The focus of the story would thus be the clash between tradition and innovation, and not between reasoning and prophecy. For an opposite reading see R. Nissim Gerondi, *Derashot ha-Ran*, L. Feldman, ed. (Jerusalem: Shalem Institute, 1973), *Derashah* 7, and also R. Aryeh Leib Ha-Kohen's introduction to *Kzot ha-Choshen* (New York, 1984). Nachmanides' interpretation is rightly questioned by Y. Silman in "Torat Israel le-Or Hidusheiah—Beirur Phenomenology," *American Academy for Jewish Research* 37 (1990–91), pp. 52–53, n. 9. For an extensive discussion of the different approaches to this story see Y. Englard, "Tanur shel Achna'i—Perusheah shel Aggada," *Shnaton ha-Mishpat ha-Ibri* 1 (1974), pp. 45–56.

9. See Babylonian Talmud, *Gitin* 6b and *Baba Mezia* 86a; *Pesikta De Rav Kahana*, Mendelbaum, ed. (New York: Beit ha-Midrash le-Rabanim, 1982), p. 73; *Bamidbar Rabah* 19:7; *Tanhuma Shemot* 18.

10. On the conception of the inspired reader in the Dead Sea Scrolls and the difference between that conception and the rabbinic one, see J. M. Baumgarten, *Studies in Qumran Law* (Leiden: Brill, 1977), pp. 13–35. The use of elaborate prophetic techniques in interpretation was also revived in some trends of Kabbalah; see M. Idel, *Kabbalah: New Perspectives*, pp. 234–49

11. R. Yehudah's attempt to canonize the Mishnah might not have met with full success. Alongside the Mishnah we find other compilations of Tanaitic materials, such as the *Tosefta*, which may have challenged the exclusivity of the Mishnah. Nor does the Talmud always follow the ruling preferred in the Mishnah by R. Yehudah. Concerning the reception of the Mishnah, see D. Weiss Halivni, "The Reception Accorded to Rabbi Judah's Mishnah," in *Jewish and Christian Self-Definition*, pp. 204–12.

12. On the calendar of the Judean Desert sects see S. Talmon, "The Calendar Reckoning of the Sect from the Judean Desert," *Scripta Hierosalymitana* (1958), vol. 4, pp. 162–99.

13. See Mishnah, *Yebamot* 1:4.

14. Maimonides contends that the second view in the Mishnah accords with

the first, for they pertain to different cases (a tactic frequently used in the Talmud to reconcile apparent differences of opinion). The first applies to minority views that were not totally rejected; the second to minority opinions that were rejected. See *Perush ha-Mishnah, Eduyot* 1:5. From the language of the *Tosefta* it seems that the two opinions did not agree. See *Tosefta, Eduyot* 1:4.

15. See *Tosefta Eduyot* 1:4.

16. This passage may be understood in two ways. Either there had been no controversies and there was an agreement in all matters of the law before there was a number of disciples of Shammai and Hillel who did not serve their master adequately; or there had been controversies even before that time, but the Houses of Hillel and Shammai refused to accept a single authority. Such a reading is preferred by E. E. Urbach, *Ha-Halakhah Mekorotehah ve-Hitpatchutah* (Jerusalem: Massadah, 1984), p. 64. The other opinion is supported in *Igeret Rav Shrira Gaon*, B. M. Levin, ed. (Jerusalem: Makor, 1972), p. 8.

17. *Tosefta, Sotah* 7:12; Babylonian Talmud, *Hagigah* 3b; *Bamidbar Raba* 15:22; see also Babylonian Talmud, Tractate *Erubin* 13b.

18. See D. Weiss Halivni's extensive analysis of the idea of revelation as including multiple meanings; see his *Peshat and Derash* (Oxford: Oxford University Press, 1990), pp. 112–119.

19. Jerusalem Talmud, *Sanhedrin* 2:2; *Shir ha-Shirim Rabah*, ch. 2; *Bamidbar Rabah* 2:3; *Midrash Tehilim* 12:4; *Pesikta Rabati* 21, and *Masekhet Sofrim* 16:5.

20. On the idea of the revealed Oral Law and its effects on canon formation, see D. Kraemer, "The Formation of Rabbinic Canon: Authority and Boundaries," in *Journal of Biblical Literature*, pp. 613–30. See also J. Neusner, *The Authority and Uses of the Hebrew Bible in the Torah of Formative Judaism* (Minneapolis: Fortress, 1989) and the critique of Neusner's view in D. F. Morgan, *Between Text and Community: The Writings in Canonical Interpretation* (Minneapolis: Fortress, 1990), pp. 106–07.

21. For the background of Karaite polemics on Ibn Daud's view see G. Cohen, *Introduction to Sefer ha-Kabbalah* (Philadelphia, 1967), and B. M. Levin, *Igeret Rab Shrira* Gaon (Jerusalem: Makor, 1972), pp. 3–7.

22. See ibid., pp. 6–8, and also the material from the Geonim quoted in nn. 3, 6.

23. See ibid., pp. 18–19.

24. In his introduction to *Mafteach le-Man'ulei ha-Talmud*, R. Nissim Gaon follows the same line of argument: "We have no need to bring evidence which proves the authenticity of the Sages' tradition (Kabbalah) . . . since our predecessors made it clear, but I will clarify the time in which the Mishnah and the Talmud were written and I will show that the preserved Kabbalah and tradition never faded from the nation." R. Nissim then describes the Mishnah in the following terms: "He (R. Yehudah the Prince) made up his mind to gather everything they had in their hands from the tradition." *Mafteach le-Man'ulei ha-Talmud* (Jerusalem: Makor, 1971), p. 2b.

25. *Sefer ha-Kabbalah*, pp. 3–4.

26. For Karo's view see *Kesef Mishneh, Hilchot Mamrim* 2:1.

27. For an extensive discussion of the complicated problem of intergenerational authority in Halakhah see I. Ta-Shma, "Halakhah ke-Batrai," *Shnaton ha-Mishpat ha-Ivri*, vols. 6–7 (1979–1980), and I. Yubal, "Rishonim ve-Achronim," *Zion* 57 (1992) pp. 369–94. For a modern debate on the source of the authority of the Talmud see R. Elchanan Vasseman, *Kovetz Shiurim, Divrei Sofrim* (Tel Aviv, 1963), pp. 96–97, versus Hazon Ish, *Kovetz Inyanim* (Bnei Brak, 1975), pp. 194–97. For an extensive discussion on the problem see S. Z. Havlin, "Al ha-Chatimah ha-Sifrutit," in *Mechkarim ba-Sifrut ha-Talmudit* (Jerusalem: Ha-Akademia ha-Israelit le-Mada'im, 1983), pp. 148–92.

28. Newman, *Arians*, p. 237.

29. Sahl is cited in S. Pinsker, *Likutei Kadmoniyot* (Vienna, 1969), pp. 32–35, and in *Karaite Anthology*, trans. by L. Nemoy (New Haven: Yale University Press, 1953), pp.118–19. For a similar Karaite view expressed by Daniel Alkamasi see J. Mann, "Tract by an Early Karaite," *JAR* 12 (1921–22), p. 275.

30. See *Karaite Anthology*, p. 249.

31. For a Karaite formulation of what makes an authoritative reader, see ibid., pp. 247–50.

32. The innovative nature of Maimonides compared to that of the Geonim was pointed out by C. Tchernowitz, *Toldot ha-Halkhah* (New York, 1948), vol. I, p. 88; see also the extensive discussion by I. Twersky, *Introduction to the Code of Maimonides (Mishneh Torah)* (New Haven: Yale University Press, 1980), pp. 62–74.

33. Maimonides repeats this point in his introduction to the commentary of the Mishnah and to the *Mishneh Torah.* In the latter he describes this category as follows: "The norms that were innovated in each generation—laws that were not received by tradition but [were derived] through a *midah* of the thirteen *midot."*

34. On the comparison of Ibn Daud's account of the controversy and Maimonides'see D. Hartman, *Maimonides: Torah and Philosophic Quest* (Philadelphia: Jewish Publication Society, 1976), pp. 112–16.

35. On the nature of interpretation as derivation and rules of interpretation as rules of inference, and the implications of this for controversy, see M. Halbertal, "Sefer ha-Mitzvot la-Rambam," *Tarbiz* 59 (1990), pp. 457–80.

36. On notions of halakhic truth, see the important discussion by A. Sagi, "Halakhic Praxis and the Word of God: A Study of Two Models," in *Jewish Thought and Philosophy* (1992), vol. 1, pp. 305–29.

37. See also Ramban, *Hasayot le-Sefer ha-Mitzvot shel ha-Rambam*, Hasagah le-Shoresh Rishon.

38. *Hidushei ha-Ritba, Erubin* 13b.

39. *Derashot ha-Ran, Derashah* 7 and 5 (second version).

40. R. Samson of Sens expresses the same view of the open-ended revelation: "Although an individual's claims may not have been accepted at first and many disagreed with him, at other times many may come to agree with his reasons and Halakhah will follow them. The whole Torah was given to Moses with aspects

of purity and aspects of impurity, and when they asked him how long they should continue to debate, he said to them, 'Follow the many, but both are the words of the living God.' " *Tosafot Shantz, Eduyot* 1:5. Another medieval author who subscribes to the same model was R. Jacob of Marvege, *Shelot u-Tshubot min ha-Shamaim*, R. Margaliyot, ed. (Jerusalem: Mosad ha-Rav Kook), p. 3. The same idea is expressed in kabbalistic terminology. See for example Meir Ibn Gabai, *Avodat ha-Kodesh* (Cracow, 1576), *Helek ha-Tachlit*, ch. 23; Shlomoh Luria, *Yam shel Shlomoh* (Bnei Brak, 1959–60), introduction to Tractate *Hulin;* and R. Shmuel be-Rabi Izhak, *Midrash Shmuel* (Cracow, 1593), *Avot* 5:19. In the sixteenth century R. Shlomoh Ephraim of Lunzeiz made a bold analogy between the revelation at Sinai and the structure of the Mishnah. Like the Mishnah, the revelation was handed to Moses complete with counterarguments, with the intention that future generation can rely upon those who overrule the existing law according to the need of the hour; the Torah itself was revealed as a flexible canon. See *Amudei Shesh* (Prague, 1607), ch. 20.

41. For an extensive and important discussion on the attitude towards open-ended revelation and controversy see A. Sagi, *Elu va-Elu* (Tel Aviv: Ha-Kibbutz ha-Meuchad, 1996).

42. Unlike Ritba and Ran, the author of *Sefer ha-Chinuch*, a disciple of Nachmanides, uses Nachmanides' terminology in a nonconstitutive fashion. According to *Sefer ha-Chinuch*, "the intention of the Torah was handed to the Sages of Israel." But such a privilege is merely procedural and not constitutive. The Sages have to be obeyed even if they are mistaken, since a legal system cannot allow anarchy: "it is better to endure one mistake, and keep everybody obedient to their [the Sages'] opinion, which is usually correct, and not that each will follow his own opinion, which will result in the destruction of the law and the division of the heart of the people and the complete loss of the nation. Because of such considerations the intention of the Torah was handed to the Sages of Israel." *Mitzvah* 508.

43. Introduction to *Igrot Moshe* (New York, 1959).

44. See D. Hartman, *A Living Covenant* (New York: Free Press, 1985), 46–57. See also an elaborate and interesting discussion on the topic by D. Weiss Halivni, "On Man's Role in Revelation," in J. Neusner and E. S. Ferichs, eds., *From Ancient Israel to Modern Judaism, Essays in Honor of Marvin Fox*, vol. 1 (Atlanta, 1989).

45. R. Yair Bakhrakh, *Responsa Havot Yair* (Frankfurt, 1698), p. 192.

46. The same ontological conception of Halakhah is present in Yehudah ha-Levi's *Kuzari.* Ha-Levi (who also uses the medical metaphor) attempts to minimize the human innovation in Halakhah and relies heavily on the concept of received tradition. See *The Kuzari*, trans. by H. Hirschfeld (New York: Schocken Books, 1964), pp. 3, 39.

47. See above, note 40, for such formulations, many of which are cast in kabbalistic language.

48. For a very helpful phenomenological analysis of certain notions of the Oral

Law and their relation to problems of authority and innovation, see Y. Silman, "Torah Elohit sh'lo ba-Shamaim—Beirur Tipologi," *Sefer Bar Ilan* 22–23 (Ramat Gan: University of Bar-Ilan Press, 1988), pp. 261–86.

49. For an important discussion of the methodology of talmudic reasoning and its relation to the Mishnah, see M. Fisch, *Rational Rabbis: Science and Talmudic Culture* (Bloomington: Indiana University Press, forthcoming), pt. 2, chaps. 2–3. Concerning the normative canonization of the Talmud by the Geonim and its use as a source of Halakhah, see L. Ginzberg, *Geonica* (New York, 1909), vol. 1, p. 73. See also S. Assaf, *Tekufat ha-Geonim ve-Safruta* (Jerusalem: Mosad ha-Rav Kook, 1976), p. 147.

50. The canonization of the Mishnah, implicit in the rule that an Amora cannot dispute with a Tana, occurred after the production of the Mishnah. Indeed some of the talmudic Sages in the first generation disagree with mishnaic Sages; see, for example, Babylonian Talmud, *Shabbat* 64b, 61a; *Ketubot* 8a.

51. See C. Tchernowitz (Rav Zair), *Toldot ha-Poskim* (New York: Jubilee Committee, 1947), vol. 3, pp. 73–137; M. Elon, *Jewish Law* (Philadelphia: Jewish Publication Society, 1994), vol. 3, pp. 1367–1422; *Sifrei Deuteronomy*, p. 154.

52. The complaint raised by the Rosh that Maimonides does not mention his sources comes up in earlier criticism of the *Mishneh Torah* as well. The Rabad, the greatest of Maimonides' critics, claims that Maimonides' omission of his sources and his expecting that his word be accepted solely on the basis of his authority was counterproductive. A reader who disagrees with Maimonides would never be convinced to change his mind and accept Maimonides' ruling without any of his reasons and sources. On these earlier criticisms see I. Kahana, "Ha-Pulemus mi-Sabib le-Kebia't ha-Halachah keha-Rambam," *Sinai* 36 (1953), pp. 391–11, 530–37, and I. Twersky, "The Beginnings of Mishneh Torah Criticism," in *Biblical and Other Studies*, A. Altmann, ed. (Cambridge Mass.: Harvard University Press, 1963), pp. 161–82, and especially nn. 47–55. In the context of halakhic ruling from the *Mishneh Torah* see also *Responsa, Ribash* 44. An early defense of Maimonides' position appears in a letter written by Sheshet ha-Nasi of Saragoza, Spain, a leading aristocrat of the first half of the thirteenth century; see A. Marx in *Jewish Quarterly Review* 25 (1935), p. 427. Sheshet's argument was that scholars attacked Maimonides' code and prohibited ruling from it because it undermined the dependency of lay people on scholars and also allowed public exposure of the scholars' shortcomings. For another defense see A. S. Halkin, "Sanegoriya al Sefer Mishneh Torah," *Tarbiz* 25 (1956), pp. 413–28. On an earlier debate concerning ruling directly from responsa of the Geonim, see r. 110 of R. Platoi bar R. Abayye in *Hemdah Genuzah* (Jerusalem, 1862); S. Assaf, *Teshubot ha-Geonim* (Jerusalem: Darom Press, 1929), r. 158, p. 81. R. Platoi objected to ruling from the variety of responsa and codes of his predecessors. For an opposite opinion see *Responsa Yosef Migash* (Jerusalem: Lev Sameach, 1991), r. 114. According to Yosef Migash it is preferable to rule from the Geonims' responsa since it is very difficult to derive rulings directly from the Talmud. Similarly, it would be preferable to rule directly from the *Mishneh Torah*. For a slightly dif-

ferent understanding of Rosh's statement, see Yosef Kapach, *Sefer ha-Mada* (Jerusalem: Machon Mishnat ha-Rambam, 1984), pp. 18–22.

53. For the sixteenth-century rabbinic criticism of ruling from the *Shulchan Arukh* see R. Yosef Ibn Leb in *Shem ha-Gedolim* (Frankfurt, 1812), *Maarechet Sefarim* 2:59; Shmuel Abuhab, *Responsa Dehar Shmuel* (Venice, 1702), r. 355; R. Yom Tov Zahalon, *Responsa Marytaz* (Jerusalem, 1985), p. 77; R. Shmuel Eliezer Idels, *Hidushei Halachot ve-Agadot ha-Maharsha*, Sotah 22a; R. Meir Ben Gedaliah of Lublin, *Responsa Maharam me-Lublin* (Venice, 1617), p. 135; R. Yom Yob Lipman Heler, Introduction to *Ma'danei Yom Tob*; R. Mordechai Yafeh, Introduction to *Ha-Lebush*; R. Yehoshua Falk, Introduction to *Sefer Meirat E'nayim*, Hoshen Mishpat; R. Yoel Sirkis, *Responsa Bach (ha-Yeshanot)*, r. 80, and *(ha-Chadashot)* (Jerusalem, 1980), r. 42. For a discussion on Karo's intention that the *Shulchan Arukh* be used as a code and not merely as a reminder or a short version of his *Beit Yosef*, see M. Benayahuh, "A'l Shum Mah Chiber Maran et ha-Shulchan Arukh ule-Shem Mi Chibro," *Asufot* 3 (Jerusalem: Yad ha-Rav Nissim, 1989), pp. 263–74. For a different approach claiming that Karo did not intend his *Shulchan Arukh* to be a code from which a *halakhah* may be derived independently, see E. Shochetman, "Al ha-Stirot ba-Shulchan Arukh ve-al Mahuto shel ha-Chibur u-Matrotav," ibid., pp 323–30.

54. Letter to Pinchas ha-Dayan, pp. 444–45.

55. See I. Twersky, *Introduction to the Code of Maimonides*, pp. 62–74.

56. Introduction to *Shulchan Arukh* (Venice 1565).

57. Another codification in the sixteenth century mentions the emergence of print as a motivation for establishing a fixed code. In his *Torat Hatat* R. Moshe Isserles codified ritual law in a conclusive manner, thus diverging from the Ashkenazic tradition of not creating fixed codes (see also below, n. 60). One of the most important books for ruling on such matters in Ashkenaz was *Sharei Dura*, a kind of handbook for scholars. Isserles claims that it was the source of many errors since it was short and inconclusive and fell into the hands of incompetent scholars who derived wrong conclusions from it. He therefore intended to replace *Sharei Dura* with an organized conclusive code. (He was harshly criticized for that.) In his introduction he mentions printing as a new factor that endangered the stability of Halakhah, thus motivating him to codify it: "How much more so now in this last generation that [*Sharei Dura*] was copied and printed several times since every person desires it because of its shortness and wishes to study all ritual law on one foot. And through print those books have fallen into the hands of many small and great, and they added many interpretations to them. Time perishes, and their words do not perish. . . and afterward these books themselves [the interpretations of *Sharei Dura*] are printed and the one who reads them claims that they are all given in Sinai and rules according to them mistakenly, since those books are meant to be short and clear, and they distorted them." *Torat Hatat* (Cracow, 1569), introduction.

58. Another difficulty with Maimonides' explanation stems from the fact that he faced as many controversies as did R. Yehudah, controversies that grew out of

disparities in understanding the Talmud and post-Talmudic customs. Maimonides decided to resolve those controversies rather than leave them as they had been left in the Mishnah. The argument that the Talmud settled the controversies in the Mishnah does not apply to those that developed in the centuries that elapsed between the canonization of the Talmud and Maimonides' code.

59. On the rejection of the authority of *Shulchan Arukh* against a local and established tradition see, for example, R. Yosef Molcho, *Shulchan Gavoah* (Jerusalem, 1990), *Klalei ha Shulchan Arukh* 15, and also R. Chaim David Azulai, *Chaim Shal* (Jerusalem, 1980), pt. 2, 35:2. On the reception of the *Shulchan Arukh* see J. Faur, "Yahas Chachmei ha-Sefaradim le-Samchut Maran ke-Posek," in *Rabbi Yosef Karo*, I. Refael, ed. (Jerusalem: Mosad ha-Rav Kook, 1969), pp. 189–97; I. Ta-Shma, "R. Yosef Karo—Bein Sefarad le-Ashkenaz," *Tarbiz* 59 (1990), pp. 153–70.

60. Quoted in *Responsa Rama* (Jerusalem, 1971), p. 25.

61. On the decentralized form of Halakhah in Ashkenaz relative to Spain and the tendency in Ashkenaz to avoid codes see I. Ta-Shma, "Kavim le-Ofiah shel Safrut ha-Halakhah be-Ashkenaz ba-Meot ha-13 -14," *A'lei Sefer* 4 (1977), pp.32–34, and "Halakhah ke-Batrai," *Shnaton ha-Mishpat ha-Ivri* 6–7 (1979–80), p. 408 n. 16.

62. See Sheshet's statement in note 51.

63. *Ari Noem* (Jerusalem, 1929), p. 51.

64. On Maharshal's approach to the Talmud as the only authoritative text in relation to the development of print and its effects on the Ashkenazi canon, see E. Rainer, "Temurot be-Yeshivot Polin ve-Ashkenaz ba-Meot ha 16–17 ve-ha-Vikuach al ha-Pilpul," in *Ke-Minhag Ashkenaz ve-Polin Sefer ha-Yovel le-Chone Shmeruk, I.* Bartal, H. Tornianski, E. Mendelson, eds. (Jerusalem: Zalman Shazar Center, 1993), pp. 57–60.

65. Concerning the rejection of codification in principle see also R. Yehudah ben Bezalel in *Netivot Olam* (London, 1961), *Netib ha-Torah* 15.

66. *Sifrei Deuteronomy*, p. 154.

67. Jerusalem Talmud, *Horayot* 1:1.

68. This view was raised in the seventeenth century by R. Issachar Baer Eilinburg. See *Sefer Beer Shev'a* (Warsaw, 1890), p. 7. For the same approach see the commentary of Yechiel Epstein, *Torah Temimah Deuteronomy* 17:10. Such a reading is more plausible in a different version of the *Sifrei*, which instead of saying "mar'in be-einekha" [show you], states "domeh be-einekha" [seems to you]. See *Sifrei*, Finkelstein edition, p. 207. Significantly, in the version that appears in another Tanaitic *midrash* to Deuteronomy, the words "before your own eyes" are completely omitted. See *Midrash Tanaim, Deuteronomy* 17:10; see also Rashi's quotation of this source in his commentary to Deuteronomy. For an extensive analysis see J. Blidstein, "Afilu Omer Lekha al-Yamim Shehu Smol," in *Mechkarim ba-Halakhah ube-Machshevet Israel*, M. Baer, ed. (Ramat Gan: Bar Ilan Press, 1994), pp. 221–41.

69. This view was stated by Nachmanides in his *Hasagot le-Sefer ha-Mitzvot shel ha-Rambam*, Shoresh Rishon. For an attempt to reconcile Nachmanides' view with

Eilinburg's see R. Chaim Yosef David Azulai, *Sha'ar Yosef* (Livorno, 1747), pp. 10–11. For a contrary view see R. Elchanan Wasserman, *Kuntres Divrei Sofrim* (Tel Aviv, 1963), pp. 107–08. Chaim ben Atar offers another view to reconcile the problem in his *Chefetz ha-Shem* (Amsterdam, 1768), p. 82, whereby an expert in the law is obligated to follow his own opinion when disobeying the court will prevent an active transgression. For other efforts to reconcile the contradiction between the *Sifrei* and *Horayot* see R. Chaim Falag'i, *He-Chafetz Chaim* (Izmir, 1863), sec. 76. For a general extensive discussion of the scope and source of the court's authority see A. Sagi, "Models of Authority and the Duty of Obedience in Halakhic Literature," *Association of Jewish Studies Review* 20 no.1 (1995), p. 1.

70. Nachmanides' Commentary on Deuteronomy 17:11.

71. One of the most prominent authorities of Halakhah in this century advanced the same argument concerning the source of the authority of the Mishnah and the Talmud. See Hazon Ish, *Kovetz Igrot* (Bnei Brak, 1957), pp. 42–43.

72. The understanding of the court's privilege as procedural seems to be the explanation for why the Mishnah says that the passage in Deuteronomy prohibits the elder from ruling against the court's decision but still allows him to teach his opinion publicly. The court therefore has a priority in defining what should be done but not in determining the truth of the matter. The elder may object to the opinion of the court on a theoretical level as long as he does not rule or act against the opinion of the court. For the distinction between ruling and teaching see Mishnah *Sanhedrin* 11:2. See also *Tosafot Shantz, Eduyot* 1:5.

73. *Sefer ha-Chinuch, Mitzvah* 508. For other medieval thinkers who believed in the procedural priority of the court see Hisdai Crescas, *Or ha-Shem* (Jerusalem: Makor, 1983), Ma'amar 3, 5:2; R. Yosef Albo, *Sefer ha-Ikarim* (Tel Aviv: Ha-Menorah, 1981), 3:23. Nissim Gerondi expresses a similar view: " 'Even if he tells you that right is left and left is right,' meaning even if it is clear to you that the truth is not in accord with the rulings of the court, you ought to listen to them. This is God's commandment that we should follow the court in regard to Torah and its commandments whether they agree with the truth or not." For an extensive discussion of this debate see Y. Silman, "Torah Elohit she'Lo ba-Shamaim —Beirur Tipologi," pp. 274–79.

74. For the distinction between being in authority and being an authority on see R. S. Peters, "Authority," in *Proceedings of the Aristotelian Society* (1958), vol. 32, pp. 207–24.

75. Nachmanides, *Commentary on Deuteronomy* 17:11.

76. See O. W. Holmes, "The Path of the Law," in *Collected Legal Papers* 173 (New York: Harcourt Brace, 1920).

77. For a thorough criticism of Holmes's position see H. L. A. Hart, *The Concept of Law* (Oxford: Clarendon Press, 1961).

78. Mishnah Tractate *Rosh ha-Shanah.* For discussion of the struggle for monopoly over the calendar in that period see Gedalia Allon, *The Jews in Their Land in the Talmudic Age* (Jerusalem: Magnes Press, 1984), vol. 1, pp. 237–48.

79. Abravanel claims that the court is privileged to rule against the general

rules of the Halakhah since particular cases do not always fit general rules. See also Yizhak Arama, *Akedat Yizhak*, J. Polak, ed. (Pressburg, 1849), Shemot chap. 43. For an extensive discussion on the treatment of this problem by medieval Jewish authors see S. Rosenberg, "Od al-Derekh ha-Rov," *Manhigut Ruchanit be-Israel*, E. Belfer, ed., pp. 103 ff., and I. Englard, "The Problem of Equity in Maimonides," *Israel Law Review* 3–4 (1986), pp. 296–332.

3. Canon and Curriculum

1. See L. Wittgenstein, *On Certainty* (Oxford: Blackwell, 1974).

2. See E. A. Havelock, *Preface to Plato* (Cambridge, Mass.: Harvard University Press, 1963), chaps. 3–5.

3. The centrality of shared narrative varies from one society to another. People can share a national narrative and yet have different religious or secular narratives. In societies whose heterogeneity is pronounced, the constitutive narrative may reflect a tension between two or more elements in the society. The War of Independence is thus a constitutive narrative for the Jewish citizens of Israel, but it is a narrative of defeat and humiliation for its Arab citizens.

4. On the effects of communal customs on Talmudic interpretation in Ashkenaz, see C. Soloveitchik, "Religious Law and Change: The Medieval Ashkenazic Example," *AJS Review* 12:2 (Fall 1987), pp. 205–21. Soloveitchik points to the difference between the Ashkenazic halakhists and those of Spain and Provence concerning the weight of a community's customs. For the Ashkenazic rabbinic authorities the will of God is manifest in both the canonized text of the Talmud and in the practice of the holy community. An interesting example on the effect of custom on halakhic interpretation is J. Katz, *Halakhah ve-Kabbalah* (Jerusalem: Magnes Press, 1984), pp. 175–201. For a general discussion on Ashkenaz and the effect of custom see I. Ta-Shma, *Minhag Ashkenaz ha-Kadmon* (Jerusalem: Magnes Press, 1992), pp. 13–108. He makes an interesting point about the effect of customs not only in rereading the text but also in rewriting it. The text was not considered to be fully closed or sealed in Ashkenaz. Hence it was adapted to harmonize with custom. In Spain, however, custom was not considered a reliable source for justifying textual change. This is one of the major reasons for the superiority of Sefardic manuscripts over the Ashkenazic ones. For an important discussion concerning text and tradition in modern day ultra-orthodox practice, see C. Soloveitchik, "Rupture and Reconstruction: The Transformation of Contemporary Orthodoxy," *Tradition* 28:4 (1994), pp. 64–130.

5. On the canonization of the Zohar see G. Scholem, *Major Trends in Jewish Mysticism* (New York: Schocken Books, 1974), pp. 156–243, and Y. Tishbi, *The Wisdom of the Zohar*, trans. D. Goldstein (Oxford: Oxford University Press, 1989). For the date in which the Zohar became canonical see Scholem, ibid. p. 156. On the normative status of the Zohar as a source for Halakhah see J. Katz, *Halakhah ve-Kabbalah* (Jerusalem: Magnes Press, 1986), pp. 52–70; M. Halamish, "Kabbalah ba-Psikah shel R. Yosef Karo," *Da'at* 21 (1988), pp. 85–102; I. Ta-Shma,

"Rabbi Yosef Karo Bein Ashkenaz le-Sfarad le-Cheker Hitpashtut Sefer ha-Zoar," *Tarbiz* 59 (1990), pp. 153–70. See also B. Huss, "Sefer ha-Zohar as a Canonical, Sacred, and Holy Text," *Journal of Jewish Thought and Philosophy* (forthcoming).

6. On the biblical idea of the study of Torah see Chapter 1 above.

7. Babylonian Talmud, *Megillah* 3b.

8. Babylonian Talmud, *Menachot* 110a and also *Sifrei Devarim* 41, Finkelstein, ed., p. 87.

9. See Mishnah, *Avot* 3:2.

10. See for example the detailed analogy between the temple and the Torah in Isaac Duran (Efodi), *Ma'aseh Efod* (Vienna, 1865), pp. 11–12.

11. See for example the debate in the Babylonian Talmud, *Berachot* 25a, and *Mekhilta de-Rabi Ishmael Beshalach*. For a detailed discussion see E. E. Urbach, *The Sages: Their Concepts and Beliefs*, trans. I. Abrahms (Jerusalem: Magnes Press, 1975), pp. 593–603. M. Baer, "Talmud Torah ve-Derekh Eretz," *Bar Ilan Annual* 2 (1964). On later debates concerning earning money from the study of Torah see Maimonides, *Perush ha-Mishnah Avot* 4:7. He condemns harshly the prevailing opinion that a scholar is allowed to be supported by the community and may even make a claim on the community to support him. See also his *Mishneh Torah*, Laws of Talmud Torah 3:10–11, and Yosef Karo's detailed arguments against Maimonides' position in *Kesef Mishneh*, Laws of Talmud Torah 3:10. Besides the issue of whether scholars should earn money from Torah, there are other questions related to the privileges of the scholar class, such as exemption from payment of taxes. The Talmud mentions such a privilege in Tractate *Baba Batra* 7b–8a, but the scope of this privilege and its actual enforcement were subjects of perennial debate centering on the question of who is a scholar: someone who devotes himself totally to the study of Torah with no other occupation (the income for taxation being inheritance or the support he receives for his scholarship), or someone who has other occupations besides the study of Torah, if these are restricted to providing his livelihood and not to the accumulation of wealth? On the definition of a scholar see the statement of Yosef Ibn Migash, *Baba Batra* 8a, and *Teshubot ha-Rosh* (New York, 1992), 15:8–9. The second subject that was debated was the scope of the exemption. Does it include only taxes that are set on the whole community, or does it extend to any kind of tax, even levies on individual property or person? For an example of such debate see Maimonides, *Mishneh Torah*, Laws of Talmud Torah 6:10, and Nachmanides in *Hidushei ha-Ramban*, *Baba Batra* 8a. On the distance between the privilege and its actual application see M. Baer, "Le-She'elat Shichruram shel Amoraei Bavel me-Tashlum Misim u-Meches," *Tarbiz* 33 (1965), pp. 247–58. For the different traditions in Spain and Ashkenaz concerning the taxation of scholars see I. Ta-Shma, "Al Petur Talmidei Chakhamim me-Misim be-Yimei ha-Benaim," in *Iyunim be-Sifrut Hazal be-Mikrah ube-Toldot Israel Mukdash le-Professor Ezrah Zion Melamed* (Ramat Gan: Bar Ilan University Press, 1982) pp. 312–22, and Y. Haker, "Petur Chakhamim me-Misim ba-Meah ha-Shesh Esreh," pt. 4 (Jerusalem: Yad Ben-Zvi, 1984), pp. 63–113.

12. On this tension between study and action see Mishnah, *Peah* 1:1; *Sifrei Devarim* 41, Finkelstein, ed., pp. 84–86; Babylonian Talmud, *Kiddushin* 40b; *Ketubot* 17a; Jerusalem Talmud, *Hagigah* 1:7; Babylonian Talmud, *Moed Katan* 9b; *Shabbat* 11a; and Jerusalem Talmud, *Shabbat* 1:2. For a general discussion see E. E. Urbach, *The Sages*, pp. 603–20.

13. On the authority of the Talmud see above ch. 2 note 49.

14. This point is emphasized by A. Grossman, "Ha-Zikah bein ha Mivneh ha-Chevrati la-Yezirah ha-Ruchanit be-Kehilot Israel be-Tekufat ha-Geonim," *Zion* 53 (1988), pp. 259–72. See also A. Grossman, *Chakhmei Zarfat ha-Rishonim* (Jerusalem: Magnes Press, 1995), pp. 427–39.

15. On the Tosafists and their enormous impact see E. E. Urbach, *Ba'alei ha-Tosafot* (Jerusalem: Bialik, 1968), chaps. 1, 13. Chaim Soloveichik described powerfully the impact of the innovations of the Tosafists on Ashkenazic culture and the pietistic response to it in "Three Themes in Sefer Hasidim," *AJS Review* 1 (1976), pp. 311–61, and also I. Ta-Shma, "Mitzvat Talmud Torah be Sefer Hasidim," *Bar Ilan Annual* 14:15 (1977), pp. 98 ff.

16. See I. Ta-Shma, "Shiput Ivri u-Mishpat Ivri ba-Mehot ha-11 veha-12 be-Sfarad (Lidiat Mazav Limud ha-Torah al-pi Shu't ha-Ri'f)," *Shenaton ha-Mishpat ha-Ivri* 1 (1974), pp. 353–72. See also the remarks of H. Z. Dimitrovsky in *Mechkarim be-Madaei ha-Yahadut*, M. Bar-Asher, ed. (Jerusalem, 1986), pp. 262–65. For a different opinion concerning the study of Torah in Spain at that period see *Sefer ha-Kabbalah le-Rabbi Abraham Ibn Daud*, G. Cohen, ed. (Philadelphia, 1967), p. 135. For an interesting description of curriculum and teaching methods in the tenth and eleventh centuries see S. D. Goiten, *Sidrei Hinuch* (Jerusalem, 1962), pp. 143–69.

17. For Maimonides' remarks on the situation of the study of Halakhah in Spain see introduction to the *Mishneh Torah*, and Maimonides' letter to Yonatan ha-Cohen and his colleagues in *Igrot ha-Rambam*, I. Sheilat, ed. (Jerusalem: Ma'aliyot, 1987), vol. 2, pp. 558–59.

18. The growth and depth of the study of Talmud in Provence in the twelfth century is described vividly in Maimonides' letter to Lunel. See B. Benedict, "Le Toldotav shel Merkaz ha-Torah be-Provence," *Tarbiz* 22 (1951), pp. 85–109; I. Twersky, "Aspects of the Social and Cultural History of ProvenÁal Jewry," *Journal of World History* 11 (1968), pp. 185–207.

19. See Babylonian Talmud, *Kiddushin* 30a and *Avodah Zarah* 19b. For other formulations of the relationship between different elements in the curriculum see also Babylonian Talmud, *Hagigah* 10a, and *Baba Mezia* 33ab.

20. See Rashi, *Hagigah* 10a (me-Talmud le-Mishnah).

21. See *Tosafot, Kiddushin* 30a (Lo zrikha le-yomei); and *Tosafot, Sanhedrin* 24a, Belulah. See also a similar approach in *Machzor Vitri*, S. H. Horovitz, ed. (Nirenberg, 1925), p. 26. *Shibolei ha-Leket*, S. Minshi, ed. (Jerusalem: Sura Publishers, 1966), sec. 44.

22. For Maimonides' formulation see n. 41 below.

23. See Abravanel's *Nachalat Avot* (New York, 1953). See also an opposite

interpretation of the Mishnah by R. Yosef Hayun cited by S. Assaf, *Mekorot le-Toldot ha-Chinukh be-Israel* (Tel Aviv: Devir, 1941), vol. 2, p. 87

24. Yehudah ben Asher's will is printed in *Beit Talmud*, (Berlin, 1891), vol. 4, p. 344.

25. See *Ma'aseh Efod* (Vienna, 1873), p. 41. Abraham Grossman shows that Efodi's criticism is not relevant to earlier periods in Ashkenaz and argues that the criticism is exaggerated even for Efodi's own time. See A. Grossman, *Chakhmei Zarfat ha-Rishonim*, p. 463 n. 14. For earlier criticism of the neglect of Bible study see Abraham Ibn Ezra, *Yesod Mora* (N.J.: Jason Aronson, 1995), chap. 1, and *Shirei Ibn-Ezra*, Kahana, ed. (Academiya ha-Leumit ha-Israelit le Madaim, 1975), pp. 25–27.

26. On Maharal's reform see "Derush al ha-Torah" in *Sefer Derashot Maharal me-Prag* (Jerusalem, 1981), pp. 3–50. For an extensive discussion on Maharal's educational approach see A. Kleinberg, *Ha-Machahbah ha-Pedagogit shel ha-Maharal mi-Prag* (Jerusalem, 1962). On the historical context of these reforms see A. Kulkah, "Ha-Reka ha-Histori shel Mishnato ha-Leumit ve-ha-Chinukhit shel ha-Maharal mi-Prag," *Zion* 50 (1985), pp. 277–320; and E. Reiner, "Temurot be Yeshivot Polin ve-Ashkenaz ba-Meot ha 15 ve ha 16," in *Ke-Minhag Ashkenaz u-Polin: Sefer ha-Yovel le-Chone Shmeruk* (Jerusalem: Merkaz Shazar, 1993), pp. 60–68. For other members of Maharal's circle see R. Ephraim Luntshits, *Amude Shesh* (Prague, 1618) (conclusion); R. Yeshahyahu Horwitz, *Shlah*, Masechet Shavuot, and his son S. Sheftel, *Vavei ha-Amudim* Amud ha-Torah (Jerusalem, 1963), ch. 5. For the attempt to model this reform on the Sefardi practice see S. Assaf, *Mekorot le-Toldot ha-Chinukh be-Israel*, vol. 1, pp. 20–22.

27. Quoted by J. Elboim, *Petichut ve-Histagrut* (Jerusalem: Magnes Press, 1990), p. 160.

28. See R. Shlomoh ben Mordechai, *Mizbach ha-Zahav* (Basel, 1604), 12a. For a discussion of the attitude to the study of Bible in sixteenth-century Poland see J. Elboim, *Petichut*, pp. 93–95. For an attack on R. Land and his father-in-law, R. Yosef Ashkenazi, see S. Assaf, *Mekorot*, pp. 189–190.

29. The Talmudic statement appears in the Babylonian Talmud, *Berachot* 28b. In some versions a similar statement appears in Babylonian Talmud, *Sanhedrin* 96a.

30. The statement of Zemach Platoi is quoted in R. Abraham Zakut, *Yohasin ha-Shalem* (London, 1857), p. 124. A similar interpretation appears in Rabbi Natan's *Arukh Erekh* (hak). The author claims that the Talmud warns against interpreting the verse according to its literal meaning. See also *Teshubot ha-Geonim*, Harkabi, ed. (Berlin, 1897), p. 144. In the Geonic period the term *higayon* began to take on a new meaning of logic. In accordance with this new use, the statement was understood by some opponents of the study of philosophy as a warning against it. For a thorough discussion of the history of the interpretations of this Talmudic statement and its implications see M. Breuer, "Min'u Bneikhem Min ha-Higayon," in *Mikhtam le-David: Sefer Zichron ha-Rav David Oks* (Ramat Gan: Bar Ilan University Press, 1978), pp. 242–61.

31. Babylonian Talmud, *Menachot* 96b. The argument refers to the obligation of an ongoing study of Torah and not to the inherent danger of "Greek wisdom." Other sources seem to address the problem of "Greek wisdom" itself. The Babylonian Talmud, *Sotah* 49b, says: "Cursed is the man who will teach his son Greek Wisdom." See also Mishnah, the end of Tractate *Sota*; *Tosefta, Avoda Zarah* 1:20; and *Tosefta*, *Sota* 15:8. Saul Lieberman tries to narrow the prohibition of the study of Greek wisdom in these sources to the prohibition against fathers teaching Greek wisdom to their young children. See S. Lieberman, *Hellenism in Jewish Palestine* (New York: Jewish Theological Seminary, 1950), pp. 100–05. For earlier attempts to minimize the prohibition see Maimonides, *Perush ha-Mishnah*, *Sotah* 4:14; Meiri, *Beit ha-Behirah*, *Baba Kamah* 83a. Yitzhak ben Sheshet (Ribash) continues this line of interpretation. He does not identify philosophy with Greek wisdom but forbids the study of philosophy on other grounds. *Responsa Ribash* (Jerusalem, 1975), p. 45.

32. For talmudic sources which claim that the obligation to study the Torah day and night can be fulfilled by reciting the Shema once in the morning and once at night, see Babylonian Talmud, *Menachot* 99b, and Midrash, *Shocher Tov Tehilim*, chap. 1.

33. I. Twersky, "Talmudists, Philosophers, Kabbalists: The Quest for Spirituality in the Sixteenth Century," in B. Cooperman, ed., *Jewish Thought in the Sixteenth Century* (Cambridge, Mass.: Harvard University Press, 1983), pp. 431–59.

34. See I. Abrahams, *Hebrew Ethical Wills* (Philadelphia: Jewish Publication Society, 1926), vol. 1, pp. 138–39; On Joseph Ibn Kaspi's attitude to Talmud study see I. Twersky, "Joseph Ibn Kaspi: Portrait of a Medieval Jewish Intellectual, in *Studies in Medieval Jewish History and Literature*, I. Twersky, ed. (Cambridge, Mass.: Harvard University Press, 1979), pp. 243 ff.; B. Herring, *Joseph Ibn Kaspi's Gevia' Kesef* (New York: Ktav, 1982), pp. 64–65.

35. For a more detailed analysis see the section on "Codification and Decanonization" below.

36. It is clear that affecting the curriculum was not Maimonides' only purpose in codifying the Halakhah. For a presentation of Maimonides' complex motivations and a survey of opinions concerning these motivations see I. Twersky, "Sefer Mishneh Torah la-Rambam—Megamato ve-Tafkido," *Dibrei ha-Akademiah ha-Leumit ha-Israelit le-Madaim* 5 (1972). Twersky tends to minimize the effect of the code on the curriculum.

37. See letter to Pinchas ha-Dayan, in *Igrot ha-Rambam*, Y. Sheilat, ed. (Jerusalem: M'aliyot, 1987), vol. 1, pp. 438–39. See also pp. 502–03.

38. Ibid., letter to R. Joseph, pp. 257–59.

39. Ibid., letter to R. Joseph ben Yehudah, p. 302.

40. Ibid., pp. 312–13. See also the interesting testimony of Maimonides' son Abraham, quoted by one of his students. In answer to some student's query, Maimonides replied: "If our aim in writing this book was to interpret the Talmud we would have not written this book." See *Tarbiz* 25, p. 424.

41. In fact Maimonides himself reinterprets the Talmudic statement con-

cerning the threefold division of the curriculum. He considers that the threefold division is only for beginners, and those who are already learned should devote their time to the study of Talmud. But the Talmud is redefined as legal reasoning (and not the text of Talmud). Maimonides maintains that "The subjects styled Pardes are included in Talmud" (Laws of Talmud Torah 1:12). The study of philosophy is therefore integrated in the curriculum through the reinterpretation of the threefold division and the concept of Talmud. The *Mishneh Torah* itself is mainly for beginners, since Maimonides defines the *Mishneh Torah* as the summary of all the Oral Law, and devoting equal time to the study of the Oral Law and the Written Law which is not the Talmud is only for beginners. On Maimonides' ruling see I. Twersky, *Introduction to the Mishneh Torah of Maimonides* (New Haven: Yale University Press, 1977), ch. 6.

It seems that Maimonides' radical ambition was to have the *Mishneh Torah* achieve authority as a code, not only because it was recognized as the best summary of the Halakhah, but because all of Israel would accept the *Mishneh Torah* as their norm. In this respect the *Mishneh Torah* would have the same ground of authority as the Talmud itself, since the Talmud's own authority, according to Maimonides, is derived from its being widely disseminated and accepted by all Jews. In the introduction to the *Mishneh Torah* Maimonides claims that unlike the Talmud, which is binding upon all the communities of Israel since it was accepted by all Israel, the rulings of the post-Talmudic Sages bind only their own communities since the rulings were accepted only locally. Maimonides mourns that situation and seems to imply that the *Mishneh Torah* will unify the diverse halakhic rulings that developed after the Talmud was accepted and sealed. The rationale for the authority of the Talmud that Maimonides provides in his introduction is the same as that for the authority of his own code, the *Mishneh Torah*.

42. See *Guide of the Perplexed*, III, 51.

43. Maimonides, *Mishneh Torah*, *Yesodei ha-Torah* 4:13. Maimonides identifies Ma'aseh Merkabah with philosophy and the discussions of Abaye and Raba with the Talmud; thus he claims that philosophy is a great thing and the Talmud a small one. This infuriated various commentators whose relationship to philosophy was more complicated. See, for example, *Hidushei ha-Ritba*, *Sukah* 28a, and Yosef Karo in the *Kesef Mishneh*, *Yesodei ha-Torah* 4:13. Karo claims that although the subject matter of Talmud is small, the reward for its study is great, and the text is more important than Ma'aseh Merkabah. For a similar approach see Shlomo Luria, *Yam shel Shlomoh*, *Sukah* 28a. Other commentators suggested that the disputes of Abaye and Raba do not refer to the Talmud since Talmudic discussions could not be called "small things." See R. Meir Aldabi, *Shbilei Emunah* (Lebob, 1823), p. 99b; Yehoshua Ibn Shueib, *Derashot al ha-Torah* (Jerusalem, 1969), pp. 39a–39b. An interesting interpretation that glorifies small things was offered by R. Chaim ben Bezalel, in *Sefer ha-Haim 'Sefer Zekhuyot'* (p. 5b). According to R. Chaim the talmudist is like a servant who serves the king with attention to the small details of the palace and is greater than the servant who praises the king only concerning the great matters.

44. *Sefer ha-Mevakesh* (Warsaw, 1884), p. 102. Falaquera describes a philosophically oriented scholar and a pietist as follows: "The one was a pietist who meditated day and night on the Law, who engaged always in the study of Scripture, who negotiated in the disputes of Abaye and Rabba and made a path in the mighty waters of these difficulties. . . The second was a scholar, who at times engaged in the study of the Law and at times in the study of science, who divided his time between reading about what is forbidden and permitted and reading the books of the scholars who endeavored to investigate the secrets of wisdom and who looked into the philosophical books." *Epistle of the Debate*, trans. by S. Harvey (Cambridge, Mass.: Harvard University Press, 1987), p. 16. Besides the obvious point that the scholar and pietist differ in their attitude to philosophy, their study of the Law is described by Falaquera in different terms. The pietist delved in the disputes of Abaye and Rabba, i.e., talmudic deliberations; in contrast, the scholar read only the rules prescribing what is forbidden and permitted (the specific law). For earlier criticisms of the exclusive place of Talmud in the curriculum in the philosophical tradition see Bachya Ibn Pakudah, *Hobot ha-Lebabot* (Kapach edition), pp. 24, 28–29; Abraham Ibn Daud, *Sefer ha-Emunah ha-Ramah*, trans. S. Weil (Jerusalem, 1967), pp. 45–46; and Abraham Ibn Ezra, *Yesod Mora* (introduction). For the connection to Islamic philosophy see J. Gutmann, *Die Religions Philosophie des Abrahm Ibn Daud aus Toledo* (Gottingen, 1879), p. 117 n. 1, and U. Simon, *Arb'a Gishot le-Sefer Tehilim* (Ramat Gan: Bar Ilan University Press, 1982), pp. 182–83.

45. *Mishneh Torah*, Laws of Teshubah 10:6; *Yesodei ha-Torah* 4:12.

46. See *Mishneh Torah*, Laws of Teshubah 3:7.

47. For Maimonides' formulation of the afterlife as the eternity of the active intellect see ibid., 8:2–3.

48. Maimonides is continuing a tradition that stressed the importance of philosophy for religious perfection. See Bachya Ibn Pakudah, *Hobot ha-Lebabot* (introduction); Abraham Ibn Ezra, *Yesod Mora*, introduction and ch. 1. For a general analysis of this subject see H. A. Davidson, "The Study of Philosophy as a Religious Obligation," *Religion in a Religious Age*, S. D. Goiten, ed. (Cambridge, Mass.: Harvard University Press, 1974), pp. 52–68.

49. *Minhat Kenaot*, in *Teshuvot ha-Rashba*, H. Dimitrovsky, ed. (Jerusalem: Mossad ha-Rav Kook, 1990), p. 473. This stereotype of the Zarfatim as backward is quite common among the Spanish elite. See E. E. Urbach's discussion, "What's a Frenchman Doing in the House of Poetry," in *Ba'alei ha-Tosafot*, p. 94. See also the satirical poem on R. Moses the Frenchman in Schirman, *Ha-Shirah ha-Ivrit be-Sfarad ube-Provance* (Jerusalem: Bialik, 1957), vol. 2, p. 440. For an interesting discussion on Provençal Jews' perception of the Jews of northern France see B. Septimus, *Hispano-Jewish Culture in Transition* (Cambridge, Mass.: Harvard University Press, 1982), p. 64.

50. *Minhat Kenaot*, p. 596.

51. Ibid., pp. 479, 467.

52. On the Maimonidean debate in the thirteenth century see B. Septimus,

Hispano-Jewish Culture in Transition, ch. 4. For the vast literature on the subject see ibid., p. 147 n.1.

53. For a detailed account of the events and negotiations that led to the clash see Y. Baer, *A History of the Jews in Christian Spain* (Philadelphia, 1961), pp. 289 ff. Baer explains that the underlying problem for the conflict in Provence and Shlomo Ibn Adret's involvement in it was the widespread study of philosophy in Spain. It has also been argued that philosophy was actually declining in Spain and the real problem was the popularity of philosophy in Provence. See C. Touati, "La Controverse de 1303–1306 autour d'études philosophiques et scientifiques," *REJ* 127 (1968), p. 34. See also J. Schatzmiller, "Bein Aba Mari la-Rashba—ha-Masa u-Matan sh-Kadam la-Herem be-Barzelonah," in *Mechkarim be-Toldot Am Israel ve-Eretz Israel*, B. Oded, ed. (Haifa, 1975), pp. 121–37; "In Search of the Book of Figures: Medicine and Astrology in Montpellier at the Turn of the Fourteenth Century," *AJS Review* 7:8 (1982–83), pp. 387–407; "Zurat Aryeh le-Klayot veha-Machloket al Limudei ha-Chokhmot be-Reshit ha-Meah ha-14," in *Sefer ha-Yobel le-Shlomo Pines Bimlot lo Shmonim Shanah*, Mechkerei Yerushalaim be-Machshevet Israel, vol. 9 (1990), pp. 397–408. For an analysis of Meiri's philosophical background and the debate over philosophy see M. Halbertal, "R. Menachem ha-Meiri, Bein Torah le-Chokhmah," *Tarbiz* 73 (1994), pp. 63–118, and G. Stern, "Menachem ha-Meiri and the Second Controversy over Philosophy" (Ph.D. diss., Harvard University, 1995).

54. Allegory was also used by commentators who were not philosophers, even by the Rashba. Thus the issue was not allegorical interpretation as such, but the extent of its use and the weight given to the direct meaning of the biblical story and to the communal tradition. The Rashba did apply the allegorical method when the simple meaning of the verse was unclear. For example, anthropomorphic descriptions of God must be understood allegorically. But he rejected allegorical interpretation that attempted to downplay the miraculous elements of biblical stories and to minimize direct intervention of God in nature. With respect to miracles, the Rashba thought that readers should give priority to the accepted tradition of Israel rather than to the reasoned argument of the philosophers. For his allegorical method see *Hidushei ha-Rashba Perushei ha-Hagadot*, L. A. Feldman, ed. (Jerusalem: Mossad ha-Rav Kook, 1991), pp. 102–10. On the use of allegory even in nonphilosophical circles see A. H. Halkin, "Yedaiah Bedershi's Apology," in A. Altman, ed., *Jewish Medieval and Renaissance Studies* (Cambridge, Mass.: Harvard University Press, 1967), pp. 165–84.

55. For a detailed description of the allegories that were practiced see *Hoshen Mishpat* in *Zunz Jubelschrift* (Berlin, 1894), pp. 158–59. One of the important questions Halkin raises is whether the allegories of the philosophers suppress the simple meaning of the text or simply add a layer of meaning to the conventional, ordinary meaning of the text. When the philosophers of Provence defended their allegorical readings, they insisted that they never intended to suppress the simple meanings of the biblical stories. See the arguments of Yedaiah Bedershi in *Teshubot ha-Rashba* 419:67a–75b and of Yaacob ben Machir in *Minhat Kenaot*, p. 511.

56. *Minhat Kenaot*, p. 412. There is no clear evidence that the spread of phi-

losophy caused any laxity in the observance of Halakhah. The supporters of philosophical learning in Provence pointed to extreme piety prevalent there and to the advantages of the study of philosophy for religious perfection. The attacks on the supposedly corrupting role of philosophy on the observance of Halakhah culminated in the accusation made by some fifteenth- and sixteenth-century authors that Jews in Spain converted to Christianity because of the impact of philosophy on Spanish Jewry. Philosophy was already in decline in Spain in the fourteenth and fifteenth centuries, however. On the accusations see Shlomo Ela'mi, *Igeret Musar*, A. M. Haberman, ed. (Jerusalem, 1946), pp. 41–43; Isaac A'ramah, *Hazut Kashah*, chaps. 8, 9; Yosef Ya'vetz, *Or ha-Chaim*, introduction and chaps. 3–10. On the discrepancy between the attacks on philosophy and the decline of philosophy, see H. H. Ben Sasson, *Retzef u-Temurah* (Tel Aviv: Am Oved, 1984), pp. 198–238. Concerning the place of philosophy in fifteenth-century Spain see also Y. Haker, "Mekomo shel R. Abraham Biba'g ba-Machloket al Limud ha-Philosophiah u-Ma'madah bi-Sfarad ba-Meah ha-15," in *Divrei ha-Kongress ha-Olami ha-Chamishi le-Mada'ei ha-Yahdut* (Jerusalem, 1969), 3:157–51. For a recent attempt to identify neo-Platonists active in fourteenth-century Spain who were the targets of the polemic against philosophy, see D. Schwartz, "Ha-Yeridah ha-Ruchanit-Datit shel ha-Kehilah ha-Yehudit bi-Sfarad be-Sof ha-Meah ha-14," in *Pea'mim* 46:7 (1991), pp. 92–114.

57. *Minhat Kenaot*, p. 412.

58. Ibid., pp. 414–419.

59. Ibid., p. 473.

60. Ibid., p. 440.

61. Ibid., pp. 515, 542.

62. Ibid., pp. 480, 515. On Maimonides' own position that the study of philosophy is not suitable for the young see the *Guide of the Perplexed* I, 34. The prohibition against teaching is therefore accepted in philosophical circles and has its roots in that tradition. Ironically, among those who recommended the limitation of study was Levi ben Hayim, one of the targets of the Rashba's struggle. On this subject see M. Idel, " Le-Toldot ha-Isur Lilmod Kabbalah," *AJS Review* 5 (1980), pp. 1–20, and nn. 25, 26. One of the interesting claims Idel makes is that the Rashba himself strictly prohibited the teaching of Kabbalah before the age of forty, which legitimated the extension of the restriction to philosophy.

63. *Minhat Kenaot*, p. 479.

64. Ibid., p. 509.

65. *Hoshen Mishpat*, pp. 145, 151.

66. Ibid., p. 151.

67. Ibid., p. 162.

68. Ibid., p. 172.

69. Ibid., p. 156. Meiri pointed out that the ban was formulated so as to allow the study of the philosophical sermons of the Tibonites and Anatoli but to prohibit study of the philosophical corpus itself. This formulation made no sense to him if the ban was aimed not against philosophy but against its popularization.

70. *Hoshen Mishpat*, p. 170.

71. Ibid., pp. 163–64.

72. Ibid., pp. 168–69.

73. Aba Mari's own world view is deeply influenced by Maimonidean ideas. See for example *Minhat Kenaot*, pp. 237–48.

74. Ibid., p. 835.

75. On the debate concerning the printing of the *Zohar* see I. Tishbi, "Ha-Pulmus al Sefer ha-Zohar ba-Meah ha-Shes Esreh be-Italyah," *P'raqim* 1 (1967–68), pp. 131–182.

76. See Rashba's reference to those figures as strict Talmudists in *Minhat Kenaot*, pp. 478, 384. For an extreme formulation of esotericism concerning Kabbalah see *Teshubot ha-Rashba* I, 94. Concerning esotericism in the Kabbalah of the Rashba's teacher, Nachmanides, see M. Idel, "We Have No Kabbalistic Tradition on This," in I. Twersky, ed., *Rabbi Moses Nahmanides: Explorations in His Religious and Literary Virtuosity* (Cambridge, Mass.: Harvard University Press, 1983).

77. *Minhat Kenaot*, p. 387. Samuel the Sulami sheltered the scholar Levi ben Hayim, who was suspected of heretical philosophical teachings. There is nothing particularly heretical in his book, *Livyat Chen*, however, so some scholars wonder why this individual was persecuted by the Rashba. The Rashba urged Samuel to expel Levi from his house, to abstain from further study of philosophy, and to concentrate on Talmud alone. In this context the Rashba mentioned the Narbonne tradition of the study of Kabbalah but did not recommend the study of Kabbalah as an alternative to philosophy.

78. *Sefer ha-Kanah* (Cracow, 1854), pp. 7b–8a. *Sefer ha-Pliah Karetz* (1744), p. 4a. See J. Katz, "Halakhah ve-Kabbalah ke-Nosei Limud Mitcharim," in his *Halakhah ve-Kabbalah* (Jerusalem: Magnes Press, 1984), pp. 82–83.

79. See Zohar III, 153a. For other examples see also *Tikunei Zohar* 73b and *Zohar Hadash* 93b. The complicated nature of the criticism of talmudism in the *Tikunei Zohar* and *Rahayah Meimanah* is debated among scholars. The perplexity arises from the author's contradictory statements concerning Halakhah and its value. Scholem thought that his antinomianism was utopian, meaning that in the messianic era the present Halakhah will be abolished. Tishbi, however, claimed that his antinomianism was, to a small degree, present-oriented. See G. Scholem, *On the Kabbalah and Its Symbolism*, trans. D. Manheim (New York: Schocken Books, 1965), pp. 77–80, and Y. Tishbi, *The Wisdom of the Zohar*, trans. D. Goldstein (Oxford: Oxford University Press, 1989), vol. 3, pp. 1089–112. For a more moderate view see E. Gotlib, *Mechkarim be-Sifrut ha-Kabbalah* (Tel Aviv: Tel Aviv University Press, 1976), pp. 545–50.

80. For such formulations see Shlomo Cordovero, *Or Ne'erav* I, ch. 1–5; Yeshayahu Horowitz, *Shnei Luchot ha-Berit* (Jerusalem, 1963), Mashecht Shbuot 31b; Maamar Rishon 30b. For a more extreme formulation that permits a person to study Kabbalah even if he is unable to master the traditional talmudic curriculum see Chaim Vital, *Etz Chaim*, introduction. On these authors see J. Katz, *Halakhah ve-Kabbalah*, pp. 89–92, 94–96, 97–99.

81. See J. Katz, "Halakhah ve-Kabbalah ke-Nosei Limud Mitcharim," in *Halakhah ve-Kabbalah*, pp. 70–101. For additional sources on the subject see

J. Elboim, *Petichut ve-Histagrut*, pp. 183, 208–22. See also M. Idel, " 'Echad me-I'r u-Shnayim me-Mishpachah'—I'yun Mechadash be-Bea'yat Tefutzatah shel Kabaalat haari ve-ha-Shabtaut," *Pea'mim* 44 (1990), p. 12 n. 30.

82. See M. Idel, *Kabbalah: New Perspectives* (New Haven: Yale University Press, 1988).

83. On the mystical meaning of Talmud Torah in the first generation of Hasidut see Y. Weiss, "Talmud Torah le-Shitat R. Israel Ba'al Shem Tov," in *Tiferet Israel Lichvod ha-Rav ha-Rashi ha-Rav Israel Brody* (London, 1963), pp. 151–69. (See Dov Baer of Mezirech, *Zava'at ha-Rivash*, pp. 29, 41, 54, 117.) For a detailed technique of study see *Magid Dvarav le-Ya'acov*, R. Shatz Upenheimer, ed. (Jerusalem: Magnes Press, 1976) sec. 66, 177, and especially 192. On the importance of the shape of the white spaces within a Torah scroll and the identification of the Torah with God's own body see M. Idel, "Hearot Rishonyot al ha-Parshanunt ha-Kabalit le-Sugeiyah," in *Sefer ha-Yovel la-Rav Mordechai Broier* (Jerusalem: Akademon Press, 1992), pp. 773–83.

84. On Abraham Abulafia see M. Idel, *The Mystical Experience in Abraham Abulafia* (New York: SUNY Press, 1988).

85. See A. Jellinek, *Philosophie und Kabbalah* (Leipzig, 1854), pp. 33–38.

86. On the concept of Torah in Kabbalah see G. Scholem, *On the Kabbalah and Its Symbolism*, pp. 32–86; M. Idel, "Tfisat ha-Torah be-Sifrut ha-Heiochalot ve-Gilguleiah ba-Kabbalah," *Mechkarei Yerushalaim be-Machshevet Israel* 1 (1981), pp. 23–84.

87. On Chaim of Volozhin's understanding of Torah study and his integration of the traditional form of study into a kabbalistic conception see E. Etkes, "Shitato u-Po'olo shel R. Hayim me-Volozhin ke-Tkuvaht ha-Chevrah ha-'Mitnagdit' la-Chasidut," *PAAJR* (1972), pp. 21–31; N. Lamm, *Torah Lishmah in the Works of Rabbi Hayyim of Volozhin and His Contemporaries* (Hoboken, N.J.: Ktav, 1989).

88. *Nefesh ha-Haim*, 4:10.

89. *Magid Mesharim* 40a.i (Amsterdam, 1708). See R. J. Z. Werblowsky, *Joseph Karo, Lawyer and Mystic* (Philadelphia: Jewish Publication Society, 1977), pp. 157–60.

90. *Or ha-Emet*, pp. 15b–17a.

91. On the technique of *devekut* among the hasidim and its implications on the linguistic function of the Torah see M. Idel, *Hasidism Between Ecstasy and Magic* (New York: SUNY Press, 1995), pp. 171–88.

92. Babylonian Talmud, *Sanhedrin* 59a.

93. *Psikta Rabbati* 5.

94. See M. Hirschman, *A Rivalry of Genius*, trans. B. Stein (Albany: SUNY Press, 1996), pp. 17–18.

95. Maimonides, *Guide of the Perplexed* III, and Meiri, *Hoshen Mishpat*, p. 162. For a discussion of this aspect of Maimonides' thought see D. Hartman, *Maimonides: Torah and Philosophical Quest* (Philadelphia: Jewish Publication Society, 1976).

96. The Rosh's responsum appears in *Shelot u-Teshubot ha-Rosh*, 55:3. For a

detailed analysis see I. Ta-Shma, "Shikulim Philosophyim be-Achra'at halakhah," *Sefunot* 16 (1985) pp. 99–110. The responsum was quoted in a sixteenth-century version of the earlier medieval debates over the study of Maimonides and the study of philosophy, in which the theme of the legitimacy of philosophy against the self-contained canon resurfaced. The dispute erupted between the two distinguished rabbis of sixteenth-century Poland: R. Moshe Isserles, known as the Rama, and R. Shlomo Luria, known as Maharshal. In one of his halakhic exchanges with the Maharshal, the Rama supported a legal opinion with a quote from Aristotle (*She'elot u-Teshubot ha-Rama* 7:8). This enraged Maharshal, who claimed that philosophers' opinions are irrelevant to halakhic discussion and proceeded to attack the study of Aristotle. The Rama answered that his study of philosophy was legitimate and offered three arguments: first, even the Rashba permitted it, provided it was undertaken after age twenty-five. Second, what is dangerous in Aristotelianism is the metaphysics, and Rama cited the physics. Third, his Aristotelianism is totally derived from the reading of Jewish authors, mainly Maimonides, and this was never prohibited. According to the Rama's testimony, he had never read Aristotle. In an attempt to shift the burden to Maharshal, Rama questioned whether the study of Kabbalah did not prove even more problematic than philosophy. Kabbalah, in the Rama's eyes, was more dangerous to the unprepared student. What is important for the purpose of our discussion is Maharshal's insistence that the study of Talmud cannot be supported or clarified through Greek wisdom. On this debate see J. Elboim, *Petichut ve-Histagrut*, pp. 156–65.

Conclusion

1. Some features of text-centeredness were challenged among the Jews before the end of the eighteenth century. For example, the hasidic movement challenged the connection between scholarship and authority, and the hasidic *zaddik* arose as an authority figure already at the beginning of the eighteenth century. Nevertheless this was not a complete shift in the nature of the community as text-centered.

2. See M. Mendelssohn, *Jerusalem*, trans. A. Arkush (Hanover, N.H.: University Press of New England, 1983).

3. See N. H. Wessely, *Divrei Shalom ve-Emet*, First Letter, chaps. 3, 5, and 7 (Berlin, 1782; Warsaw, 1886).

4. B. Mossinson, "Ha-Tanach be-Beit ha-Sefer," *Ha-Chinuch* 1 (1910), p. 118. See also J. Schoneveld, *The Bible in Israeli Education* (Assan: Van Gorcum, 1976), pp. 27–33.

5. Ah'ad Ha'am, "Ha-Gimnasiah ha-Ivrit be-Yaffo," *Kol Kitbei Ah'ad Ha'am* (Tel Aviv, 1965), p. 420. See also Schoneveld, p. 33–38.

6. See, for example, E. Schweid, "Horaat Miktzoot ha-Yahadut be-Beit ha-Sefer ha-Tikhon be-Medinat Israel," *Petachim* 3 (1972), pp. 6–18, and also B. Kurzweil, "Mahutah u-Mekoroteiah shel Tenua'at ha-I'vrim ha-Tzei'rim ('Kena'anim')," *Luach ha-Aretz* 12 (1953), pp. 107–29.

7. D. Ben Gurion, *I'yunim ba-Tanakh* (Tel Aviv, 1970) p. 47.

8. Ibid., pp. 48–49.

Appendix

1. On this theme see L. Strauss, "How to Study Spinoza's Theologico-Political Treatise," *Persecution and the Art of Writing* (Chicago: University of Chicago Press, 1988), pp. 142–201.

2. Thomas Hobbes, *Leviathan* (London: Penguin Books, 1988), p. 427.

3. Ibid., p. 544.

4. Ibid., p. 547.

5. Ibid., p. 548.

6. Ibid., pp. 500–501.

7. Benedict de Spinoza, *A Theologico-Political Treatise*, trans. R. H. M. Elwes (New York: Dover, 1951), p. 119.

8. Ibid., p. 194.

9. S. Pines, *Bein Machshevet Israel le-Machshevet ha-Amim* (Jerusalem: Bialik, 1977), pp. 306–41.

Index

The terms Bible, Halakhah, Midrash, Mishnah, Sages, Scripture, Talmud, and Torah are used so frequently throughout the text that they have not been listed in the index.